Anthropology 1AB3

Introduction to Anthropology:
Race, Religion and Conflict

NELSON
EDUCATION

ISBN-13: 978-0-17-674330-7
ISBN-10: 0-17-674330-8

Consists of Selections from:

Anthropology: The Human Challenge, 14th Edition
William A. Haviland,
Harald E.L. Prins,
Dana Walrath,
Bunny McBride
ISBN 10: 1-1339-4132-X, © 2014

Cultural Anthropology: A Problem-Based Approach, Second Canadian Edition
Richard H. Robbins, Sherri N. Larkin, Maggie Cummings, Karen McGarry
ISBN 10: 0-17-650272-6, © 2013

Cultural Archaeology: The Human Challenge, 14th Edition
William A. Haviland,
Harald E.L. Prins,
Dana Walrath,
Bunny McBride
ISBN 10: 1-1339-5742-0, © 2014

Cover Credit:

Pichugin Dmitry/Shutterstock

Brief Contents

The Essence of Anthropology

The Anthropological Perspective

Anthropology is the study of humankind in all times and places. Of course, many other disciplines focus on humans in one way or another. For example, anatomy and physiology concentrate on our species as biological organisms. The social sciences examine human relationships, leaving artistic and philosophical aspects of human cultures to the humanities. Anthropology focuses on the interconnections and interdependence of all aspects of the human experience in all places, in the present and deep into the past, well before written history. This unique, broad **holistic perspective** equips anthropologists to address that elusive thing we call *human nature*.

Anthropologists welcome the contributions of researchers from other disciplines, and in return offer their own findings to these other disciplines. An anthropologist may not know as much about the structure of the human eye as an anatomist or as much about the perception of color as a psychologist. As a synthesizer, however, the anthropologist seeks to understand how anatomy and psychology relate to color-naming practices in different societies. Because they look for the broad basis of human ideas and practices without limiting themselves to any single social or biological aspect, anthropologists can acquire an especially expansive and inclusive overview of human biology and culture.

Keeping a holistic perspective allows anthropologists to prevent their own cultural ideas and values from distorting their research. As the old saying goes, people often see what they believe, rather than what appears before their eyes. By maintaining a critical awareness of their own assumptions about human nature—checking and rechecking the ways their beliefs and actions might be shaping their research—anthropologists strive to gain objective knowledge about human beings. With this

anthropology The study of humankind in all times and places.

holistic perspective A fundamental principle of anthropology: The various parts of human culture and biology must be viewed in the broadest possible context in order to understand their interconnections and interdependence.

IN THIS CHAPTER YOU WILL LEARN TO

Describe the discipline of anthropology and make connections among its four fields.

Compare anthropology to the sciences and the humanities.

Identify the characteristics of anthropological field methods and the ethics of anthropological research.

Explain the usefulness of anthropology in light of globalization.

3

in mind, anthropologists aim to avoid the pitfalls of **ethnocentrism**, a belief that the ways of one's own culture are the only proper ones.

To some, an inclusive, holistic perspective that emphasizes the diversity within and among human cultures can be mistaken as shorthand for liberal politics among anthropologists. This is not the case. Anthropologists come from many different backgrounds, and individuals practicing the discipline vary in their personal, political, and religious beliefs (**Figure 1.1**). At the same time, they apply a rigorous methodology for researching cultural practices from the perspective of the culture being studied—a methodology that requires them to check for the influences of their own biases. This is as true for an anthropologist analyzing the culture of the global banking industry as it is for one investigating trance dancing among contemporary hunter-gatherers. We might say that anthropology is a discipline concerned with unbiased evaluation of diverse human systems, including one's own. At times this requires challenging the status quo that is maintained and defended by the power elites of the system under study.

While other social sciences have predominantly concentrated on contemporary peoples living in North American and European (Western) societies, anthropologists have traditionally focused on non-Western peoples and cultures. Anthropologists work with the understanding that to fully access the complexities of human ideas, behavior, and biology, *all* humans, wherever and whenever, must be studied. A cross-cultural and long-term evolutionary perspective distinguishes anthropology from other social sciences. This approach guards against theories about the world and reality that are **culture-bound**—based on the assumptions and values that come from the researcher's own culture.

As a case in point, consider the fact that infants in the United States typically sleep apart from their parents. To people accustomed to multibedroom houses, cribs, and car seats, this may seem normal, but cross-cultural research shows that *co-sleeping,* of mother and baby in particular, is the norm (**Figure 1.2**). Further, the practice of sleeping apart favored in the United States dates back only about 200 years.

Recent studies have shown that separation of mother and infant has important biological and cultural consequences. For one thing, it increases the length of the infant's crying bouts. Some mothers incorrectly interpret crying as an indication that the baby is not receiving sufficient breast milk and consequently switch to using bottled formula, which has been shown to be less healthy. In extreme cases, a baby's cries may provoke physical

ethnocentrism The belief that the ways of one's own culture are the only proper ones.

culture-bound A perspective that produces theories about the world and reality that are based on the assumptions and values from the researcher's own culture.

© Documentary Educational Resources

Figure 1.1 Anthropologist Jayasinhji Jhala Anthropologists come from many corners of the world and carry out research in a huge variety of cultures all around the globe. Dr. Jayasinhji Jhala, pictured here, hails from the old city of Dhrangadhra in Gujarat, northwestern India. A member of the Jhala clan of Rajputs, an aristocratic caste of warriors, he grew up in the royal palace of his father, the maharaja. After earning a bachelor of arts degree in India, he came to the United States and earned a master's in visual studies from MIT, followed by a doctorate in anthropology from Harvard. Currently a professor and director of the programs of Visual Anthropology and the Visual Anthropology Media Laboratory at Temple University, he returns regularly to India with students to film cultural traditions in his own caste-stratified society.

abuse. But the benefits of co-sleeping go beyond significant reductions in crying: Infants who are breastfed receive more stimulation important for brain development, and they are apparently less susceptible to sudden infant death syndrome (SIDS or "crib death"), which occurs at a higher rate in the United States than in any other country. There are benefits to the mother as well: Frequent nursing prevents early ovulation after childbirth, promotes weight

VISUAL COUNTERPOINT

Figure 1.2 Sleeping Habits across Cultures Although infants in the United States typically sleep apart from their parents, cross-cultural research shows that co-sleeping, particularly of mother and baby, is the rule. Without the breathing cues provided by someone sleeping nearby, an infant is more susceptible to sudden infant death syndrome (SIDS), a phenomenon in which a 4- to 6-month-old baby stops breathing and dies while asleep. The highest rates of SIDS are found among infants in the United States. The photo on the right shows a Nenet family sleeping together in their *chum* (reindeer-skin tent). Nenet people are Arctic reindeer pastoralists living in Siberia.

loss to shed pregnancy pounds, and allows nursing mothers at least as much sleep as mothers who sleep apart from their infants (McKenna & McDade, 2005).

Why do so many mothers continue to sleep separately from their infants? In the United States, the cultural values of independence and consumerism come into play. To begin building individual identities, babies are provided with rooms (or at least space) of their own. This room also gives parents a place to stow the toys, furniture, and other paraphernalia associated with good and caring childrearing in the United States.

Although the findings of anthropologists have often challenged the conclusions of sociologists, psychologists, and economists, anthropology is absolutely indispensable to those in other disciplines because it is the only consistent check against culture-bound assertions. In a sense, anthropology is to these disciplines what the laboratory is to physics and chemistry: an essential testing ground for their theories.

Anthropology and Its Fields

Individual anthropologists tend to specialize in one of four fields or subdisciplines: cultural anthropology, linguistic anthropology, archaeology, and physical (biological) anthropology (**Figure 1.3**). Some anthropologists consider

archaeology and linguistics to be part of the broader study of human cultures, but archaeology and linguistics also have close ties to physical anthropology. For example, while linguistic anthropology focuses on the social and cultural aspects of language, it has deep connections to the evolution of human language and to the biological basis of speech and language studied within physical anthropology.

Researchers in each of anthropology's fields gather and analyze data to explore similarities and differences among humans, across time and space. Moreover, individuals within

Figure 1.3 The Four Fields of Anthropology Note that the divisions among the fields are not sharp, indicating that their boundaries overlap. Note also that all four include the practice of applied anthropology.

BIOCULTURAL CONNECTION

The Anthropology of Organ Transplantation

In 1954, the first organ transplant occurred in Boston when surgeons removed a kidney from one identical twin to place it inside his sick brother. Today, transplants between unrelated individuals are common, so much so that organs are trafficked in the black market, often across continents from the poor to the wealthy. Though some transplants rely upon living donors, routine organ transplantation depends largely upon the availability of organs obtained from individuals who have died. To reduce illegal traffic, several European countries have enacted policies that assume that any individual who is "brain dead" is automatically an organ donor unless the person has "opted out" ahead of time.

A practice like organ transplantation can exist only if it fits with cultural beliefs about death and the human body. The North American and European view—that the body is a machine that can be repaired much like a car—makes a practice like organ transplantation acceptable. But this is not the view shared by all societies. Anthropologist Margaret Lock has explored differences between Japanese and North American acceptance of the biological state of brain death and how it affects the practice of organ transplantation.

The diagnosis of brain death relies upon the absence of measurable electrical currents in the brain and the inability to breathe without technological assistance. The brain-dead individual, though attached to machines, still seems alive with a beating heart and normal skin coloring. Part of the reason most North Americans find organ transplantation tolerable with the determination of brain death is that personhood and individuality are culturally ascribed to the mind, and thus located in the brain. North Americans' acceptance of brain death has allowed for the "gift of life" through sometimes anonymous organ donation and subsequent transplantation.

By contrast, in Japan, the concept of brain death is hotly contested, and organ transplants are rarely performed. The Japanese idea of personhood does not incorporate a mind–body split; instead, a person's identity is tied to the entire body rather than solely to the brain. Consequently, the Japanese reject that a warm body is a corpse from which organs can be harvested. Further, organs cannot be transformed into "gifts" because anonymous donation is incompatible with Japanese social patterns of reciprocal exchange.

Organ transplantation involves far greater social meaning than the purely biological movement of an organ from one individual to another. Cultural and biological processes are tightly woven into every aspect of this new social practice.

BIOCULTURAL QUESTION

What criteria do you use for death, and is it compatible with the idea of organ donation? Do you think that donated organs are fairly distributed in your society or throughout the globe?

For more on this subject, see Lock, M. (2001). Twice dead: Organ transplants and the reinvention of death. Berkeley: University of California Press.

---

each of the four fields practice **applied anthropology**, which entails the use of anthropological knowledge and methods to solve practical problems. Most applied anthropologists actively collaborate with the communities in which they work—setting goals, solving problems, and conducting research together. In this book, the Anthropology Applied features spotlight how anthropology contributes to solving a wide range of challenges.

applied anthropology The use of anthropological knowledge and methods to solve practical problems, often for a specific client.

medical anthropology A specialization in anthropology that brings theoretical and applied approaches from cultural and biological anthropology to the study of human health and disease.

cultural anthropology The study of patterns in human behavior, thought, and emotions, focusing on humans as culture-producing and culture-reproducing creatures. Also known as *social* or *sociocultural anthropology*.

An early example of the application of anthropological knowledge to a practical problem was the international public health movement that began in the 1920s. This marked the beginning of **medical anthropology**—a specialization that brings theoretical and applied approaches from cultural and biological anthropology to the study of human health and disease. The work of medical anthropologists sheds light on the connections between human health and political and economic forces, both locally and globally. Examples of this specialization appear in some of the Biocultural Connections featured in this text, including the one presented on this page, "The Anthropology of Organ Transplantation."

Cultural Anthropology

Cultural anthropology (also called *social* or *sociocultural anthropology*) is the study of patterns in human behavior, thought, and emotions. It focuses on humans as culture-producing and culture-reproducing creatures. To understand the work of the cultural anthropologist, we must clarify the meaning of **culture**—a society's shared and socially transmitted ideas, values, emotions, and perceptions, which are used to make sense of experience and which generate behavior and are reflected in that behavior. These are the (often unconscious) standards by which societies—structured groups of people—operate. These standards are socially learned, rather than acquired through biological inheritance. The manifestations of culture may vary considerably from place to place, but no individual is "more cultured" in the anthropological sense than any other.

Integral to all the anthropological fields, the concept of culture might be considered anthropology's distinguishing feature. After all, a biological anthropologist is distinct from a biologist *primarily* because he or she takes culture into account. Cultural anthropologists may study the legal, medical, economic, political, or religious system of a given society, knowing that all aspects of the culture interrelate as part of a unified whole. They may focus on divisions in a society—such as by gender, age, or class—factors we will explore in depth later in this text. But it is also worth noting the significance of these same categories to the archaeologist who studies a society through its material remains, to the linguistic anthropologist who examines ancient and modern languages, and to the biological anthropologist who investigates the physical human body.

Cultural anthropology has two main components: ethnography and ethnology. An **ethnography** is a detailed description of a particular culture primarily based on **fieldwork**, which is the term all anthropologists use for on-location research. Because the hallmark of ethnographic fieldwork is a combination of social participation and personal observation within the community being studied and interviews and discussions with individual members of a group, the ethnographic method is commonly referred to as **participant observation** (Figure 1.4). Ethnographies provide the information used to make systematic comparisons among cultures all across the world. Known as **ethnology**, such cross-cultural research allows anthropologists to develop theories that help explain why certain important differences or similarities occur among groups.

Ethnography

Through participant observation—eating a people's food, sleeping under their roof, learning how to speak and behave acceptably, and personally experiencing their habits and customs—the ethnographer seeks to gain the best possible understanding of a particular way of life. Being a participant observer does not mean that the anthropologist must join in battles to study a culture in which warfare is prominent; but by living among a warring people, the ethnographer should be able to understand how warfare fits into the overall cultural framework.

The ethnographer must observe carefully to gain an overview without placing too much emphasis on one

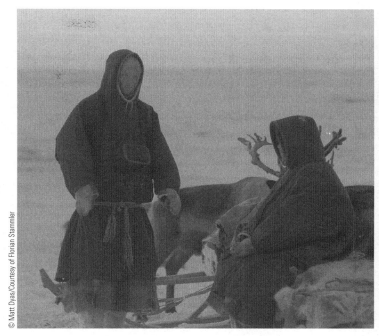

Figure 1.4 Fieldwork in the Arctic British anthropologist Florian Stammler engages in participant observation among Sami reindeer nomads in Siberia. Specializing in Arctic anthropology, particularly in the Russian far north, Stammler coordinates the anthropology research team at the University of Lapland's Arctic Centre. His interests include Arctic economy, human–animal relations, and the anthropology of place and belonging.

cultural feature at the expense of another. Only by discovering how *all* parts of a culture—its social, political, economic, and religious practices and institutions—relate to one another can the ethnographer begin to understand the cultural system. This is the holistic perspective so basic to the discipline.

The popular image of ethnographic fieldwork is that it occurs among hunters, herders, fishers, or farmers who live in far-off, isolated places. To be sure, much ethnographic work has been done in the remote villages of Asia, Africa, or Latin America, islands of the Pacific Ocean, deserts of Australia, and so on. However, as the discipline developed after the mid-1900s with the demise of colonialism, industrialized societies

culture A society's shared and socially transmitted ideas, values, and perceptions, which are used to make sense of experience and which generate behavior and are reflected in that behavior.

ethnography A detailed description of a particular culture primarily based on fieldwork.

fieldwork The term anthropologists use for on-location research.

participant observation In ethnography, the technique of learning a people's culture through social participation and personal observation within the community being studied, as well as interviews and discussion with individual members of the group over an extended period of time.

ethnology The study and analysis of different cultures from a comparative or historical point of view, utilizing ethnographic accounts and developing anthropological theories that help explain why certain important differences or similarities occur among groups.

and neighborhoods in modern cities have also become a significant focus of anthropological study.

Ethnographic fieldwork has transformed from expert Western anthropologists studying people in "other" places to a collaborative approach among anthropologists from all parts of the world and the varied communities in which they work. Today, anthropologists from around the globe employ the same research techniques that were used in the study of non-Western peoples to explore diverse subjects such as religious movements, street gangs, refugee settlements, land rights, conflict resolution, corporate bureaucracies, and health-care systems in Western cultures.

Ethnology

Largely descriptive in nature, *ethnography* provides the raw data needed for *ethnology*—the branch of cultural anthropology that involves cross-cultural comparisons and theories that explain differences or similarities among groups. Intriguing insights into one's own beliefs and practices may come from cross-cultural comparisons. Consider, for example, the amount of time spent on domestic chores by industrialized peoples and traditional food foragers—people who rely on wild plant and animal resources for subsistence.

Anthropological research has shown that food foragers work far less time at domestic tasks and other subsistence pursuits compared to people in industrialized societies. Despite access to "labor-saving" appliances such as dishwashers, washing machines, clothes dryers, vacuum cleaners, food processors, and microwave ovens, urban women in the United States who are not working for wages outside their homes put 55 hours a week into their housework. In contrast, aboriginal women in Australia devoted 20 hours a week to their chores (Bodley, 2008, p. 67). Nevertheless, consumer appliances have become important indicators of a high standard of living in the United States due to the widespread belief that household appliances reduce housework and increase leisure time.

By making systematic comparisons, ethnologists seek to arrive at scientific explanations of cultural features and social practices in all times and places. (The Biocultural Connection you read on page 6 is one of countless examples of anthropological insights gained through comparative research.)

Applied Cultural Anthropology

Today, cultural anthropologists contribute to applied anthropology in a variety of contexts ranging from business to education to health care to governmental interventions to humanitarian aid. For example, anthropologist Nancy Scheper-Hughes has taken her investigative work on the global problem of illegal trafficking of organs and used it to help found Organs Watch, an organization dedicated to solving this human rights issue (see the Globalscape later in this chapter).

Linguistic Anthropology

Perhaps the most distinctive feature of the human species is language. Although the sounds and gestures made by some other animals—especially by apes—may serve functions comparable to those of human language, no other animal has developed a system of symbolic communication as complex as that of humans. Language allows people to create, preserve, and transmit countless details of their culture from generation to generation.

Linguistic anthropology is the branch of anthropology that studies human languages; it investigates their structure, history, and relation to social and cultural contexts. Although it shares data, theories, and methods with the more general discipline of linguistics, it differs in that it includes distinctly anthropological questions, such as, how does language influence or reflect culture? And how does language use differ among distinct members of a society?

In its early years, linguistic anthropology emphasized the documentation of languages of cultures under ethnographic study—particularly those whose future seemed precarious due to colonization, forced assimilation, population decimation, capitalist expansion, or other destructive forces. When the first Europeans began to colonize the world five centuries ago, an estimated 12,000 distinct languages existed. By the early 1900s—when anthropological research began to take off—many languages and peoples had already disappeared or were on the brink of extinction. Sadly this trend continues, with predictions that nearly half of the world's remaining 6,000 languages will become extinct over the next hundred years (Crystal, 2002; Knight, Studdert-Kennedy, & Hurford, 2000).

Linguistic anthropology has three main branches: descriptive linguistics, historical linguistics, and language in relation to social and cultural settings. All three yield valuable information about how people communicate and how they understand the world around them.

Descriptive Linguistics

This branch of linguistic anthropology involves the painstaking work of dissecting a language by recording, delineating, and analyzing all of its features. It leads to a deeper understanding of a language—its structure (including grammar and syntax), its unique linguistic repertoire (figures of speech, word plays, and so on), and its relationship to other languages.

Historical Linguistics

While descriptive linguistics focuses on all features of a particular language at any one moment in time, historical

---

linguistic anthropology The study of human languages—looking at their structure, history, and relation to social and cultural contexts.

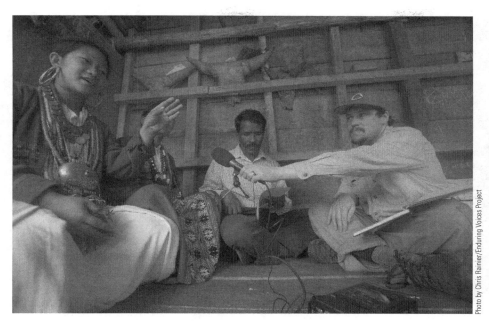

Figure 1.5 Preserving Endangered Languages Linguistic anthropologist David Anderson (right) has devoted his career to documenting and saving indigenous languages. He founded and heads the Living Tongues Institute for Endangered Languages and works throughout the globe to preserve languages that are dying out at a shocking rate of about one every two weeks. Here he is recording for the first time the language of Koro, spoken by some 1,000 people in India's remote northeastern state, Arunachal Pradesh. Situated near India's contested border with China, this region is considered a black hole in the study of languages.

Photo by Chris Rainier/Enduring Voices Project

linguistics deals with the fact that languages change. In addition to deciphering "dead" languages that are no longer spoken, specialists in this field examine interrelationships among different languages and investigate earlier and later forms of the same language. Their findings make significant contributions to our understanding of the human past. By working out relationships among languages and examining their spatial distributions, they may estimate how long the speakers of those languages have lived where they do. By identifying those words in related languages that have survived from an ancient ancestral tongue, they can also suggest not only where, but how, the speakers of the inherited language lived. Such work shows linguistic ties between geographically distant groups such as the Navajo in Arizona's desert and the Gwich'in above the Arctic Circle in Alaska, or between the Magyars in Hungary and the people of Finland.

Language in Its Social and Cultural Settings

Some linguistic anthropologists study the social and cultural contexts of a language. For example, they may research how factors such as age, gender, ethnicity, class, religion, occupation, or financial status affect speech. Because members of any culture may use a variety of different registers and inflections, the ones they choose (often unconsciously) to use at a specific instance convey particular meanings.

Scientists in this branch of linguistics also look into the dynamic relationship between language and culture—investigating to what degree they mutually influence and inform each other. In this vein, they may investigate how a language reflects culturally significant aspects of a people's environment or values.

Linguistic anthropologists may also focus on the socialization process through which an individual becomes part of a culture, moves up in social status, or takes on a new professional identity. First-year medical students, for example, amass 6,000 new terms and a series of linguistic conventions as they begin to take on the role of a physician. Individuals training for any specialized career, from lawyer to chef, face similar challenges in quickly expanding their vocabularies.

Applied Linguistic Anthropology

Linguistic anthropologists put their research to use in a number of settings. Some, for example, have collaborated with recently contacted cultural groups, small nations (or tribes), and ethnic minorities in the preservation or revival of languages suppressed or lost during periods of oppression by dominant societies. Their work has included helping to create written forms of languages that previously existed only orally. This sort of applied linguistic anthropology represents a trend in mutually useful collaboration that is characteristic of much anthropological research today (**Figure 1.5**).

Archaeology

Archaeology is the branch of anthropology that studies human cultures through the recovery and analysis of material remains and environmental data. Such material products include tools, pottery, hearths, and enclosures that remain as traces of cultural practices in the past, as well as human, plant, and marine remains, some of which date back 2.5 million years. The arrangement of these traces, as much as the traces themselves, reflects specific human ideas and behavior. For example, shallow, restricted concentrations of charcoal that include oxidized earth, bone fragments, and charred plant

archaeology The study of cultures through the recovery and analysis of material remains and environmental data.

Figure 1.6 **Analyzing Human Remains in a Bioarchaeology Laboratory** Bioarchaeology graduate students J. Marla Toyne and Mellisa Lund Valle are conducting a skeletal inventory and checking for pathological conditions in human remains from a 14th-century mass execution and sacrifice site at Punta Lobos in the Huarmey River Valley in northern Peru. Their work is part of a research project directed by Dr. John Verano of Tulane University, New Orleans.

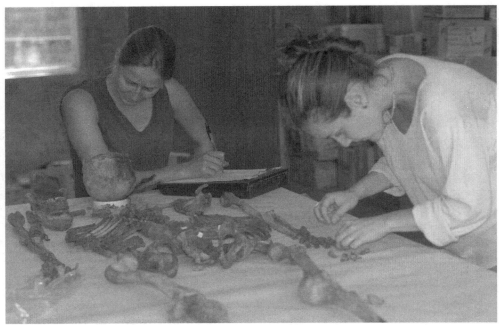

Courtesy of John Verano

remains, located near pieces of fire-cracked rock, pottery, and tools suitable for food preparation, indicate cooking and food processing. Such remains can reveal much about a people's diet and subsistence practices.

In addition to specific questions about a single group of people at a particular place and time, archaeologists use material remains to investigate broad questions, including settlement or migration patterns across vast areas, such as the spread of the earliest humans from Africa or the first peopling of the Americas. Together with skeletal remains, material remains help archaeologists reconstruct the biocultural context of past human lifeways and patterns. Archaeologists organize this material and use it to explain cultural variability and change through time.

Because archaeological research is explicitly tied to unearthing material remains in particular environmental contexts, a variety of innovations in the geographic and geologic sciences have been readily incorporated into archaeological research. Innovations such as geographic information systems (GIS), remote sensing, and ground-penetrating radar (GPR) complement traditional explorations of the past through archaeological digs.

Although archaeologists tend to specialize in particular culture zones or time periods that are connected with particular regions of the world, a number of topical subspecializations also exist. We turn now to these.

---

historical archaeology The archaeological study of places for which written records exist.

bioarchaeology The archaeological study of human remains—bones, skulls, teeth, and sometimes hair, dried skin, or other tissue—to determine the influences of culture and environment on human biological variation.

Historical Archaeology

Archaeologists can reach back for clues to human behavior far beyond the maximal 5,000 years to which historians are confined by their reliance on written records. Calling this time period "prehistoric" does not mean that these societies were less interested in their history or that they did not have ways of recording and transmitting history. It simply means that written records do not exist.

That said, archaeologists are not limited to the study of societies without written records; they may study those for which historic documents are available to supplement the material remains. **Historical archaeology**, the archaeological study of places for which written records exist, often provides data that differ considerably from the historical record. In most literate societies, written records are associated with governing elites rather than with farmers, fishers, laborers, or slaves, and therefore they include the biases of the ruling classes. In fact, according to James Deetz, a pioneer in historical archaeology of the Americas, in many historical contexts, "material culture may be the most objective source of information we have" (Deetz, 1977, p. 160).

Bioarchaeology

Bioarchaeology is the study of human remains—bones, skulls, teeth, and sometimes hair, dried skin, or other tissue— to determine the influences of culture and environment on human biological variation. Whether mummified (as in the dry deserts of northwestern China, Egypt, or Peru) or not, human remains excavated at archaeological sites provide valuable clues about the lifestyle and health of prehistoric peoples, including information about activity, physiological stress, nutrition, disease, and social rank (Figure 1.6).

For example, mummified skeletal remains from the Andean highlands in South America not only reveal this burial practice but also provide evidence of some of the earliest brain surgery ever documented. In addition, these bioarchaeological remains exhibit skull deformation techniques that distinguish nobility from other members of society.

Some archaeologists specialize in *ethnobotany*, studying how people of a given culture made use of indigenous plants. Others specialize in *zooarchaeology*, tracking the animal remains recovered in archaeological excavations. Still others, maritime archaeologists, may research submerged sites or old sailing vessels sunk to the bottom of a sea, lake, or river hundreds or even thousands of years ago.

Contemporary Archaeology

Although most archaeologists concentrate on the past, some study material objects in contemporary settings, and that includes garbage dumps. Just as a 3,000-year-old shell mound (*midden*) on the seacoast of Denmark, New England, or Tiera del Fuego offers significant clues about prehistoric communities living on mussels, oysters, fish, and other natural resources, modern garbage dumps provide evidence of everyday life in contemporary societies. For large cities like New York, the accumulation of daily garbage is staggering. In just a few centuries, millions of inhabitants have dumped so much trash that this urban area has been physically raised 6 to 30 feet—primarily from discarded newspapers and rubble from demolition and building construction, but also from huge amounts of plastic and household and office supplies and equipment (Rathje & Murphy, 2001).

Among the first anthropologists to study modern garbage was William Rathje, who founded the Garbage Project at the University of Arizona in 1973. The project began with a study of household waste of Tucson residents and later expanded to other cities. When surveyed by questionnaires, only 15 percent of households reported consuming beer, and none reported an intake of more than eight cans a week. Analysis of garbage from the same area showed that 80 percent of the households consumed some beer, and 50 percent discarded more than eight cans per week (Rathje & Murphy, 2001).

Beyond providing data on beer consumption, the Garbage Project has tested the validity of research survey techniques, upon which sociologists, economists, other social scientists, and policymakers rely heavily. The tests show a significant difference between what people *say* they do and what the garbage analysis shows they *actually* do.

Applied Archaeology

The Garbage Project also gives us a fine example of applied archaeology producing useful, thought-provoking information about contemporary social issues. Its program of excavating landfills in different parts of North America, initiated in 1987, produced the first reliable data on what materials actually go into landfills and what happens to them there. Again, common beliefs turned out to be at odds with the actual situation. For example, when buried in deep compost

landfills, biodegradable materials such as newspapers take far longer to decay than anyone had expected. This kind of information is a vital step toward solving waste disposal problems. The data gathered from the Garbage Project's landfill studies on hazardous wastes and rates of decay of various materials play a major role in landfill regulation and management today (Rathje & Murphy, 2001).

Cultural Resource Management

While archaeology may conjure up images of ancient pyramids and the like, much archaeological fieldwork is carried out as **cultural resource management**. What distinguishes this work from traditional archaeological research is that it is a legally required part of any activity that might threaten important aspects of a country's prehistoric and historic heritage. Many countries, from Chile to China, use archaeological expertise to protect and manage their cultural heritage.

In the United States, for example, if a construction company plans to replace a highway bridge, it must first contract with archaeologists to identify and protect any significant prehistoric or historic resources that might be affected by this new construction. And when cultural resource management work or other archaeological investigation unearths Native American cultural items or human remains, federal laws come into the picture again. The Native American Graves Protection and Repatriation Act (NAGPRA), passed in 1990, provides a process for the return of these remains, especially human bones and burial gifts (such as copper jewelry, weapons, and ceramic bowls), to lineal descendants, culturally affiliated Indian tribes, and Native Hawaiian organizations.

In addition to working in all the capacities mentioned, archaeologists also consult for engineering firms to help them prepare environmental impact statements. Some of these archaeologists operate out of universities and colleges, while others are on the staff of independent consulting firms. When state legislation sponsors any kind of archaeological work, it is referred to as *contract archaeology*.

Physical Anthropology

Physical anthropology, also called *biological anthropology*, focuses on humans as biological organisms. Traditionally, physical anthropologists concentrated on human evolution, primatology, growth and development, human adaptation, and forensics. Today, **molecular anthropology**, or the anthropological study of genes

---

cultural resource management A branch of archaeology concerned with survey and/or excavation of archaeological and historical remains that might be threatened by construction or development; also involved with policy surrounding protection of cultural resources.

physical anthropology The systematic study of humans as biological organisms; also known as *biological anthropology*.

molecular anthropology The anthropological study of genes and genetic relationships, which contributes significantly to our understanding of human evolution, adaptation, and diversity.

and genetic relationships, contributes significantly to our understanding of human evolution, adaptation, and diversity. Comparisons among groups separated by time, geography, or the frequency of a particular gene can reveal how humans have adapted and where they have migrated. As experts in the anatomy of human bones and tissues, biological anthropologists lend their knowledge about the body to applied areas such as gross anatomy laboratories, public health, and criminal investigations.

Paleoanthropology

Dealing with much greater time spans than other branches of anthropology, **paleoanthropology** is the study of the origins, predecessors, and early representatives of the present human species. Focusing on long-time biological changes (evolution) paleoanthropologists seek to understand how, when, and why we became the species we are today. In biological terms, we humans are *Homo sapiens,* a species in the larger order of primates, one of the many kinds of mammals. Because we share a common ancestry with other primates (monkeys and apes), paleoanthropologists look back to the earliest primates (about 65 million years ago, abbreviated mya) or even to the earliest mammals (225 mya) to reconstruct the intricate path of human evolution. At times, paleoanthropologists take a **biocultural** approach, focusing on the interaction of biology and culture.

Paleoanthropologists compare fossilized skeletons of our ancestors to other fossils and to the bones of living members of our species. Combining this knowledge with biochemical and genetic evidence, they strive to scientifically reconstruct the complex course of human evolutionary history. With each new fossil discovery, paleoanthropologists have another piece to add to the puzzle still far from fully solved. Further on in this text, we discuss how, genetic evidence establishes the close relationship between humans and ape species—chimpanzees, bonobos, and gorillas. Genetic analyses indicate that the distinctively human line split from the apes sometime between 5 and 8 million years ago.

Primatology

Studying the anatomy and behavior of the other primates helps us understand what we share with our closest living relatives and what makes humans unique. Therefore, **primatology**, or the study of living and fossil primates, is a vital part of physical anthropology. Primates include the

Penelope Breese/Liaison/Getty Images

Figure 1.7 Primatologist Jane Goodall Nearly forty-five years ago Jane Goodall began studying chimpanzees to shed light on the behavior of our distant ancestors. The knowledge she has amassed reveals striking similarities with our species. Goodall has devoted much of her career to championing the rights of our closest living relatives.

Asian and African apes, as well as monkeys, lemurs, lorises, and tarsiers.

Biologically, humans are members of the ape family—large-bodied, broad-shouldered primates with no tail. Detailed studies of ape behavior in the wild indicate that the sharing of learned behavior is a significant part of their social life. Increasingly, primatologists designate the shared, learned behavior of nonhuman apes as *culture.* For example, tool use and communication systems indicate the elementary basis of language in some ape societies.

Primate studies offer scientifically grounded perspectives on the behavior of our ancestors, as well as greater appreciation and respect for the abilities of our closest living relatives. As human activity encroaches on all parts of the world, many primate species are endangered. Primatologists, such as Jane Goodall (**Figure 1.7**), strongly advocate for the preservation of primate habitats so that these remarkable animals will be able to continue to inhabit the earth with us.

Human Growth, Adaptation, and Variation

Some physical anthropologists specialize in the study of human growth and development. They examine biological mechanisms of growth as well as the impact of the environment on the growth process. For example, Franz Boas, a pioneer of American anthropology of the early 20th century (see the Anthropologists of Note feature on the next page) compared the heights of immigrants who spent their

---

paleoanthropology The anthropological study of biological changes through time (evolution) to understand the origins and predecessors of the present human species.

biocultural An approach that focuses on the interaction of biology and culture.

primatology The study of living and fossil primates.

ANTHROPOLOGISTS OF NOTE

Franz Boas (1858–1942) • Matilda Coxe Stevenson (1849–1915)

Franz Boas on a sailing ship, about 1925.

Franz Boas was not the first to teach anthropology in the United States, but it was Boas and his students, with their insistence on scientific rigor, who made anthropology courses common in college and university curricula. Born and raised in Germany where he studied physics, mathematics, and geography, Boas did his first ethnographic research among the Inuit (Eskimos) in Arctic Canada in 1883 and 1884. After a brief academic career in Berlin, he came to the United States where he worked in museums interspersed with ethnographic research among the Kwakiutl (Kwakwaka'wakw) Indians in the Canadian Pacific. In 1896, he became a professor at Columbia University in New York City. He authored an incredible number of publications, founded professional organizations and journals, and taught two generations of great anthropologists, including numerous women and ethnic minorities.

As a Jewish immigrant, Boas recognized the dangers of ethnocentrism and especially racism. Through ethnographic fieldwork and comparative analysis, he demonstrated that white supremacy theories and other schemes ranking non-European peoples and cultures as inferior were biased, ill informed, and unscientific. Throughout his long and illustrious academic career, he promoted anthropology not only as a human science but also as an instrument to combat racism and prejudice in the world.

Among the founders of North American anthropology were a number of women, including **Matilda Coxe Stevenson**, who did fieldwork among the Zuni Indians of Arizona. In 1885, she founded the Women's Anthropological Society in Washington, DC, the first professional association for women scientists. Three years later, hired by the Smithsonian's Bureau of American Ethnology, she became one of the first women in the world to receive a full-time official position in science. Along with several other pioneering female anthropologists in North America, she was highly influential among women's rights advocates in the late 1800s. The tradition of women building careers in anthropology continues. In fact, since World War II more than half the presidents of the now 12,000-member American Anthropological Association have been women.

Matilda Coxe Stevenson in New Mexico, about 1900.

Recording observations on film as well as in notebooks, Stevenson and Boas were also pioneers in visual anthropology. Stevenson used an early box camera to document Pueblo Indian religious ceremonies and material culture, while Boas photographed Inuit and Kwakiutl Indians from the early 1890s for cultural as well as physical anthropological documentation. Today, their early photographs are greatly valued not only by anthropologists and historians, but also by indigenous peoples themselves.

childhood in the "old country" (Europe) to the increased heights reached by their children who grew up in the United States. Today, physical anthropologists study the impact of poverty, pollution, and disease on growth. Comparisons between human and nonhuman-primate growth patterns can provide clues to the evolutionary history of humans. Detailed anthropological studies of the hormonal, genetic, and physiological bases of healthy growth in living humans also contribute significantly to the health of children today.

Studies of human adaptation focus on the capacity of humans to adapt or adjust to their material environment—biologically and culturally. This branch of physical anthropology takes a comparative approach to humans living today in a variety of environments. Human beings are the only primates to inhabit the entire earth. Although biological adaptations make it possible for people to live in environmentally extreme regions, cultural adaptations also contribute to our survival in places that are dangerously cold, hot, or of high altitude.

Some of these biological adaptations are built into the genetic makeup of populations. The long period of human growth and development provides ample opportunity for the environment to shape the human body. *Developmental adaptations* are responsible for some features of human variation, such as the enlargement of the right ventricle of the heart to help push blood to the lungs among the Aymara Indians of the Bolivian altiplano—an extensive area of high plateau at the widest part of the Andes. *Physiological adaptations* are short-term changes in response to a particular environmental stimulus. For example, if a woman who normally lives at sea level flies to La Paz, a large Bolivian city in the altiplano at an altitude of 3,660 meters (nearly 12,000 feet), her body will undergo a series of physiological responses, such as increased production of the red blood cells that carry oxygen. These kinds of biological adaptation contribute to present-day human variation.

Genetically based human differences include visible traits such as height, body build, and skin color, as well as biochemical factors such as blood type and susceptibility to certain diseases. Still, we remain members of a single

ANTHROPOLOGY APPLIED

Forensic Anthropology: Voices for the Dead

The work of Clyde C. Snow, Michael Blakey, and Amy Zelson Mundorff

Forensic anthropology is the analysis of skeletal remains for legal purposes. Law enforcement authorities call upon forensic anthropologists to use skeletal remains to identify murder victims, missing persons, or people who have died in disasters, such as plane crashes. Forensic anthropologists have also contributed substantially to the investigation of human rights abuses in all parts of the world by identifying victims and documenting the cause of their death.

Among the best-known forensic anthropologists is Clyde C. Snow. He has been practicing in this field for over forty years, first for the Federal Aviation Administration and more recently as a freelance consultant. In addition to the usual police work, Snow has studied the remains of General George Armstrong Custer and his men from the 1876 battle at Little Big Horn, and in 1985 he went to Brazil, where he identified the remains of the notorious Nazi war criminal Josef Mengele.

Snow was also instrumental in establishing the first forensic team devoted to documenting cases of human rights abuses around the world. This began in 1984 when he went to Argentina at the request of a newly elected civilian government to help with the identification of remains of the *desaparecidos*, or "disappeared ones," the 9,000 or more people who were eliminated by death squads during seven years of military rule. A year later, he returned to give expert testimony at the trial of nine junta members and to teach Argentineans how to recover, clean, repair, preserve, photograph, x-ray, and analyze bones. Besides providing factual accounts of the fate of victims to their surviving kin and refuting the assertions of revisionists that the massacres never happened, the work of Snow and his Argentinean associates was crucial in convicting several military officers of kidnapping, torture, and murder.

Since Snow's pioneering work, forensic anthropologists have become increasingly involved in the investigation of human rights abuses in all parts of the world, from Chile to Guatemala, Haiti, the Philippines, Rwanda, Iraq, Bosnia, and Kosovo. Meanwhile, they continue to do important work for more typical clients. In the United States these clients include the Federal Bureau of Investigation and city, state, and county medical examiners' offices.

Forensic anthropologists specializing in skeletal remains commonly work closely with forensic archaeologists. The relation between them is rather like that between a forensic pathologist, who examines a corpse to establish time and manner of death, and a crime scene investigator, who searches the site for clues. While the forensic anthropologist deals with the human remains—often only bones and teeth—the forensic archaeologist controls the site, recording the position of relevant finds and recovering any clues associated with the remains.

In Rwanda, for example, a team assembled in 1995 to investigate mass murder (genocide) for the United Nations, which included archaeologists from the U.S. National Park Service's Midwest Archaeological Center. They performed the standard archaeological procedures of mapping the site, determining its boundaries, photographing and recording all surface finds, and excavating, photographing, and recording buried skeletons and associated materials in mass graves.[a]

In 1991, in another part of the world, construction workers in New York City discovered an African burial ground from the 17th and 18th centuries.

species. Physical anthropology applies all the techniques of modern biology to achieve fuller understanding of human variation and its relationship to the different environments in which people have lived. Physical anthropologists' research on human variation has debunked false notions of biologically defined races, a belief based on widespread misinterpretation of human variation.

Forensic Anthropology

One of the many practical applications of physical anthropology is **forensic anthropology**—the identification of human skeletal remains for legal purposes. In addition to helping law enforcement authorities identify murder victims, forensic anthropologists investigate human rights abuses such as systematic genocide, terrorism, and war

crimes. These specialists use details of skeletal anatomy to establish the age, sex, population affiliation, and stature of the deceased. Forensic anthropologists can also determine whether the person was right- or left-handed, exhibited any physical abnormalities, or had experienced trauma.

While forensics relies upon differing frequencies of certain skeletal characteristics to establish population affiliation, it is nevertheless false to say that all people from a given population have a particular type of skeleton. (See the Anthropology Applied feature to read about the work of several forensic anthropologists and forensic archaeologists.)

forensic anthropology The identification of human skeletal remains for legal purposes.

AP Images/Rodrigo Abd

The excavation of mass graves by the Guatemalan Foundation for Forensic Anthropology (Fernando Moscoso Moller, director) documents the human rights abuses committed during Guatemala's bloody civil war, a conflict that left 200,000 people dead and another 40,000 missing. In 2009, in a mass grave in the Quiche region, Diego Lux Tzunux uses his cell phone to photograph the skeletal remains believed to belong to his brother Manuel who disappeared in 1980. Genetic analyses allow forensic anthropologists to confirm the identity of individuals so that family members can know the fate of their loved ones. The analysis of skeletal remains provides evidence of the torture and massacre sustained by these individuals.

Ground Project provided incontrovertible evidence of the horror of slavery in North America, in the busy northern port of New York City. The more than 400 individuals, many of them children, were worked so far beyond their ability to endure that their spines were fractured.

A decade after construction workers happened upon the African Burial Ground, terrorists attacked the World Trade Center in lower Manhattan. Amy Zelson Mundorff, a forensic anthropologist for New York City's Office of the Chief Medical Examiner, was injured in the September 11 attack. But two days later she returned to work where she supervised and coordinated the management, treatment, and cataloguing of people who lost their lives in the tragedy.

Thus, several kinds of anthropologists analyze human remains for a variety of purposes. Their work contributes to the documentation and correction of violence committed by humans of the past and present.

Researchers used a bioarchaeological rather than a strictly forensic approach to examine the complete cultural and historical context and lifeways of the entire population buried there. Directed by Michael Blakey, the African Burial

[a]Haglund, W. D., Conner, M., & Scott, D. D. (2001). The archaeology of contemporary mass graves. *Historical Archaeology 35* (1), 57–69.

Anthropology, Science, and the Humanities

Anthropology has sometimes been called the most humane of the sciences and the most scientific of the humanities—a designation that most anthropologists accept with pride. Given their intense involvement with people of all times and places, anthropologists have amassed considerable information about human failure and success, weakness and greatness—the real stuff of the humanities.

Anthropologists remain committed to the proposition that one cannot fully understand another culture by simply observing it; as the term *participant observation* implies, one must *experience* it as well. This same commitment to fieldwork and to the systematic collection of data, whether qualitative or quantitative, is also evidence of the scientific side of anthropology. Anthropology is an **empirical** social science based on observations or information taken in through the senses and verified by others rather than on intuition or faith. But anthropology is distinguished from other sciences by the diverse ways in which scientific research is conducted within the discipline.

Science, a carefully honed way of producing knowledge, aims to reveal and explain the underlying logic, the structural processes that make the world tick. The creative scientific endeavor seeks testable explanations for observed phenomena, ideally in terms of the workings of hidden but unchanging principles or laws. Two basic ingredients are essential for this: imagination and skepticism. Imagination, though having the potential to lead us astray, helps us recognize unexpected ways phenomena might be ordered and to think of old things in new ways. Without it, there can be no science. Skepticism allows us to distinguish fact (an observation verified by others) from fancy, to test our speculations, and to prevent our imaginations from running away with us.

In their search for explanations, scientists do not assume that things are always as they appear on the surface. After all, what could be more obvious to the scientifically uninformed observer than the earth staying still while the sun travels around it every day?

Like other scientists, anthropologists often begin their research with a **hypothesis** (a tentative explanation or hunch) about the possible relationships between certain observed facts or events. By gathering various kinds of data that seem to ground such suggested explanations on evidence, anthropologists come up with a **theory**, a coherent statement that provides an explanatory framework for understanding; an explanation or interpretation supported by a reliable body of data. In their effort to demonstrate links between *known* facts or events, anthropologists may discover *unexpected* facts, events, or relationships. An important function of theory is that it guides us in our explorations and may result in new knowledge. Equally important, the newly discovered facts may provide evidence that certain explanations, however popular or firmly believed, are unfounded. When the evidence is lacking or fails to support the suggested explanations, promising hypotheses or attractive hunches must be dropped. In other words, anthropology relies on empirical evidence. Moreover, no scientific theory—no matter how widely accepted by the international community of scholars—is beyond challenge. That includes the findings of some of anthropology's earliest and most respected scholars.

It is important to distinguish between scientific theories—which are always open to challenges born of new evidence or insights—and doctrine. A **doctrine**, or dogma, is an assertion of opinion or belief formally handed down by an authority as true and indisputable. For instance, those who accept a creationist doctrine on the origin of the human species as recounted in sacred texts or myths do so on the basis of religious authority, conceding that such views may be contrary to genetic, geological, biological, or other explanations. Such doctrines cannot be tested or proved one way or another: They are accepted as matters of faith.

Straightforward as the scientific approach may seem, its application is not always easy. For instance, once a hypothesis has been proposed, the person who suggested it is strongly motivated to verify it, and this can cause one to unwittingly overlook negative evidence and unanticipated findings. This is a familiar problem in all science as noted by paleontologist Stephen Jay Gould: "The greatest impediment to scientific innovation is usually a conceptual lock, not a factual lock" (Gould, 1989, p. 226). Because culture provides humans with concepts and shapes our very thoughts, it can be challenging to frame hypotheses or to develop interpretations that are not culture-bound. However, by encompassing both humanism and science, the discipline of anthropology can draw on its internal diversity to overcome conceptual locks.

empirical An approach based on observations of the world rather than on intuition or faith.

hypothesis A tentative explanation of the relationships among certain phenomena.

theory A coherent statement that provides an explanatory framework for understanding; an explanation or interpretation supported by a reliable body of data.

doctrine An assertion of opinion or belief formally handed down by an authority as true and indisputable.

culture shock In fieldwork, the anthropologist's personal disorientation and anxiety that may result in depression.

CULTURE
AND MEANING

© iStockphoto/Thinkstock

As noted in the epigraph from Rupert Ross, it is nearly impossible to accurately interpret people's acts when we do not understand the meanings they attribute to those acts. Egyptian hieroglyphics provide an apt metaphor for potential pitfalls of misinterpretation. What do you see when you look at this hieroglyph? How do you make sense of it? Unless you are well versed in Egyptian myth and history, it is likely that your interpretation says more about your own cultural context than that of the ancient Egyptians. Understanding human beliefs and behaviours requires a similar attention to meaning in context.

Acts are never merely acts. They are also signals of attitude. Those signals, however, are often culture specific. When acts are seen, but their signal-content misinterpreted, it is impossible to avoid forming inaccurate interpretations of others. Until we understand what particular acts mean to the other, we will continually ascribe motivations and states of mind that are well off the mark.

Rupert Ross, Dancing with a Ghost

PROBLEM 1

How can people begin to understand beliefs and behaviours that are different from their own?

INTRODUCTION

The World Behind Everyday Appearances

In **sociocultural anthropology** we strive to look beyond the world of everyday experiences to discover the patterns and meanings that lie behind that world. Take, for example, the typical classroom chair with attached desk.

In our taken-for-granted, everyday world, this piece of furniture is a utilitarian object: something to sit on, or to write on, or even to put our feet on. But for the sociocultural anthropologist, the classroom chair tells some interesting tales and poses some interesting questions. For example, why do we have chairs at all? Many societies don't; instead, people sit or squat on the ground or the floor or sit on stools or benches. Historically, the chair likely first appeared in Europe or the Near East, but it wasn't common even in Europe until the 18th century. Another question: Why does the classroom chair take the form it does? Why don't we sit on stools? One feature of the chair that anthropologists might explore as they try to decipher the meaning of the classroom chair and desk is the erect position into which it forces the body, compelling it, in effect, to "pay attention." We might take a clue from the French philosopher Michel Foucault, who refers to the shaping of the human body as a "political anatomy." By this, he means that people's bodies are controlled by others to operate with the necessary speed and efficiency. Political anatomy produces, he says, "docile bodies."

> **sociocultural anthropology**
> An anthropological approach that retains the British focus on social anthropology at the same time as it adds the American focus on culture to produce something slightly different from either one.

Sociocultural anthropologists find patterns of meaning even in objects as simple as a classroom chair.

© Ursula Alter/iStockphoto

An anthropologist might suggest that the classroom chair and desk are part of the political anatomy of educational settings—part of the system of relations that gives meaning to the classroom. In other words, this piece of furniture forms the body into a shape that prepares it (or forces it) to attend to a teacher and not to others in the same room. Moreover, it is appropriate to its unique setting in the classroom, as are other objects of furniture. Imagine, for example, replacing classroom chairs with bar stools, whose main purpose is to promote bodily mobility and conversation with others.

Once alert to the idea that the classroom chair might serve as an instrument of control, we might notice other ways in which classroom design serves as a mode of discipline. The distribution of people in space, with each person in a particular "spot" in neat, ordered rows, serves to discipline people to "pay attention" to the classroom centre and not to others around them. We might also notice the distinctive ordering of time and the use of clocks, bells, and whistles to control the movement and activities of people in school settings. We can even take our analysis a step further and examine the discipline of the school setting sequentially, from kindergarten through high school. Contrast, for example, the wide-open space of the kindergarten classroom,

with its open, movable chairs and tables and teacher's desk set off to the side, with the enclosed, partitioned space of a second- or third-grade classroom, with its neatly arranged desks facing the centred desk of the teacher. This is the evolution of classroom discipline.

Students, of course, do not always obey the subtle commands that direct their bodies to do certain things at certain times. One only has to examine the strange bodily contortions of students as they resist the form into which the classroom chair tries to force them. We also try, occasionally, to resist the isolation imposed by the arrangement of classroom furniture or the timetables set by clocks, bells, and whistles.

The ways in which specific societies order behaviour through the arrangement of space and time is but one small area examined by sociocultural anthropology, but it serves as an example of how, from an anthropological perspective, we cannot take anything about even our own beliefs and behaviour for granted, let alone the behaviour and beliefs of those whose backgrounds and histories differ from our own.

This book is about how sociocultural anthropology can help us see beyond our taken-for-granted world. We will be examining how sociocultural anthropology helps us understand others and, in the process, better understand ourselves. We will also be examining how knowledge of others and ourselves is relevant to careers in social and economic development, public policy and planning, education, medicine, and conflict resolution.

What Makes Sociocultural Anthropology Unique?

The term "anthropology" comes from two Greek words: *anthropos*, meaning "human beings," and *logia*, meaning "the study of" or "the knowledge of." This study of, or knowledge of, human beings includes everything that humans do currently or have done in the past. It also includes collecting evidence of how and when we became human and comparing humans to other organisms in the world. If asked to describe a typical anthropologist, you might envision an intrepid explorer, like Indiana Jones, searching for priceless artifacts or painstakingly excavating ancient fossils. But it would be more realistic to imagine a sociocultural anthropologist equipped with a notebook and a voice recorder rather than a shovel or a trowel. The kind of knowledge about human beings that sociocultural anthropologists are interested in is acquired by spending time with people, talking to them, observing what they do, and trying to understand their lives—as anthropologist Bronislaw Malinowski aptly put it—"from the native's point of view" (see section 1.2).

In North America, anthropology is divided into four different approaches to the study of humans. Although these four subdisciplines address some of the same questions about what it means to be human, they focus on different aspects of the anthropological question (hence the differences among the tools—notebooks versus shovels—used by different kinds of anthropologists). The subdisciplines are biological anthropology, archaeology, linguistic anthropology, and sociocultural anthropology (known as cultural anthropology in the United States and social anthropology in Britain). To understand what makes sociocultural anthropology unique among the subdisciplines (and among the social sciences in general), it is important first to understand the points of convergence and divergence among these subdisciplines.

Biological anthropology, the oldest of the four subdisciplines, focuses on human beings as one of a great multitude of organisms that inhabit the earth. Some biological anthropologists specialize in paleoanthropology, which is the study of fossil remains of the earliest humans, and attempt to understand the history of human biological evolution. Other biological anthropologists specialize in primatology, or the study of our closest nonhuman relatives. The newest branch of biological anthropology is forensic anthropology, which is the study of human remains for identification and cause of death.

Archaeology is the branch of anthropology that studies human history and its artifacts. Archaeologists typically look at the material remains of human groups in order to learn how people lived.

Tools, pottery shards, and other artifacts offer clues about the social and cultural lives of societies that existed thousands of years ago.

Linguistic anthropologists examine the relationship between language and culture. They are interested in how people use language, both in a physical sense with regard to how communication is structured, and in a historical sense with regard to how different languages have developed and spread throughout history.

Finally—and most importantly for our purposes in this text—*sociocultural anthropologists* look at how societies are structured and how cultural meanings are created. Although these anthropologists are interested in differences among peoples throughout the world, they also look for similarities in how people construct their own versions of what it means to be human. Sociocultural anthropologists, then, explore both the universal and the particular, moving back and forth between these two levels of inquiry and analysis in their work. They do fieldwork (see section 1.2) among the societies and cultures they study, gathering data by talking to people and by participating in and observing their day-to-day lives.

This focus on social structures and cutural meanings, in all their forms, is what makes sociocultural anthropology unique among the sudisciplines. Many people—including some anthropologists themselves—wonder whether sociocultural anthropology should be characterized as a science or as one of the humanities. At its best, sociocultural anthropology incorporates aspects of both: the methodological and analytical rigour of the sciences, and the interpretive insights and nuances of the humanities. Eminent anthropologist Eric Wolf (1964, 88) perhaps put it best when he described anthropology as "the most scientific of the humanities, [and] the most humanistic of the sciences." This combination of versatility and breadth is precisely what makes anthropology such an interesting and dynamic discipline.

Moreover, the unique perspective on humanity provided by sociocultural anthropology is well suited to thinking about the complexity of the contemporary world and the human condition. This book is organized around eight general problems that arise from the human condition—problems such as how to understand people with different beliefs and behaviours; why ways of life change; how people justify violence; and whether it is possible to solve problems of social inequality. These problems concern everyone, not just sociocultural anthropologists, but definitive solutions are not possible. So the goal, instead, is to achieve a greater understanding of why those problems exist and what might be done to address them. Sociocultural anthropologists can ask specific questions concerning them, applying their unique disciplinary perspective and methodologies. We will be focusing on these eight general problems in this text. At various points you will be asked to supply your own answers to questions and, perhaps, to discuss your answers with others.

Understanding others requires you to recognize that your behaviours and beliefs, as well as those of people in other societies, are socially patterned and constructed. For that reason, you will find in this text many comparisons between North American life and life in other societies. Whether or not you pursue a career in anthropology, or a career that explicitly requires anthropological expertise, learning to approach and understand human beliefs and behaviour from an anthropological perspective is a valuable skill in the contemporary world.

QUESTIONS

1.1 Why do human beings differ in their beliefs and behaviours?

1.2 How do anthropologists learn about culture?

1.3 Is it possible to see the world through the eyes of others?

1.4 How can the meanings that others find in experience be interpreted and described?

1.5 What can learning about other peoples tell anthropologists about their own societies?

1.6 How can an anthropological perspective be used outside of academia?

QUESTION 1.1: WHY DO HUMAN BEINGS DIFFER IN THEIR BELIEFS AND BEHAVIOURS?

From an anthropological perspective, members of a society view the world in a similar way because they share the same **culture**; people differ in how they view the world because their cultures differ. What do anthropologists mean by culture? A good place to start to understand the concept of culture is with the fact that members of all human societies experience specific life events such as birth, death, and the quest for food, water, and shelter. All societies have what are for them appropriate rules for courtship, ideas about child rearing, procedures for exchanging goods, methods of food production, techniques for building shelters, and so on. But from one society to the next, the meanings people assign these events differ. We learn these meanings from, and teach these meanings to, other members of our culture. Our working definition of culture, therefore, is as follows: "culture is the system of meanings about the nature of experience that is shared by a people and passed from one generation to another." This definition encompasses the meanings that people give to things, events, activities, and people. As we will see in section 1.2, throughout the history of the discipline, anthropologists have debated—and often disagreed about—the substance of culture and the best ways to study it. Our working definition of culture highlights those aspects of this complicated and contentious term upon which most anthropologists *can* agree: culture is about meaning; cultural meanings must be learned; and, once learned, meanings are shared by members of a particular

culture
The system of meanings about the nature of experience that are shared by a people and passed on from one generation to another, including the meanings that people give to things, events, activities, and people.

culture. Culture enables human beings to make sense of their life experiences and to understand those experiences as meaningful in particular ways. All human beings share certain basic experiences: hunger, sex, and death, for example. Why, though, do people from different backgrounds understand these experiences in different ways? Thinking about culture begins to suggest an answer to this question.

Attitudes toward death provide one example. For some people, death marks the passage of a person from one world to another. For others, death is an ending, the final event in a life span; and still others view death as part of a never-ending cycle of birth, death, and rebirth. The Kwakwaka'wakw of British Columbia, for example, believe that when a person dies, the soul leaves the body and enters the body of a salmon. When a salmon is caught and eaten, a soul is released and is free to enter the body of another person.

Some societies fear the dead; others revere them. In rural China until recently, each household contained a shrine to the family ancestors. Before any major family decision, the head of the household addressed the shrine to ask the ancestors' advice, thus making the dead part of the world of the living. In southern Italy, by contrast, funeral customs were designed to *discourage* the dead from returning. Relatives placed useful objects such as matches and small change near the body to placate the soul of the deceased and to ensure that it did not return to disturb the living.

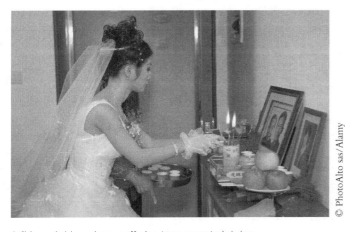

A Chinese bride makes an offering to an ancestral shrine.

© PhotoAlto sas/Alamy

In some societies, death is accepted as natural and inevitable; in others, death is always attributed to the malevolent act of some person, often involving sorcery. In these societies, every death elicits suspicion and a demand for vengeance. Still other societies require great demonstrations of grief and mourning for the deceased. Thus, the Dani of New Guinea require a close female relative of a recently deceased person to sacrifice part of a finger. When the Wari' in of western Brazil still lived independent of Western civilization, they disposed of the bodies of their dead by eating the roasted flesh, certain internal organs, and sometimes the ground bones. They ate the dead not because they needed the meat or because they liked the taste of human flesh, but rather out of a respect and compassion for the dead person and the dead person's family (we will explore this example in section 1.3). In southern Europe, widows were required to shave their heads; at one time in India, widows were cremated alive at their husbands' funerals, a practice known as *sati*. In most North American societies, survivors of the deceased are expected to restrain their grief almost as if it were a contagious disease. To many North Americans, the sight of southern Italian women pulling their hair and being restrained from flinging themselves into an open grave is as bewildering as their own restraint of grief would be to southern Italians.

Food provides another telling example of how a culture takes the "raw materials" of human life and makes them meaningful. All humans need to eat; however, no society accepts all items in their edible universe as "good to eat." Only a relatively few items are so designated. Insects such as grubs, beetles, and ants are acceptable fare in some societies, while people in others are horrified by the thought of eating insects. North Americans generally do not define insects as food (although U.S. federal regulations do allow a certain percentage of insect matter to be included in processed food). Most North Americans like and are encouraged to drink milk, yet some people in China consider milk undrinkable. Conversely, the Chinese raise dogs for meat—something that would horrify most

North Americans. North American children who have raised pet guinea pigs would have a hard time accepting the Peruvian practice of raising guinea pigs for food. Of all the two million or so species of living organisms that inhabit the earth, only humans dwell largely in worlds that they themselves have created by giving meanings to things. This creation is what anthropologists mean by the term "culture." Human beings are cultural animals; they ascribe meanings of their own creation to objects, persons, behaviours, emotions, and events and then proceed to act as if those meanings are real. All facets of their lives—death, birth, courtship, mating, food acquisition and consumption—are suffused with meaning.

Clifford Geertz suggests that human beings are compelled to impose meaning on their experiences because without those meanings to help them comprehend experience and impose an order on the universe, the world would seem a jumble, "a chaos of pointless acts and exploding emotions" (1973, 46). Geertz writes that human beings are "incomplete or unfinished animals who complete themselves through culture—not culture in general, but specific forms of it": Balinese, Italian, Ilongot, Chinese, Kwakiutl, Canadian, and so on (1976, 49). When people share the meanings they give to experiences, they share and participate in the same culture.

Differences in culture arise in part from the fact that different groups of human beings, for various reasons, create, share, and participate in different realities; as a consequence, they assign different meanings to death, birth, marriage, and food. Objects, persons, behaviours, emotions, and events in a human world have meanings ascribed to them by those who share, use, or experience them. The clothes people wear, the foods they eat (or refuse to eat), even their gender, are defined through the meanings that people give them. Understanding culture, and the culturally situated meanings that flourish in various cultural contexts, is therefore the main object of anthropological study. In the next section, we will explore how anthropologists have approached the study of culture and how unique research methods have emerged as the discipline of anthropology has developed.

EXERCISE 1.1

Mere edibility is not enough to determine what counts as food. Food is a cultural creation; that is, human beings define what is and what is not food. Consider, for example, the items listed below, all of which serve as food among one group of people or another. Which of these would you eat, and which would you not eat? If there are any you would not eat, explain why.

	Yes	No
eel		
kangaroo tail		
dog		
guinea pig		
raw squid		
sea urchin (sea slugs)		
ants		
monkey brains		
grubs		
opossum		
rattlesnake		
iguana		
horse		
dolphin		
pickled pig's feet		
haggis (stuffed intestines)		
cow brains		
blood sausage		
raw steak		
rotten meat		
armadillo		

QUESTION 1.2: HOW DO ANTHROPOLOGISTS LEARN ABOUT CULTURE?

The Formative Years of Anthropology

Anthropology began at a particular time in history: "the Age of Exploration," which was launched by Christopher Columbus when he arrived in the Americas in 1492 and which lasted until the early 17th century. It was during these centuries that Europeans first encountered people who looked and behaved very differently (Barrett 1996, 3). Travellers and explorers returned home with stories about the seemingly "strange" people they had met in faraway places, sometimes bringing back live native "specimens" as well. Those at home debated at length whether these beings were actually human. European countries established colonies throughout the world, often sending missionaries along to "civilize" the strange people; those missionaries then documented their encounters. One of the most famous of these accounts is the *Jesuit Relations*, first published in 1632, which describes the interactions between the Jesuit missionaries and the indigenous peoples in southern Ontario. These missionaries' writings were a type of proto-anthropology, though it must be added that missionaries and anthropologists today have very different motivations for the work they do.

Notwithstanding these early cross-cultural interactions, anthropology did not emerge as a formal discipline until 1883, when Edward Tylor was appointed to the first position of anthropology in Britain. Decades later, in 1925, Thomas F. McIlwraith became the first anthropology appointment at the University of Toronto. Canada's first Department of Anthropology was founded at the same university in 1936.

In the late 1800s, as anthropology grew in popularity throughout Europe and North America, many early anthropologists like Tylor were **armchair anthropologists**. That is, instead of visiting various peoples and conducting their own first-hand research, they stayed at home and amassed diaries, reports, and various documents written by others who had come in contact with various non-Western peoples. Sitting in their "armchairs," or perhaps at their university office desks, these anthropologists applied a comparative method to explore differences and similarities in social institutions and belief systems in a variety of societies. Based on their comparisons, armchair anthropologists would attempt to make cross-cultural generalizations about such things as warfare, family structures and marriage, religion, and other phenomena.

Tylor relied on the accounts provided by travellers and missionaries as sources of information for his book, *Primitive Culture*. But he did so uncritically—that is, he did not acknowledge the inherent biases in their writings, instead taking their work at face value (as did many other armchair anthropologists of his day). It is worth noting the ways in which Tylor's own 1871 definition of culture reflected the methodological approach that he shared with his fellow armchair anthropologists. According to Tylor, "culture or civilization, taken in its wide [comparative] ethnographic sense, is that complex whole which includes knowledge, belief, art, morals, law, custom, and any other capabilities and habits acquired by man as a member of his society" (1871, 1). As in our working definition of culture outlined in section 1.1, Tylor's definition emphasized the shared and learned aspects of culture. However, he and other Victorian anthropologists wrote about culture in the singular, believing that some peoples or cultural groups might have more or less culture or civilization than others. In this sense, both their methodology and their understanding of culture were not merely comparative, but hierarchical as well. Contemporary anthropologists remain interested in the differences and similarities between cultures, but they no longer resort to hierarchies when comparing human beliefs and behaviours.

> **armchair anthropologist**
> Refers to an approach to the study of various societies that dominated anthropology in the late 1800s. It involved the collection, study, and analysis of the writings of missionaries, explorers, and colonists who had sustained contact with non-Western peoples. Armchair anthropologists used these documents to make comparisons and generalizations about the ways of life of various groups.

CULTURE AND MEANING   9

Ethnographic Fieldwork

Anthropologists such as Bronislaw Malinowski and Franz Boas (often regarded as the "fathers" of social and cultural anthropology, respectively) would soon move beyond the armchair anthropology of Tylor and his contemporaries. In the United States, Boas sought firsthand knowledge among the Inuit and the Kwakwaka'wakw. After Malinowski went to live in the Trobriand Islands during the First World War, extended periods of fieldwork became the required methodology of sociocultural anthropology.

Anthropologists, like other social scientists, use surveys, written documents, historical accounts, and questionnaires as part of their research toolbox. But the unique feature of sociocultural anthropology is the **ethnographic method**—investigators immerse themselves in the lives of the people they are trying to understand and thereby attain some level of understanding of the meanings those people ascribe to their existence. This immersion process entails **participant observation**, defined as the active participation of observers in the lives of their subjects.

The ethnographic method is only part of the anthropological enterprise. The anthropologist also seeks to explain why people view the world as they do and to contribute to the understanding of human behaviour in general. But this enterprise begins with fieldwork, which involves the meeting of at least two cultures: that of the researcher, and that of the people the researcher is trying to understand. Anthropological researchers must set aside their own views of things and attempt to see the world in a new way. In many respects, they must assume the demeanour and status of children who must be taught by their elders the proper view of the world.

Bronislaw Malinowski (1884–1942), Polish-born and British-trained, was one of the first anthropologists to abandon the armchair approach. He would revolutionize anthropology by stressing the primacy of **fieldwork**. In Malinowski's time, fieldwork usually involved conducting first-hand, long-term, qualitative research with a group of people. This meant that anthropologists had to get out of their armchairs and travel to live among non-Western (usually indigenous) peoples. Having arrived at their research site, they would spend at least a year carrying out fieldwork—conducting interviews and surveys, taking photographs, and recording songs and oral narratives, among other things. In 1915, Malinowski arrived in the Trobriand Islands as the guest of British colonial officials. Soon after his arrival, he concluded that it would be necessary to spend each day with the Trobrianders if he hoped to obtain a comprehensive understanding of their daily lives. So he left the comfort of his colonial household, acquired a

Bronislaw Malinowski in the Trobriand Islands. Malinowski was one of the first anthropologists to conduct long-term fieldwork.

ethnographic method
The immersion of researchers in the lives and cultures of the peoples they are trying to understand in order to comprehend the meanings these people ascribe to their existence.

participant observation
An element of fieldwork that can involve participating in daily tasks, and observing daily interactions among a particular group.

fieldwork
Anthropologists engage in long-term interactions (usually a year or more) with various groups of people. This often involves living with people, observing and contributing to daily chores and tasks (participant observation), and conducting interviews. Most fieldwork in anthropology has historically been qualitative in nature.

tent, and set up camp in a nearby Trobriand village. By living with Trobrianders, observing and participating in their daily tasks, and learning their language, he established the importance of participant observation as a fieldwork strategy.

Participant observation requires long-term engagement with a group of people and their daily lives. This may involve living with them as well as observing and participating in daily tasks, no matter how mundane. This fieldwork technique would become a defining feature of contemporary anthropological fieldwork. Even today, anthropologists regularly observe and participate in such things as gardening, harvesting, cooking, recreation, and various rituals and ceremonies.

Malinowski took detailed field notes by hand during his interactions with Trobriand Islanders. In the evenings, he typed up his notes. Later, he would transform these into an **ethnography**, defined as a written description and analysis of an anthropologist's experiences and interactions with a group of people. In essence, the ethnography is the end product of a fieldwork experience.

Malinowski felt that by carefully documenting their experiences and observations with field notes, and combining this with participant observation and other qualitative fieldwork techniques, anthropologists would be able to obtain "the native's point of view" (Malinowski 1961, 25). This approach, also referred to as the "emic" or "insider" perspective, implies that the goal of anthropology is to understand people's beliefs and culture *from their own perspective*. Until Malinowski's time, armchair anthropologists had tended to privilege "etic" or "outsider" explanations for human behaviour. The categories of "insider versus outsider" have been challenged in recent years as a result of globalization's destabilizing impact on unitary identities such as "insider" and "outsider" (see, for example, Narayan 1993). This does not at all detract from Malinowski's contribution, for he was instrumental in establishing the importance of long-term fieldwork for understanding various cultures, and in challenging the cultural generalizations that the

comparative, armchair approach tended to produce. The differences between Edward Tylor's definition of culture and Malinowski's reflect the differences between armchair anthropology and ethnographic fieldwork. Malinowski was less interested in hierarchical comparisons than in understanding each culture on its own terms. His view was that cultures arise in order to meet the particular needs of specific peoples. Culture, in this sense, can be understood as plural. For Malinowski, culture was

the integral whole consisting of implements and consumers' goods, of constitutional charters for the various social groupings, of human ideas and crafts, beliefs, and customs. Whether we consider a very simple or primitive culture or an extremely complex and developed one, we are confronted by a vast apparatus, partly material, partly human, and partly spiritual, by which man is able to cope with the concrete, specific problems that face him. (1944, 36)

Changing Notions of Fieldwork

Malinowski's insistence on long-term fieldwork and participant observation would have lasting effects on the discipline. These days, PhD students in anthropology are still required to spend at least a year in the field, and they often incorporate participant observation as a fieldwork technique. However, fieldwork has also changed over the last century, and many of Malinowski's original ideas about fieldwork have been challenged.

In the late 19th century, anthropology was about the study of non-Western peoples and places. Most anthropologists were upper-class, educated, white men from Europe, Australia, Canada, and the United States. From their perspective, indigenous peoples were the most

ethnography
A written description and analysis of a particular group of people, usually based upon anthropological fieldwork.

appropriate subjects of study. In a somewhat paternalistic way, these early anthropologists viewed indigenous peoples as groups in need of "rescue." Thus, a great deal of early-20th-century anthropology in North America was an outgrowth of salvage anthropology—an idea espoused by Franz Boas, among others, who felt that indigenous peoples throughout the world were undergoing rapid assimilation and would eventually disappear. He thus felt that anthropologists had an obligation to document and collect the various traditions and cultures of these groups. Boas and his students began documenting Inuit and Northwest Coast indigenous cultures so to "preserve" them before they disappeared (which they never did). Museums at the time took on the same task. Indeed, museums became integral to this culture of collecting and would play a prominent role in the development of Canadian anthropology. In 1911, the Anthropology Division of the Geological Survey of Canada was established, with Edward Sapir, Marius Barbeau, and Diamond Jenness on its staff. In the 1920s, this unit became part of the National Museum of Canada, since renamed the Museum of Civilization (Ervin 2001, 15).

Regna Darnell, an anthropologist at the University of Western Ontario who has conducted extensive research on the history of Canadian anthropology, contends that although there are no features of Canadian anthropology that set it apart as utterly unique, "the national discipline combines features of disciplinary organization and historical context in patterns that *are* unique" (1998, 155). It is difficult to define exactly what is "Canadian" about Canadian anthropology,

but Darnell has an interesting suggestion: "In Canada, a critical mass of First Nations languages and cultures maintains them with a saliency in the national forum unparalleled in the United States" (2000, 170). Many Canadian anthropologists focus on First Nations peoples, but they also conduct research in Latin America, the Caribbean, Asia, Africa, Europe (Eastern and Western), New Zealand, Australia, Melanesia, Polynesia, and the Middle East. Throughout this book, we will be looking at the work of many Canadian anthropologists as well as that of anthropologists in other places in the world.

Many anthropologists continue to focus on indigenous groups. However, ideas about appropriate "field sites" and subjects of study have changed since the days of Malinowski and Boas. Anthropologists no longer restrict themselves to the study of non-Western peoples and places. These days we are just as likely to see anthropologists studying aspects of their own culture. This shift in thinking has had consequences for how anthropologists conduct their fieldwork. The field "site" is not necessarily a faraway place. Today, anthropologists might study office culture in Vancouver, homelessness in Toronto, or separatist ideologies in Quebec. As such, they do not necessarily travel long distances for fieldwork, and many no longer live among their informants for extended lengths of time.

Globalization (which we discuss in more detail in Chapter 7) also has transformed how anthropologists perceive and study societies. Television, the Internet, and other media technologies have transformed the ways we form and maintain social relationships. Today we are creating a sense of community not only through face-to-face interactions but also through Internet sites, chat rooms, online games, Skype, and Facebook, among others. Given that our contemporary interactions are mediated by technology, we increasingly see anthropologists conducting fieldwork online as well as face to face. For example, Tom Boellstorff's ethnography, *Coming of Age in Second Life* (2008), documents his research on the three-dimensional, online gaming

---

salvage anthropology

An approach to anthropology that arose in the late 1800s when anthropologists witnessed the extinction and/or assimilation of indigenous groups throughout the world. In response, some anthropologists, such as Franz Boas, suggested that anthropologists rapidly document the oral stories, songs, histories, and other traditions of indigenous groups before they disappeared.

world of "Second Life." Boellstorff conducted all of his fieldwork online. He justified this by stating that this virtual space is a productive one for studying the unique "cultural logic" of gaming and gamers. In other words, the online communities created by gamers are just as valid an object of study as traditional face-to-face communities have been. Interestingly, Boellstorff cites Tylor's understanding of culture as a "complex whole," asking, "What is a virtual world if not a complex whole, however networked?" (2008, 66). He goes on to explain that he is not studying "virtual culture," but rather "culture in virtual worlds" (ibid.).

Given that globalization has resulted in increasingly fragmented communities and highly mobile groups, it is often no longer tenable for anthropologists to stay in one location for a long period. Malinowski advocated in-depth research in one specific location, but anthropologists today often conduct multi-locale fieldwork, or fieldwork in multiple locations. Other anthropologists advocate the use of multi-sited fieldwork, a term coined by George Marcus in 1995. **Multi-sited fieldwork** involves connecting the localized events and experiences of a community with broader regional, national, or global processes. This approach often goes hand in hand with multi-locale approaches. For instance, Canadian anthropologist Andrew

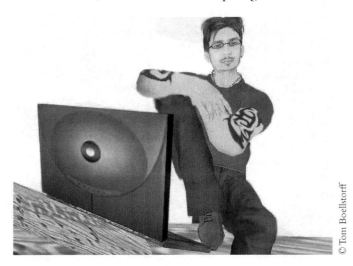

Tom Boellstorff conducted his fieldwork for *Coming of Age in Second Life* entirely online.

Walsh (2010) has studied the commodification of sapphires and the growing preference for "natural" gems (sapphires that have not been subject to heat treatment to enhance their colour) from multiple perspectives. He has interviewed Malagasy miners and local sapphire traders in Madagascar as well as gemologists and jewellers in North America. His work has taken him not only to Madagascar but also to international gemological trade shows. In essence, Walsh is attempting to track the multiple meanings and relationships that form around the international sapphire trade, and he explores how international demand for "natural" sapphires is affecting the lives of miners in local communities in Madagascar.

Fieldwork has undergone changes since Malinowski's time; but the *content* of fieldwork, or data collection, has undergone relatively few changes. Another key aspect of doing anthropology that remains relatively unchanged is that, as anthropologists, through our ethnographies we create bodies of knowledge about the people we are studying. Issues of how to accurately and ethically represent human beliefs and behaviours therefore remain central to the discipline.

Representation and Culture

Because they create knowledge about culture and relay other people's stories about themselves, anthropologists are concerned about issues of **representation.** That is why they try to think

> **multi-sited fieldwork**
> This term, coined by George Marcus in 1995, refers to the process of connecting localized experiences of fieldwork with broader, global processes. It necessitates understanding various issues from multiple "sites" or perspectives.
>
> **representation**
> The way in which a group of people is depicted in writing or through images. Anthropologists are increasingly conscious of the fact that when they write about a group of people, they are constructing particular representations that may have positive or negative long-term effects for a group of people.

critically about how they depict the people they are studying, be it in writing, photographs, art, films, and other media or on the Internet. Representations can be created by anthropologists, by the media, or by the informants themselves. Increasingly, anthropologists are speaking out against racist, sexist, or homophobic representations produced by the mass media. In the wake of 9/11, for example, many mainstream American media outlets depicted Islamic people (especially men) as violent terrorists or as "uncivilized," "backward," "primitive." The mass media have tended to resort to **essentialism** when representing particular groups. In essentialist representations, groups of people are depicted in ways that tend to homogenize and stereotype them (Mattingly, Lawlor, and Jacobs-Huey 2002). When essentialist representations are consumed by a public that is too often uncritical, racism is perpetuated, and domestic and foreign policy are affected for the worse.

With respect to representation, anthropologists also turn a critical lens upon themselves. An anthropologist who takes a photograph or writes an ethnographic account is crafting a particular representation of a group of people. This raises an important issue: Who has the right to produce representations of another group of people, and is there such a thing as a misrepresentation?

The people whom anthropologists study are becoming increasingly critical of how they are depicted. American anthropologist Margaret Mead travelled to American Samoa in 1925 to study adolescent girls' sexual habits; this led to the publication of her now famous ethnography, *Coming of Age in Samoa* (1928). Throughout her book, Mead painted a picture of Samoan society as peaceful; she also noted that the girls were free to experiment with pre-marital sex. This contrasted sharply with American attitudes at the

time regarding sexuality, where pre-marital sex was viewed as taboo. Her ethnography, which was widely read by anthropologists, students, and the mainstream public, cultivated (perhaps unintentionally) a romanticized and "exotic" representation of Samoans for a largely Western audience. Later generations of Samoans critiqued her work, often denying that teenagers engaged in gratuitous sex (Marshall 1993). Some anthropologists are quick to point out that the "missionization" of Samoans has contributed to the development of stricter moral ideals of sexuality—ideals that in turn have affected their perceptions of Mead's text. Even so, their objections raise some interesting questions for anthropology students. What if the anthropologist's interpretations of culture

© Gerard Sioen/Anzenberger/Redux

Images, like this one, that depict the Yanomamo as fierce and warlike have resulted in essentialist representations of the tribe.

essentialism
The act of creating generalizations or stereotypes about the behaviour or culture of a group of people.

differ from those of his or her informants? And what are the consequences of the representations cultivated by anthropologists?

There are no clear-cut answers for those questions, but it is worth noting that the representations crafted by anthropologists can have long-term ill consequences for the groups being depicted. For example, Napoleon Chagnon studied the Yanomami, an Amazonian indigenous group in Brazil and Venezuela. He often labelled them as "fierce" and warlike. In fact, the title of his ethnography about them is *The Yanomamo: The Fierce People* (1968). Other anthropologists who have studied the Yanomami (e.g., Ferguson 1995) have challenged his interpretation of the Yanomami as fierce. Terence Turner (2005) has argued that representations of the Yanomami as "fierce" have done them harm. For instance, in the early 1990s, the British government wanted to provide financial assistance for various Amazonian groups for education and medical clinics. But after reading Chagnon's work, they decided that the money would be better spent on reducing levels of "violence" in the community.

Clearly, representations put forward by anthropologists, the mass media, and others have social, economic, and political consequences for various groups. So it is important for anthropologists to consider the long-term impact of their work in various communities.

EXERCISE 1.2

Find a Canadian newspaper or magazine article that discusses a particular event involving a "minority" group. Outline how the author of the article represents this group. What words does the author use? What sorts of pictures (if any) are displayed? What is the tone of the article? Who was it written by, and for what audience?

QUESTION 1.3: IS IT POSSIBLE TO SEE THE WORLD THROUGH THE EYES OF OTHERS?

This question lies at the heart of the anthropological enterprise. The anthropologist must be able to look beyond everyday appearance to decipher the often hidden meanings of beliefs, objects, and behaviours, while at the same time setting aside her or his preconceptions about what is normal or proper. But in addition to that, the anthropologist must also learn one culture and then relate what he or she has learned to members of another culture in order to translate the meanings of one world into the meanings of another. Like children making their way in a world they do not fully comprehend, anthropologists often find themselves in awkward, embarrassing, or dangerous situations and must be prepared to learn from those moments.

The Embarrassed Anthropologist

Awkwardness and embarrassment are a part of fieldwork, as well as a part of the process through which the fieldworker learns about another culture. Richard Scaglion spent over a year with the Abelam of Papua New Guinea. Shortly after he arrived in the field, he observed and photographed an Abelam pig hunt in which the men set out nets and waited while the women and children made lots of noise to drive the pigs into the nets. Soon after, he was invited by the Abelam to participate in a pig hunt, and he took this as a sign of acceptance, that the people "liked him." He started to go with the men, but they told him they wanted him to go with the women and children to beat the bush, explaining, "We've never seen anyone who makes as much noise in the jungle as you." Later, wanting to redeem himself, Scaglion offered to help an Abelam who was planting crops with a digging stick. A crowd gathered to watch as he used a shovel to try to dig a demonstration hole. After he had struggled for several minutes to get the shovel into the hard-packed soil, someone handed him a digging stick, and he was amazed at how easy it was to use. Later, he found out that several Abelam had shovels but rarely used them because they didn't work.

After months of answering Scaglion's questions about their view of the natural world, such as the moon, sun, and stars, some Abelam asked him about *his* views of the universe. Feeling on safe ground, he gave the usual grade school lecture about the shape of the earth, its daily rotation, and its travels around the sun. Using a coconut, he showed them the relative positions on the earth of New Guinea, Australia, Europe, and the United States. Everyone listened intently, and Scaglion thought it had gone well—until a week later, when he overheard some elders wondering how it was that North Americans walked upside down!

Beginning again, Scaglion used the coconut to explain how, as the earth rotates, sometimes the United States is upright and New Guinea is on the bottom. The Abelam rejected this because they could see that they were *not* upside down, and no one, not even some of the old people in the community, remembered ever having walked upside down. Scaglion began to draw on the physics he had learned at university. As he tried to explain Newton's law of gravity (or "grabity," as his friends pronounced it), he suddenly realized that he didn't understand "grabity" either. It was something he had accepted since grade three, a concept that even physicists simply take for granted as a convenient concept.

EXERCISE 1.3A

Think of some awkward or embarrassing situation created by something you did or didn't do, said or didn't say. What was inappropriate about your behaviour, and why did it lead to misunderstanding or embarrassment? What did you learn from the experience about the meaning of your or others' behaviour?

Confronting Witchcraft in Mexico

Awkward or embarrassing moments in the field may help anthropologists understand a culture and even question their own view of the world. But the question of whether one can ever see the world through others' eyes remains a contentious one among anthropologists. Obviously, to communicate with anyone—even members of their own society—people must share some of the meanings they ascribe to objects, persons, behaviours, emotions, and events. What happens, then, when views of the world are completely different?

Michael Kearney travelled to the town of Santa Catarina Ixtepeji in the valley of Oaxaca, Mexico, with the intention of studying the relationship between the people's view of the world and their social arrangements and environment. He began his work secure in his knowledge of the scientific and materialist view of the world in which he was reared, but he was often fascinated by the differences between his view and that of the people of Santa Catarina Ixtepeji. Their world was controlled by mystic notions of "fate," the will of God, and

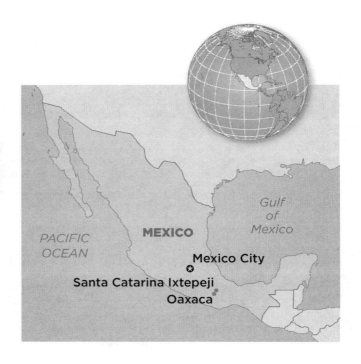

malevolent witches and other harmful and sometimes lethal spiritual forces. He became familiar with the Ixtepejanos' world view, never doubting that it was "unscientific"—albeit justified, perhaps, by a life in which suffering, disease, and death were common.

Kearney's faith in his own world view was momentarily shattered by an incident that began innocently enough. While walking to an appointment, he came upon an obviously distressed woman, Doña Delfina. She was known as a witch, and Kearney had been trying unsuccessfully to interview her. When they met she explained that her sister-in-law had a "very bad disease in her arms" and that she wanted him to help. Kearney accompanied Doña Delfina to her house, where he found that the sister-in-law's arms were ulcerated with deep, oozing lesions that looked to him like infected burns. They rejected his offer to take the sick woman to a doctor for medical treatment, so Kearney said he had some ointment that might help, and they eagerly agreed that he should use it. He got the ointment, which contained an anaesthetic, and daubed it on the woman's sores. Much to the amazement of Doña Delfina, her sister-in-law immediately felt better. By the afternoon, her arms had greatly improved; by the following morning, scabs had formed; the day after, she had completely recovered.

Kearney was credited with a "miraculous cure." But the same day, a Ixtepejano friend asked Kearney what he had done and he proudly explained. The friend replied, "Why did you do that? It was not a good thing to do." The sick woman, he said, had been the victim of black magic; another woman, Gregoria, was trying to take Delfina's brother away from his wife and was using black magic to make Delfina's sister-in-law sick. Delfina was using *her* magic to keep her brother in the household, but Gregoria was winning. Now, the friend explained to Kearney, he had intervened, tipping the balance of power back to Delfina but creating a powerful enemy in Gregoria. "Maybe you should leave town for a while until Gregoria calms down," Kearney's

friend suggested. Kearney did not take the danger seriously, and he might never have done so were it not for two incidents that occurred soon afterward.

A young doctor in town asked Kearney, who had medical training, to assist in an autopsy of a man who had died in a fall off a truck. It was a particularly long and gory autopsy accomplished only with rusty carpenter's tools in a dimly lit room. Images of the scene and the cadaver disturbed Kearney's sleep over the next few days. One night, about a week later, as the wind beat cornstalks against his house, Kearney felt an itching on his arm. Rolling up his sleeve, he discovered several angry welts that seemed to be growing as he watched them. Immediately he thought of the chancrous arms of Delfina's sister-in-law, realizing at the same time that Gregoria's house was only 50 metres from his and that she could be trying to kill him. "She got me!" he thought. The image of the cadaver on the table jumped into his mind, followed by a wish that he had got out of town while there was still time. As Kearney put it, he was witnessing the disintegration of his scientific, materialist view of the world and grappling with forces with which he was unprepared to deal.

Kearney is not sure how long his initial terror lasted—seconds, perhaps minutes. As he struggled against it, he realized that he was suspended between two worlds, his own and that of the Ixtepejanos. He was questioning a world of meanings that he had until then taken for granted. Kearney is not sure how long he was able to truly believe that the world was as the Ixtepejanos saw it, but as he retrieved his own view of the world, the Ixtepejano's world view, filled with witchcraft and magic, ceased to be only intellectually interesting. It acquired a reality and a sense of legitimacy for him that it had not had before he experienced the real fear that he had been bewitched. He came to realize through his experience that systems of belief are eminently reasonable when viewed from within that system.

The experiences of these anthropologists, Kearney and Scaglion, highlight certain features of the ethnographic method. They especially illustrate anthropologists' attempts to appreciate the views of others while at the same time questioning their own views of the world. They also illustrate what makes the ethnographic method unique: by participating in the lives of others and in their cultural practices, anthropologists can take *themselves* as subjects of investigation. Those who succeed in seeing the world as others do, if even for a brief moment, find it far easier to understand and describe that world. It also helps the anthropologist understand how others can believe what they do. Claude Levi-Strauss, one of the greatest anthropologists of the 20th century, once said that fieldwork, and anthropologists' attempts to immerse themselves in the world of others, makes them "marginal" men or women. They are never completely native because they cannot totally shed their own cultural perceptions, but they are never the same again after having glimpsed alternative visions of the world. Anthropologists are, as Roger Keesing put it, outsiders who know something of what it is to be insiders.

Scaglion and Kearney both succeeded because they were able to see things, at least temporarily, from the native's point of view or an insider's perspective. This is by no means easy, especially when we are faced with practices and beliefs that we find incredible or troublesome. We may be able to overcome our initial shock or bewilderment on confronting different cultures if we understand something about why cultural differences exist. But how should we react if the meanings that others ascribe to experiences differ from our own? It is difficult enough to look beyond everyday appearances at our own beliefs and behaviours; it is far more difficult when we confront beliefs and behaviours of others that we initially consider wrong, horrible, or bizarre. As we shall see in the next section, being able to overcome, or at last set aside, our own cultural biases is one of the major challenges that anthropologists face when they attempt to study and understand cultural beliefs and practices.

How Do People Judge the Beliefs and Behaviours of Others?

Richard Scaglion is fond of telling the story of his friend, a member of the Abelam tribe of Papua New Guinea, who was looking through an issue of *Sports Illustrated*. The friend, dressed in full ceremonial regalia with a feather through his nose, was laughing uncontrollably at a woman shown in a liquor advertisement. When he managed to stop laughing long enough to explain what he thought was so funny, he said, "This white woman has made holes in her ears and stuck things in them." When Scaglion pointed out that his friend had an ornament in his nose, the reply was "That's different. That's for beauty and has ceremonial significance. But I didn't know that white people mutilated themselves."

Scaglion's friend was confronting a problem that many do when the behaviour or beliefs of others seem to differ from their own, and his response was not unusual. He was both shocked and mystified at the strange behaviour. And this suggests a dilemma: Since there are so many versions of what the world is like, how do we go about trying to understand each of them without making positive or negative judgments? Which version of the world is correct? Are there any such versions that we *can* reject or condemn? Can we say, as so many have, that one culture is superior to another?

In the catalogue of human behaviours and beliefs, it is not difficult to find practices or ideas that may seem bizarre or shocking even to trained anthropologists. Sociocultural anthropologists have described the beliefs of the Ilongots of the Philippines, who must kill an enemy to obtain a head that they can throw away in order to diminish the grief and rage they feel at the death of a kinsman or kinswoman. They have studied the historical records of the Aztecs in Mexico, who believed that the universe underwent periodic destruction and that the only way to ward off disaster was to pluck

Abelam villager in ceremonial costume.

the hearts from live sacrificial victims to offer to the gods. They have also studied modern states that routinely engage in or sanction torture, terror, and genocide. How, then, should we react to practices and beliefs such as these?

The Ethnocentric Fallacy and the Relativist Fallacy

If we do condemn or reject the beliefs or behaviours of others, we may be embracing the **ethnocentric fallacy**, which is the idea that our beliefs and behaviours are right and true, while those of other peoples are wrong or misguided. Sociocultural anthropologists have long fought against **ethnocentrism**, that is, the tendency to judge the beliefs and behaviours of other cultures

from the perspective of one's own. They try to show that what often appears on the surface to be an odd belief or a bizarre bit of behaviour is functional and logical in the context of a particular culture. They find the ethnocentric fallacy *intellectually* and *methodologically* intolerable; if everyone everywhere thinks that they are right and that others must be wrong, an intellectual and social dead end is inevitable. Furthermore, if we, as anthropologists, assume that we have all the right answers, our study of other cultures becomes simply the study of other people's mistakes.

Because of the intellectual and methodological implications of ethnocentrism, sociocultural anthropologists emphatically reject this position. But the opposite pole to ethnocentrism, **cultural relativism**, raises issues of its own. Cultural relativism, simply stated, holds that no behaviour or belief can be judged to be odd or wrong simply because it is different from our own. Instead, we must try to understand a culture on its own terms and to understand behaviours or beliefs for the purpose, function, or meaning they have to people in the societies in which we find them. In other words, cultural relativism holds that a specific belief or behaviour can only be understood in relation to the culture—the system of meanings—in which it is embedded.

For example, according to Renato Rosaldo (1989), the ceremonies and rituals accompanying a successful headhunting expedition help the Ilongot psychologically manage their grief over the death of a kinsperson. However, relativism poses a *moral* predicament. Once we concede, say, that it is

ethnocentric fallacy
The mistaken notion that the beliefs and behaviours of other cultures can be judged from the perspective of one's own culture.

ethnocentrism
The tendency to judge the beliefs and behaviours of other cultures from the perspective of one's own culture.

cultural relativism
The attempt to understand the beliefs and behaviours of other cultures in terms of the culture in which they are found.

CULTURE AND MEANING

permissible to rip the hearts out of living human beings, provided that you believe it necessary to save the world, or that it is permissible to subject young girls to genital modification to protect family reputations, we find ourselves falling quickly into the **relativistic fallacy**, which is the idea that it is impossible to make moral judgments about the beliefs and behaviours of others. This, of course, seems morally intolerable because it implies that no beliefs or behaviours can be condemned. So we are left with two untenable positions: the ethnocentric alternative, which is intellectually and methodologically unsatisfactory, and the relativist alternative, which is morally unsatisfactory. How do we solve this problem?

Virginity Testing in Turkey and Cannibalism Among the Wari'

To illustrate further the dilemma of relativism and the difficulty of appreciating the cultures of others without making moral judgments, some time ago a human rights group based in the United States issued a report condemning the practice of virginity testing in Turkey. Traditionally, young women in Turkey, as in some other cultures, are expected to avoid sexual relations prior to marriage, although the same rule does not apply to men. In this tradition, the bride's virginity is revealed by displaying, the morning after the wedding, the sheet that was spread on the couple's wedding bed with the tell-tale hymeneal blood stain. The human rights report condemns the traditional testing as well the reported practice of forcing tests on hospital patients, students, and applicants for government jobs. As anthropologists, we must ask: Is the human rights group being ethnocentric in judging Turkish customs by North American cultural norms, or is it correctly identifying abuses of women that must be corrected? Might it help if we better understood the logic behind the belief?

In her book on Turkish village society, *The Seed and the Soil,* anthropologist Carol Delaney describes how virginity testing relates to the way in which Turkish villagers conceptualize and explain the reproductive process. They see producing children as analogous to the planting and growing of crops; the man provides the "seed" with his semen, and the woman serves as the "soil" in which the seed germinates and grows. As a metaphor for reproduction, the idea of the seed and the soil provides villagers with a way of thinking about and understanding reproduction. However, the metaphor of seed and soil has at least one very important implication; since seeds do not have a limited life span, as we know semen to have, villagers believe that once planted, the seed (semen) may grow at any time. Consequently, if a woman has had sexual relations with a man other than her husband at any time prior to her marriage, the paternity of the child will be in doubt. Since descent in traditional Turkish villages is closely tied to many things, including property rights, uncertainty about the identity of the true father can have major implications. Thus in the context of Turkish beliefs about procreation, virginity testing may be said to make sense. Furthermore, Turkish beliefs about conception are not that far removed from our own, since our language draws from the same agricultural metaphors as those of Turkish villagers to explain reproduction. We talk about women being "fertile" or "barren" and semen "fertilizing" "eggs." "Sowing one's oats" as an expression of sexual activity is still heard in parts of the United States and Canada. Furthermore, these views are reinforced by religious proscription, legitimized in the Koran and the Old Testament. Thus, before we either condemn or accept the Turkish villagers for their treatment of women, we need to examine what their beliefs tell us about our own. Ours may be equally problematical.

> **relativistic fallacy**
> The idea that it is impossible to make moral judgments about the beliefs and behaviours of members of other cultures.

But what of cannibalism, such as the Wari' practice of roasting and eating the dead? Surely there is no way to justify that. Cannibalism, as Beth Conklin points out in her study of Wari' cannibalism, *Consuming Grief*, pushes the limits of cultural relativism, guaranteeing reactions of revulsion and fascination. But in addition to that, it has political implications: for centuries, cannibalism was the ultimate smear tactic. To accuse one's enemies or people one wished to degrade or dominate of cannibalism was the ultimate justification for conquest, domination, and exploitation. In 1503, Queen Isabella of Spain decreed that Spaniards could legally enslave specifically those American Indians who were cannibals. Pope Innocent IV, in 1510, ruled that Christians could punish, by force of arms, the sin of cannibalism. By claiming moral superiority in this way, Christians were claiming the right to decide ultimately what is right and what is wrong. Armed with that power, they felt justified in imposing their own views and way of life. What Queen Isabella and Pope Innocent IV conveniently overlooked, however, was that Europeans at the time themselves practised cannibalism. As Conklin notes, medicinal cannibalism—the consumption of human body parts for curing purposes—had a long tradition in Europe. Up until two centuries ago, European physicians prescribed the consumption of human flesh, heart, bones, and other body parts as cures for such afflictions as arthritis, reproductive disorders, sciatica, warts, and skin blemishes. Human blood was thought to be a cure for epilepsy, and physicians recommended that it be drunk immediately after the supplier died. Physicians also thought that the blood of someone who died violently was particularly effective. Thus, in Denmark, epileptics would stand around the scaffolds, cups in hand, waiting to catch the blood of executed criminals. And almost every apothecary kept dried and powdered human body parts on hand for anxious customers.

The people of medieval Europe accepted in their own lives the same types of practices they condemned in others. Furthermore, they failed to understand the practices from the point of view of the others. The Wari' ate their dead, for example, because they believed it was the compassionate thing to do. As Conklin puts it, "More painful than having the corpse eaten would have been to have it *not* eaten" (2001, 81). For the Wari', a corpse left intact was a painful reminder of the deceased. People unrelated to the deceased ate the corpse, even when the smell or taste repulsed them, in the belief that it would help family members come to terms with their loss. Furthermore, the Western practice of burying the dead (which missionaries and government officials forced the Wari' to do after contact) was almost as horrific to the Wari' as their cannibalism might have been for non-Wari'. "It's cold in the earth," a father who had recently lost a two-year-old son explained to Beth Conklin. "We keep remembering our child, lying there, cold. We remember and we are sad. It was better in the old days, when the others ate the body. Then we did not think about our child's body much. We did not remember our child as much, and we were not so sad" (xv).

Burying the body also violated many fundamental Wari' values. For them, the ground was "dirty" and "polluting." They never sat directly on the dirt, and discarding things on the ground was considered disrespectful. Special ritual objects were never supposed to touch the ground.

Without a deeper understanding of Wari' culture, we cannot know how consuming the dead aligns with the meaning they impose on their world, including how they deal with their emotions. By consuming the dead, Wari' are trying to obliterate the painful memories of their loss. The memory of the body is painful, but equally painful are the material objects associated with the deceased and the very mention of the deceased's name. Thus, the Wari' not only consume the body but also burn the house and personal possessions of the deceased. And for months, they walk into the forest to find places associated with the deceased— where a hunter made a kill or a woman felled a fruit tree, or where there was something such as a favourite log on which she or he liked to sit—cut the vegetation around it, and, after it has dried, burn the spot, changing the appearance of the last earthly places to which memories of the deceased might cling. As they "sweep" (the Wari' term for it), they cry over the memories; but once done, "it is different," "there is not much sadness there." For most North Americans, a dead body is only a shell, its soul or spiritual essence gone. Thus some societies can prepare the dead to look as they did in life and think of them buried in that way. The Wari', by contrast, want to separate the dead from the living; thus, obliterating their memories is perfectly logical. And they are not the only group to do so.

There are other aspects of Wari' beliefs about consuming the dead. For example, they believe that the spirits of the dead ultimately enter the bodies of animals they depend on for food, thus creating a cycle of eating and being eaten. The point being made here is that when we impose our own meanings on practices such as cannibalism

EXERCISE 1.3B

Wari' attempt in their funeral practices to obliterate the memory of the dead, as do many other societies. Other societies, however, memorialize the dead; forgetting them would be an act of disrespect. Think about your own cultural background and whether or not you are encouraged to memorialize the dead. List the ways that you try to keep the memory of deceased persons alive, and speculate as to why you do that instead of trying to forget them. If you are encouraged to forget the dead, how is that accomplished? Why? Compare your beliefs and practices with those of your classmates.

and fail to see those practices the way others do, we miss a great deal.

But does this mean that *any* practice or belief, once we understand it from "the native's point of view," is acceptable? Does understanding the cultures of others require that we accept and justify all beliefs and practices?

Objectivity and Morality

For anthropologists, the conflict between ethnocentrism and relativism is not just a theoretical one. When choosing their research subjects, anthropologists may face this dilemma: Should they maintain a "moral distance" from those they are studying and remain "objective," or should they engage in criticizing behaviour or beliefs they encounter (e.g., virginity testing).

The contradiction between "objective" anthropology and a politically committed anthropology became apparent to Nancy Scheper-Hughes when she returned as an anthropologist to a shantytown in Brazil where, previously, she had worked as a community organizer. The women with whom she had worked in the past became angry. Why, they asked, when as a community organizer she had helped

The Taj Mahal, a monument built to honour a 17th-century Mughal emperor's wife, who died in childbirth.

them organize to fight for clean water, decent wages, and protection from police brutality, was she now, as an anthropologist, so passive, so indifferent to the destruction around her? She tried to explain that as an anthropologist her work was different—she was there now to observe, document, and write about their lives as truthfully as she could. The women refused to accept this and insisted that if they were to work with her, she would have to work with them to fight for better lives. "What," they said, "is anthropology to us?"

On the basis of that experience, Scheper-Hughes (1995, 416) now argues for a politically committed, morally engaged, and ethically grounded anthropology. "Those of us who make our living observing and recording the misery of the world," she writes, "have a particular obligation to reflect critically on the impact of the harsh images of human suffering that we foist upon the public."

Scheper-Hughes proposes what she calls a more "womanly" anthropology, one that is concerned with how people treat one another. Moral relativism, she says, is no longer appropriate to the world in which we live, and anthropology, if it is to be worth anything at all, must be "critically grounded." Anthropologists cannot ignore the massacres and disappearances of vulnerable people that often occur in the communities in which anthropologists work. Anthropologists must, she insists, serve as witnesses and reporters of human rights abuses and of the suffering of the poor and the oppressed.

But serving as a witness for the poor and oppressed can itself lead to moral dilemmas for the anthropologist when the people with whom the anthropologist works engage in behaviour that may appear morally questionable. Scheper-Hughes confronted this question when she discovered and reported that impoverished women in the Brazilian shantytowns sometimes allowed their starving infants to die in the belief that they were doomed anyway. When Philippe Bourgois studied the world of crack dealers on the Upper East Side of New York City, he worried about the negative images

he would be conveying if he reported the personal violence, sexual abuse, addiction, and alienation he witnessed. He recalled the advice of anthropologist Laura Nader, who advised others not to study the poor and powerless, because whatever you say will be used against them.

Human rights activists, in particular, are skeptical about cultural relativism. If, they say, we must tolerate the beliefs and practices of other cultures because to do otherwise would be ethnocentric, how can we ever criticize what seem to be violations of basic human rights, such as the right to bodily integrity, or the right to be free from torture, arbitrary imprisonment, slavery, and genocide? Cultural relativism, they say, makes arguments about human rights meaningless by legitimizing almost any behaviour.

Take the case of the practice in some areas of India of *sati*, the burning of a widow on her husband's funeral pyre. In 1987, Roon Kanwar, an 18-year-old girl, was burned alive on her husband's pyre. Women's rights groups protested, but relatives claimed that it is an ancient Indian custom and accused the protesters of being Western imperialists imposing their own cultural standards on them. Although India has outlawed the practice, prosecutors rarely enforce the law because of the difficulty of obtaining evidence. Would it matter if Roon Kanwar committed *sati* voluntarily? What would happen if she objected? Does it matter that it is only women who are burned? Is the purpose of *sati* to deny a widow the inheritance of her husband's family's land? Elizabeth Zechenter, who makes the argument for universal principles of human rights, says that cultural relativists are right to contend that the endorsement or rejection of some foreign customs risks imposing one's own cultural prejudices on others. But she adds that the idea that we can make no judgments without being ethnocentric is illusory: "One simply cannot avoid making judgments when faced with oppression and brutality masquerading under the guise of cultural tradition. Such a nonjudgmental tolerance of brutality is actually an ultimate form of ethnocentrism, if not an outright ethical sur-render" (1997, 336).

There is obviously no easy answer to the ques-tion of when, if ever, it is proper to judge the beliefs and practices of others to be right or wrong, or when, if ever, it is proper to work to change behaviours or beliefs judged to be wrong. Ideally, our attempts to understand what at first seemed puzzling in some cultures, and our arrival at some solution to that puzzle, should lead us to ask our-selves what made the behaviour or belief seem puzzling in the first place. We also need to bear in mind that when cultures order the world in certain ways for their members, they are in effect masking other ways of viewing things. We need to appre-ciate that there are perspectives different from our own and that our ethnocentric biases may blind us to those alternatives. In other words, while cul-ture provides us with certain meanings to give to objects, persons, behaviours, emotions, and events, it also shields us from alternative meanings. What our culture hides from us may be more important than what it reveals.

EXERCISE 1.3C

You have been doing anthropological research in Canada with a religious group that believes they must live the life described in the Christian Bible, particularly as described in the Book of Acts. They live communally, sharing all property; they believe that women should be subservient to their husbands, and they enforce rules against drinking alcoholic beverages, smoking, and so on. The group has lately come under attack by a group in the local community as being a "dangerous cult." You know that, although their beliefs and practices differ from those of the larger society around them, they are not dangerous and, in fact, lead lives of harmony. They have asked you to speak in their defence. Can you do this without sacrificing your objectivity?

QUESTION 1.4: HOW CAN THE MEANINGS THAT OTHERS FIND IN EXPERIENCE BE INTERPRETED AND DESCRIBED?

In one Sherlock Holmes detective story, Dr. Watson, Holmes's assistant, decides to teach the great detec-tive a lesson in humility. He hands Holmes a pocket watch owned by Watson's late brother and challenges Holmes to infer from the watch the character of its owner. Holmes's interpretation: "[Your brother] was a man of untidy habits—very untidy and careless. He was left with good prospects, but he threw away his chances and finally, taking to drink, he died."

Watson, astounded at the accuracy of Holmes's description of his late brother, asks if it was guess-work. "I never guess," replies Holmes:

> *I began by stating that your brother was careless. When you observe the lower part of the watch case, you notice that it is not only dented in two places, but it is cut and marked all over from the habit of keeping other hard objects, such as coins or keys, in the same pocket. Surely it is no great feat to assume that a man who treats [an expensive] watch so cavalierly must be a careless man. Neither is it a very far-fetched inference that a man who inherits one article of such value is pretty well provided for in other respects.*

"But what about his drinking habits?" asks Watson. Holmes responds:

> *Look at the innerplate which contains the keyhole [where the watch is wound]. Look at the thousands of scratches all around the hole-marks where the key has slipped. What sober man's key could have scored those grooves? But you will never see a drunkard's watch without them. He*

winds it at night, and he leaves these traces of his unsteady hand. Where is the mystery in all this?

Had Holmes been an anthropologist, he might have been tempted also to draw some inferences about the society in which the watch was manufactured, particularly about its conceptions of time. For example, in some societies time is task oriented, not clock oriented; time might be measured by how long it takes to cook rice, as in Madagascar. In other societies, time patterns depend on natural events such as the rising of the sun or the ebb and flow of tides. British anthropologist E.E. Evans-Pritchard, in his classic account of the Nuer of the Sudan, noted that

> *the Nuer have no expression equivalent to "time" in our language, and they cannot, therefore, as we can, speak of time as though it were something actual, which passes, can be wasted, can be saved, and so forth. I don't think they ever experience the same feeling of fighting against time because their points of reference are mainly the activities themselves, which are generally of a leisurely character. Events follow a logical order, but they are not controlled by an abstract system, there being no autonomous points of reference to which activities have to conform with precision. Nuer are fortunate.*

An anthropologist might also infer that clocks are instruments of discipline; they tell us when to get up, when to go to bed, when to eat, when to start work, when to stop work. Our work patterns themselves are defined by clocks, and our wages may depend on the constant repetition over time of a particular task. Historian E.P. Thompson notes that until the institution of modern notions of time and the need to measure it with clocks, work patterns were characterized by alternating bouts of intense labour and idleness, at least whenever people were in control of their own working lives. He even suggests that this pattern persists today, but only among a few self-employed professionals such as artists, writers, small farmers, and, he suggests, university students.

© SuperStock, Inc./Getty

Modern notions of clock-based time tell us a great deal about the culture we live in. What measures of time are most important in your life as a student?

Watson's brother's watch was a product of Western society, part of its culture. Holmes "read" the watch as if it were a collection of symbols or words, a **cultural text** that revealed the character of its owner. He could just as easily have viewed it as a text inscribed with the symbols that revealed the ideas about time and work that characterized the civilization that produced it.

One way to think about culture is as a text of significant symbols: words, gestures, drawings, natural objects—anything, in fact, that carries meaning. To understand another culture we must be able, as Holmes was with a pocket watch, to decipher the meanings of the symbols that comprise a cultural text. We must be able to interpret the meanings embedded in the language, objects, gestures, and activities that are shared by members of a society. Fortunately, the ability to decipher a cultural text is part of being human; in our everyday lives we both read and maintain the text that makes up our own culture. We have learned the meanings behind the

cultural text
A way of thinking about culture as a text of significant symbols—words, gestures, drawings, natural objects—that carries meaning.

symbols that frame our lives, and we share those meanings with others. Our task in understanding another culture is to take the abilities that have enabled us to dwell in our own culture and use them to understand the cultures of others.

Deciphering the Balinese Cockfight

To illustrate how an anthropologist might decipher a cultural text, imagine yourself coming upon a cockfight on the island of Bali. You see a ring in which two roosters with sharpened metal spurs attached to their legs are set at each other until one kills the other. Surrounding the fighting cocks are men shouting encouragement to their favourites, each having placed a wager that his favourite will kill its opponent.

What do you make of this? Your first reaction might be shock or disgust at the spectacle of the crowd urging the cocks to bloody combat. After a while you might begin to find similarities to events that are meaningful to you, such as some North American sports. But what if, like Sherlock Holmes (or like Clifford Geertz, from whom this example is taken), you want to understand the meaning of what is happening and what that meaning tells you about how Balinese view their world? If you assume that the cockfight is a feature of Balinese culture, a Balinese text filled with

symbols that carry meaning about what it is to be Balinese, how might you proceed to read this text?

You might begin by finding out the language the Balinese use to talk about the cockfight. You would no doubt discover that the double-entendre of cock both as a synonym for rooster and as a euphemism for penis is the same for the Balinese as it is for North Americans. The double-entendre even produces, says Geertz, the same jokes, puns, and obscenities in Bali as it does in North America. You would discover that *sabung*, the Balinese word for cock, has numerous other meanings and is used metaphorically to mean hero, warrior, champion, political candidate, bachelor, dandy, lady-killer, or tough guy. Court trials, wars, political contests,

In Balinese society, cockfighting is a major sporting event that is closely tied to cultural interpretations of manhood, competition, and status.

inheritance disputes, and street arguments are compared with cockfights. Even the island of Bali is thought of as being cock-shaped (in this case meaning the fowl). You would also find that men give their fowls inordinate attention, spending most of their time grooming them and even feeding them a special diet. As one of Geertz's Balinese informants put it, "We're all cock crazy."

Having discovered the importance of cockfights to the Balinese and the connections they make between cocks and men, you next examine the cockfight itself. You learn that cockfights are public events held in arenas of about 4.7 square metres from late afternoon until after sundown. Handlers, expert in the task, attach sharp spurs to the cock's legs; for a cock thought to be superior to an opponent, the spurs are adjusted in a slightly disadvantageous position. The cocks are released in the centre of the ring and fly at each other, fighting until one kills the other. The owner of the winning cock takes the carcass of the loser home to eat; the losing owner is sometimes driven in despair to wreck family shrines. You discover that the Balinese contrast heaven and hell by comparing them to the mood of a man whose cock has just won and the mood of a man whose cock has just lost.

You find out that while the Balinese place odds on cockfights, there are strict social conventions that dictate the wagering. For example, a man will never bet against a cock that is owned by someone of his family group or village or a friend's family group or village, but he will place large bets against a cock owned by an enemy or the friend of an enemy. Rarely is a cockfight without social significance (e.g., between two outsiders), and rarely do cocks owned by members of the same family or village fight each other. Moreover, the owners of the cocks, especially in important matches, are usually among the leaders of their communities. You might learn that cockfights come close to encouraging open expressions of aggression between village and kin-group rivals, but not quite, because the cockfight is, as the Balinese put it, "only a cockfight."

Given the social rules for betting and the ways in which odds are set, you might reason, as Geertz did, that the Balinese rarely make a profit betting on cockfights. Geertz says, in fact, that most bettors just want to break even. Consequently, the meaning of the cockfight for a Balinese has little to do with economics. The question is what meaning the cockfight *does* have for the Balinese. What is the cockfight really about, if it is not about money?

Geertz concludes that the Balinese cockfight is above all about status, about the ranking of people vis-à-vis one another. The Balinese cockfight is a text filled with meaning about status as the Balinese see it. Cocks represent men—more specifically, their owners; the fate of the cock in the ring is linked, if only temporarily, to the social fate of its owner. Each cock has a following consisting of the owner, the owner's family, and members of the owner's village, and these followers "risk" their status by betting on the cockfight. Furthermore, Geertz maintains that the more a match is between near equals, personal enemies, or high-status individuals, the more the match is about status. And the more the match is about status, the closer the identification of cock and man, the finer the cocks, and the more exactly they will be matched. The match will inspire greater emotion and absorption, and the gambling will be more about status and less about economic gain.

For Geertz, the cockfight is like any art form; it takes a highly abstract and difficult concept—status—and depicts it in a way that makes it comprehensible to the participants. The cockfight is meaningful to the Balinese because it tells them something real about their own lives, but in a way that does not directly affect their lives. They see the struggle for status that is part of everyday life vividly portrayed, even though, in the cockfight itself, no one really gains or loses status in any permanent sense.

A few words of caution are necessary concerning what we might learn about the Balinese from this particular cultural text. First, it would probably be a mistake to assume that the people

CULTURE AND MEANING   27

gain status by being on the winning side or lose it by being on the side of the loser. The status outcomes of the cockfight do not translate into real life any more than the victory of your favourite sports team increases your status. Instead, says Geertz, the cockfight illustrates what status is about for the Balinese. The cockfight is a story the Balinese tell themselves about themselves. It would also be a mistake to assume that the character of the Balinese can be read directly from the cockfight; any conclusion that the cockfight is indicative of an aggressive, competitive, violent national character would quickly be dispelled. The Balinese are shy about competition and avoid open conflict. The slaughter in the cockfight is not how things are literally, but as they could be. Finally, the cockfight reveals only a segment of the Balinese character, as Watson's brother's watch revealed only a segment of its owner's character. The culture of a people, like the possessions of a person, is an ensemble of texts—collections of symbols and meanings—that must be viewed together to achieve a full understanding.

QUESTION 1.5: WHAT CAN LEARNING ABOUT OTHER PEOPLES TELL ANTHROPOLOGISTS ABOUT THEIR OWN SOCIETIES?

Anthropologists do not limit themselves to the study of cultures that are different from their own. They often apply concepts and techniques that are useful in understanding and interpreting other cultures as a means to understand and interpret their own. One objective of studying other cultures is to help us recognize the meanings we impose on our experiences. When Renato Rosaldo asked the Ilongots why they cut off human heads, they replied that rage, born of grief, drives them to kill others; by severing the heads of their victims, they are able to throw away the anger born of bereavement. Rosaldo found it difficult to accept the idea that the death of a kinsperson could cause anger or rage and that such rage in itself could drive a person to kill another. He questioned the Ilongots further but could obtain no other reason for their headhunting; he devised other theories to explain it, but none were satisfactory. Only his own experience of grief and anger at the accidental death of his wife, Michelle, while both were doing fieldwork among the Ilongots helped him realize how grief can generate rage and how grief drove the Ilongots to hunt the heads of their enemies. At the same time that he began to understand the Ilongots, he began to understand his own grief and reaction to death.

A Balinese Anthropologist Studies Canadian Hockey

Whether we approach other cultures as anthropologists, as travellers, or as professionals who need to communicate with people of other cultures, the confrontation with other ways of believing and behaving should cause us to reflect on our way of viewing the world. To illustrate, try to step outside yourself and objectify an experience whose meaning you take for granted. Pretend you are a Balinese anthropologist who suddenly comes upon a spectacle as important in its way to Canadians as the cockfight is to Balinese: a hockey game.

As a Balinese, your first reaction to this Canadian text might be one of horror and revulsion at seeing men and women speeding from one end of an ice pad to the other with long wooden sticks in their hands, rudely pushing one another out of the way while thousands cheer them on. As you settled in, however, you would soon find some obvious similarities between the hockey game and the cockfight you are familiar with at home. Both are spectator sports in which the spectators sort themselves into supporters of one side or the other. In fact, in hockey, the sorting is even more carefully arranged, since fans of one team are often seated on one side of the arena and fans of the other on the opposite side.

Your next step (as in interpreting the cockfight) would be to examine the language Canadians use to refer to the hockey game. You discover that they use similar expressions in talking about hockey and fighting, such as *roughing* and *slashing*. Coaches talk about getting "revenge" for defeats, as generals might talk about getting revenge on battlefields. You conclude that Canadians seem to feel the same way about hockey as they do about fighting. In fact, if you attend several hockey games, you will most likely witness a scene in which players of opposing teams take off their protective gloves and actually begin to punch each other.

You soon discover that winning and losing hockey games is as important to Canadians as winning and losing cockfights is to Balinese. Winners engage in frenzied celebrations called *victory parties*, and losers are often despondent in defeat. As anthropologists know, this is not always the case in other societies. When the Gahuku-Gama of the Highlands of New Guinea started playing soccer, they always played until a committee of elders decided that the score was tied, and then the match was considered completed. So you speculate that hockey is also about the meanings that Canadians give to the idea of success. You learn that success in Canada (like status in Bali) is a highly abstract idea; because it is abstract, its meaning is embedded in activities understood by members of the society. You need to find answers to certain questions about the meaning of success in Canadian society: How is success defined? How is it obtained? Why doesn't everyone who follows all the rules for gaining success attain it?

Through your fieldwork, you find that most North Americans believe that "all men are created equal" and that every person has (or at least should have) an equal opportunity to succeed. People compete for success, and they ought to compete on an equal footing, on a "level playing field," as some put it. Success, North Americans believe, comes from hard work, sacrifice, and self-denial. But you wonder why North Americans

An anthropologist might suggest that the meaning of hockey, for North Americans, is tied to our cultural understandings of success.

© Mike Blake/Reuters

believe that hard work, sacrifice, and self-denial bring success. Aren't there instances where they do not? How do North Americans explain why women and minorities succeed less often than white males do? And why do some people achieve more success than others? You conclude that it is, in fact, impossible to prove directly in real life the correctness of this North American success model. Faith in the value of work and self-denial must be generated in other ways. As a Balinese anthropologist studying the Canadian custom of hockey, you conclude, then, that the meaning of Canadian hockey lies in its demonstration of the North American success model as it is supposed to work. But there is more to the Canadian game of hockey than simply a mirror of society: Canadian hockey is also a ritual that creates meaning.

Rituals do not just reflect society. As Yngve Lithman suggests, they also draw attention to something and provide an "explanation" for something. One of the reasons why Canadian hockey has become a national symbol is that it brings Canadians from different parts of the country together with a common focus. During the hockey season, a team from Calgary competes against a team from Montreal, a team from Vancouver plays in the same ice rink as a team from Toronto, and so on.

Anthropologist Noel Dyck points out that Canadian hockey "is not only one of Canada's proudest contributions to the world of sport but also a national passion" (2000, 10). Hockey becomes important to children very early in life, and it involves the whole family. Tiny players, called "Tim Bits," sponsored by the Tim Hortons coffee shops throughout Canada, begin their training so young that their mothers or fathers, or even their grandfathers or grandmothers, help them put on their protective clothing in the dressing rooms. Young teams of children are grouped according to age into categories such as "novice," "atom," "peewee," "bantam," and "midget," all progressing to secondary school and university teams. Those working toward professional play are called "Junior" and progress from "Junior D" to "Junior A." At the other end of the life cycle, older players have teams called "old timers," which are also grouped according to age.

Canadian hockey is also a ritual that anthropologists Peter Collings and Richard Condon suggest helps people adjust to sudden change by providing a way for players to gain status, achievement, and self-esteem. In the Kitikmeot region of the Northwest Territories, society is no longer based on hunting as a way of life, but communities are not yet fully integrated into the North American capitalist economy. In the Canadian Arctic, hockey has become a recreational activity that helps bridge this gap, and it consumes the passion of most communities.

At first, when radio and television were introduced to the Arctic, and to the community of Holman where Collings and Condon did their fieldwork in the 1980s, children played hockey on the snow-covered streets. Later, when a sporting organization in Yellowknife sent skates to Inuit communities, children started playing hockey on ice ponds. The initial hockey games were played Inuit style, with little emphasis on winning or losing, and were governed by flexible rules. Eventually, however, a league was established and competition began to take place between teams from different communities. With the formalization of hockey as a competition, violence became a standard feature of the game. Collings and Condon found that significantly more injuries were sustained playing hockey than during any other activity, including hunting, trapping, or fishing. Furthermore, being injured during a hockey game was a sure way to gain prestige, especially if an injured player returned to the ice before his injury was healed. Collings and Condon argue that the game of hockey, as it is played in Holman, models the values of achievement and self-reliance: "If achievement and self-reliance cannot be expressed in the conduct of everyday life, then it can be expressed on the ice while competing with one's peers. Status and control, so elusive to these young people in real life, become attainable goals when modeled in the context of play" (1996, 258).

Collings and Condon acknowledge the positive aspects of sports. Games such as hockey affirm the value of success, as well as a dramatic set of instructions on how it attain it. The games help build character and teach young people about cooperation. But Collings and Condon also suggest that there is a "darker side" to hockey. For some people, "games can teach violence, verbal aggression, subterfuge, cheating, poor sportsmanship, and other undesirable traits" (261). At the same time, hockey demonstrates the limits of acceptable violence. When players break the rules of how the game is supposed to be played they incur penalties, just as citizens are penalized for breaking the laws in Canada. When players score a high number of points, they are rewarded with both prestige and, in the case of professional hockey, wealth. Violence and competition are part of Canadian life, and the game of hockey shows how both are important to Canadians, but both must be controlled.

Anthropologists therefore can conclude (as did Collings and Condon) that hockey provides for Canadians, as the cockfight does for the Balinese, a small-scale rendering of a concept (status in the case of the Balinese, both status and success in the Canadian case) that is too complex to be directly comprehended.

Hockey is compelling because it is a vivid demonstration of the value of success, as well as a dramatic set of instructions on how to attain it. Consequently, the audience for a hockey game is led to believe that if the rules that govern the world of hockey are equated with the rules that govern success outside the rink, then the principles that govern success on the hockey rink must also apply in the outside world. That is, if hard work, dedication, submission to authority, and teamwork lead to success in a game, they will lead to success in real life. The rules by which success is achieved in hockey can also be applied to life to succeed in the real world.

Of course, hockey is also a game that people enjoy. Analyzing it should not reduce our enjoyment of it but rather should heighten our fascination with it. By looking at hockey from the same perspective as Geertz viewed the cockfight, we should gain an understanding of why the meaning carried by the game is important. While understanding the cockfight heightens our appreciation of the hockey game, it also helps us see similarities between Canadians and Balinese. If you were shocked by the cockfight, seeing the similarities to hockey should lessen that shock, at the same time making hockey seem just a bit more exotic.

An Anthropologist Looks at a "Happy Meal"

Nothing is too mundane to provide some insights into the culture of which it is a part. Take the "Happy Meal" advertised by one of the many fast food establishments in North America. It consists of a hamburger, French fries, a cola drink, and a plastic toy, generally a "Barbie" doll or a "Hot Wheels" car. What can we learn about the culture of North America by looking beyond the "taken for granted" quality of this meal? Among other things, we can get some idea of North American demographic and ecological patterns, agricultural and industrial history, and gender roles.

Why, for example, is meat the centre of the meal? Most cultures have diets centred on some complex carbohydrate—rice, wheat, manioc, yams, taro—or something made from these—bread, pasta, tortillas, and so on. It is the spice, vegetables, meat, or fish that when added to these foods give cuisine its distinctive taste. However, meat and fish are generally at the edge, not the centre, of the meal. Why is beef the main ingredient, rather than some other meat, such as pork?

Anthropologists Marvin Harris and Eric Ross note that one advantage of beef was its suitability for the outdoor grill, which became more popular as people moved from cities into suburbs. Suburban cooks soon discovered that pork patties crumbled and fell through the grill, whereas beef patties held together better. In addition, to reduce the risk of trichinosis, pork had to be cooked until it was grey, which makes it very tough.

In the United States, beef farmers, as well as the farmers who grew the corn fed to beef to achieve a desirable fat content, benefited from the definition of a hamburger set by the United States Department of Agriculture: "'Hamburger'" shall consist of chopped fresh and/or frozen beef with or without the addition of beef fat as such and/or seasonings, shall not contain more than 30 percent fat, and shall not contain added water, phosphates, binders, or extenders. Beef cheek (trimmed Beef cheeks) may be used in the preparation of hamburgers only in accordance with the conditions prescribed in paragraph (a) of this section" (quoted in Harris 1987, 125).

As Marvin Harris noted, we can eat ground pork and ground beef, but we can't combine them and still call it a hamburger. Even when lean, grass-fed beef is used for hamburger. Also, fat must be added as a binder, and the fat must come from beef scraps, not from vegetables or a different animal. This definition of the hamburger protects both the beef industry and the corn farmer, whose income is linked to cattle production. Moreover, it helps the fast food industry, because the definition of hamburger permits the use of inexpensive scraps of fat from slaughtered beef to make up to 30% of its hamburger. Thus an international beef patty has been created that has overcome what Harris calls the "pig's natural superiority as a converter of grain to flesh."

The cola drink that accompanies our hamburger is the second part of the fat and sugar-centred diet that has come to characterize our culture. People in Canada consume, on average, about 38.6 kilograms of sugar a year. Why so much? Sugar, as anthropologist Sidney Mintz suggests, has no nutritional properties, but it provides a quick and inexpensive energy boost for hard-working labourers with little time for a more nutritious meal. Sugar also serves as an excellent complement to the fat in hamburgers, because it has what nutritionists call "go-away" qualities that remove the fat coating and the beef aftertaste from the mouth.

We can also learn from the "Happy Meal" that the fat-and-sugar diet is highly environmentally destructive. Beef raising is among the most environmentally inefficient and destructive forms of food raising. For example, the amount of water used to produce 10 pounds of steak equals the household consumption of a family for an entire year. Thirty-three times more water is needed to produce a kilogram of beef protein than an equivalent amount of plant protein.

Cattle raising is playing a major role in the destruction of tropical forests in Brazil, Guatemala, Costa Rica, and Honduras, where forests have been levelled to create pasture for cattle. Since most of the forest is cleared by burning, the creation of cattle pasture also creates carbon dioxide and, according to some environmentalists, contributes significantly to global warming.

Sugar is no less destructive a crop. Sugar production alters the environment in a number of ways.

Forests must be cleared to plant sugar; wood or fossil fuel must be burned in the evaporation process; waste water is produced when sucrose is extracted from the sugar cane; and more fuel is burned in the refining process. Contemporary sugar production in Hawai'i has destroyed forests, and waste products from processing have severely damaged marine environments. "Big Sugar," as the sugar industry is called in Florida, is largely responsible for the pollution, degradation, and virtual destruction of the Everglades.

Thus one of the "texts" that anthropologists can read from a Happy Meal relates to the extent to which consumption patterns associated with our culture create waste and environmental damage. Because of these consumption patterns, the average child born in the United States or Canada will, in the course of his or her lifetime, do twice the environmental damage of a Swedish child, 3 times that of an Italian child, 13 times that of a Brazilian child, 35 times that of an Indian child, and 280 times that of a Chadian or Haitian child.

And what of "Barbie dolls" and "Hot Wheels"? Clearly there is a message about the definition of gender roles, as dolls are expected to be chosen by girls, and cars by boys. But one can deduce, if you look closely enough, even more about our culture from this meal.

EXERCISE 1.4

We've examined some of the lessons we can learn about our culture from the "Happy Meal." There are obviously others. See what you can deduce about the following dimensions of life in North America from the "Happy Meal."

1. What can you say about gender roles in North America?
2. What can you deduce about race relations?
3. What can you say about the physical attributes of people favoured in North America?

QUESTION 1.6: HOW CAN AN ANTHROPOLOGICAL PERSPECTIVE BE USED OUTSIDE OF ACADEMIA?

What Can You Do with a BA in Anthropology?

Students taking anthropology classes often say, "I like anthropology, but what can I do with it?" A more or less typical response is "Anything that you can do with any liberal arts major." However, that doesn't get us very far. Being a professional anthropologist—teacher, researcher, consultant—generally requires an advanced degree. However, an anthropological perspective and methodology can be invaluable in all sorts of career areas, so much so that one national newspaper recently labelled anthropology a "hot major." This does not necessarily mean that you will see scores of job postings looking specifically for candidates with an anthropology degree. However, the demand for candidates with ethnographic skills is on the rise. A recent LinkedIn search using "ethnography" as a keyword yielded many hits that included jobs at Netflix, Skype, Microsoft, VISA, and Google. These examples are all from the corporate world, but many anthropologists are employed in the public sector or by nongovernmental organizations (NGOs) as well. Why are these companies looking for ethnographers? Anthropology, like any discipline, deals with problems and questions, which is what any career or profession does. In the contemporary lingo of Human Resources departments, ethnographers "add value" to the companies they work for by bringing their unique perspective to bear on the problems and questions that they address, and they often have distinctive insights and are able to suggest innovative solutions that accountants, marketers, doctors, or lawyers cannot.

What kinds of problems can ethnographers help solve? People in management must address the problem of how to structure relationships among staff; people in government must address problems involved in designing public policy initiatives, such as reducing juvenile crime. Someone in a medical field may face the problem of how to educate the young regarding sexually transmitted disease, while someone employed in the tourist industry must address the problem of how to minimize the negative consequences of tourism for local populations. The solutions to all of these and other problems can benefit from an anthropological perspective, because all involve ways that people give meaning to their experiences. Throughout the remaining chapters of this book, we will be examining various examples of how anthropological perspectives are applied to careers outside of academia. The best way to understand what anthropology is, and the problem-solving potential of ethnographic insights, is to look at what anthropologists and ethnographers do and at how they approach various kinds of social problems. The examples below, while they are drawn from the experiences of professional anthropologists, nonetheless demonstrate the very important ways in which anthropological knowledge and ethnographic expertise matter in the "real world," and begin to suggest some of the ways that anthropology can be put to use outside of academia.

Applied Anthropology

Applied anthropology is the branch of anthropology that specializes in putting anthropological knowledge into practice outside of academia. Sociocultural anthropology is about social and cultural differences, whether they occur from one country to another or within a single classroom. The fact that different peoples assign different meanings to events, objects, individuals, and emotions is a source of considerable conflict, miscommunication, and misunderstanding. Anthropologists seek to explain this diversity, to help people understand one another better, and, in the process, to apply their experience and knowledge to solving social, economic, educational, and political problems created by diversity.

In Canada, applied anthropologists have been involved in research that has helped document the validity of First Nations land claims. Edward Hedican writes that more and more Native band administrations are employing anthropologists to conduct research in areas that the band finds useful. This makes anthropological research easier because, as Hedican suggests, "people will certainly be more willing to cooperate with researchers if they are able to see that the work has some direct relevance to their lives" (1995, 226).

Law and Society

Another important branch of sociocultural anthropology involves the area of law and society, sometimes called political anthropology. Sally Falk Moore describes this approach as one that "inquires into the context of enforceable norms: social, political, economic, and intellectual. This includes, but goes farther than, what Western governments and courts define as law. In anthropology, while the 'socio-legal' includes formal juridical institutions and their social surroundings, it also encompasses law-like activities and processes of establishing order in many other social domains, formal and informal, official and unofficial, in our own society and in others" (2005, 1).

Anthropologists who study legal issues in a particular place ask questions about power, such as "who makes the rules, who can undo them, how are they normalized and enforced, and how are they morally justified" (2). These questions were first asked in egalitarian societies where legal institutions, such as courts and police, were absent; anthropologists tried to understand what prevented total chaos. Other questions are now being asked in relation to the possible lasting effects of colonialism on "native laws," as the colonial powers enforced their own sense of what was right and just.

In his book *Culture and Power*, Stanley Barrett argues that globalization has increased conflict throughout the world and that anthropology's interest in the political is likely to grow. He suggests that "power, authority, influence, manipulation, and coercion (or force) constitute the basic terms in this field of inquiry" (2002, 19). With these concepts in mind, anthropologists have extended their interest in legal issues to include, for example, indigenous claims on the state and global human rights. They also look at global issues that involve international labour, immigration patterns and obstacles, and development schemes, continually asking, "Who is in control? Whose interests are being served?" We will touch on many of these issues in the chapters that follow.

Political Ecology

A relatively new branch of sociocultural anthropology that is gaining popularity is political ecology, defined by Blaikie and Brookfield (1987, 17) as a field of study that "combines the concerns of ecology and a broadly defined political economy." One of the directions this approach has taken has involved challenging dominant explanations for environmental degradation and contesting some of the popular solutions to environmental problems (Paulson, Gezon, and Watts 2003, 205). Analyzing the politics of environment may uncover the interests of powerful elites who profit from directing public inquiry away from their activities and toward those of less powerful peoples, such as indigenous groups, who are forced into parts of the rain forest, where they clear plots of land to grow subsistence products.

Although political ecology usually focuses on land scarcity and access to material resources, two anthropologists at McMaster University have included community identity in their study of peri-urban political ecology. Tina Moffat and Beth Finnis combine a focus on access to land with access to education in a "squatter" community of 300 people called Nayabasti, in Kathmandu, Nepal.

As in many such communities, most of Nayabasti's people lack both sewers and indoor plumbing and build houses out of rudimentary materials. The people of Nayabasti were given the land informally by the municipal government 30 years ago, but they have no legal documentation and the only improvement that has been made is the partial installation of indoor toilets (unconnected to sewers) by a Danish NGO. When the community was first formed, there were few others close by. However, the area now includes monasteries that were built by Tibetan refugees, as well as the homes of wealthy urbanites who have moved from the core of Kathmandu to the outskirts because the land is cheaper and the air is cleaner. The arrival of these newcomers, who have clear title to their land, has placed the community of Nayabasti at even more risk.

Moffat and Finnis discuss the difficulties the community has faced in its efforts to provide education for local children. In 1998, the residents pooled their resources and set about searching for a place to build their own school. After a period of negotiation with the municipal government, a plot of land was found. The community provided almost all the labour to build the school, with Lumanti, a local NGO, providing financial support. Moffatt and Finnis caution that it is still uncertain whether the school will be sustainable in the long term, but the project did reinforce community identity, and the community's "ability to get this far is evidence of the incredible capacity of slum and squatter dwellers" (2005, 465).

Medical Anthropology

Medical anthropology is another branch of anthropology in which anthropologists are able to put their ethnographic skills and perspectives to good use. According to the Society for Medical Anthropology, it is "a subfield of anthropology that draws upon social, cultural, biological, and linguistic anthropology to better understand those factors which influence health and well being (broadly defined), the experience and distribution of illness, the prevention and treatment of sickness, healing processes, the social relations of therapy management, and the cultural importance and utilization of pluralistic medical systems."

This subfield of anthropology has moved in many directions. Medical anthropologists may analyze the politics of health care access, local interpretations and experience of health and illness, the cultural and historical context of contemporary medical practice and policies, or perceptions and experiences of risk and stigma related to various illnesses. Naomi Adelson is a medical anthropologist who has done fieldwork with the James Bay Cree of northern Quebec. In her ethnography, *Being Alive Well*, she notes that the Cree do not have a word that readily translates into what we call "health" in English. Rather, they talk about *miyupimaatisiiun*, or "being alive well." For the Cree, being alive well has less to do with individuals and physiology than with social and political relations. Adelson's informants asked, rhetorically, "If the land is not healthy, than how can we be?" (2000, 1). The Cree understanding and experience of health is grounded in what it means to "be Cree," which is itself grounded in connections to the land and to the past (25). Once, the James Bay Cree travelled and hunted across a vast swath of land in northwestern Quebec, but today many live in the village of Whapmagoostui at the mouth of the Great Whale River, hunting in the bush only on weekends. Since the 1970s, the Cree have been fighting with the provincial government of Quebec over the appropriate uses of the land and its resources, most famously in the building of the James Bay I hydroelectric dam and the failed James Bay II project. While the Quebec government saw the land as underused and underpopulated and as a untapped source of wealth and power, the Cree knew that the projects would drastically alter the ecosystem surrounding Whapmagoostui, changing the migration and survival patterns of land and sea mammals, fish, and birds. What would it mean to be

Cree in the face of such changes? How could they manage to "be alive well"? Adelson argues that "all definitions of health ... are laden with ideological nuances and can never be separated from cultural norms and values" (1).

Since Adelson conducted her initial fieldwork, there has been a fusing, at the local level, of health and politics. Adelson distributed copies of her research to local political and health authorities, and her use of "being alive well" to explain Cree understandings of health has been incorporated, via *The James Bay Experience: A Guide for Health Professionals Working Among the Cree in Northern Quebec*, into the vocabulary of doctors, dentists, and other health care workers in the area (115).

THE CULTURAL CONSTRUCTION OF IDENTITY

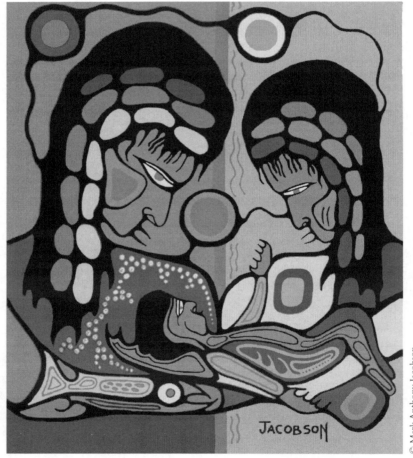

© Mark Anthony Jacobson

From the moment we are born, interactions with others are shaped by their perceptions of us. According to Goffman, who we quote in the epigraph, we use our bodies in unconscious and conscious ways to communicate information about ourselves to others. Through our speech, clothing, gestures, postures, and other phenomena, people make assumptions and often judgments about our character and our place in the world. Similarly, we often consciously manipulate our bodies to show others who we think we are. These aspects of what we call identity—including race, class, and gender—form the subject of this chapter.

When an individual enters the presence of others, they commonly seek to acquire information about him or to bring into play information about him already possessed. They will be interested in his general socioeconomic status, his conception of self, his attitude toward them, his competence, his trustworthiness, etc. Although some of this information seems to be sought almost as an end in itself, there are usually quite practical reasons for acquiring it. Information about the individual helps to define the situation, enabling others to know in advance what he will expect of them and what they may expect of him. Informed in these ways, the others will know how best to act in order to call forth a desired response from him.

Erving Goffman

PROBLEM 5

How do people determine who they are and how do they communicate who they think they are to others?

INTRODUCTION

Try to imagine a society in which every person is physically indistinguishable from every other person. How would people in such a society know how to behave toward one another? Whenever we interact with another person, the interaction must be based on some idea of who the other is: Friend? Stranger? Family member? Teacher? At the same time, the other must have some idea of who *we* are, a conception of the relationship that exists between us. The need to know the social identity of others is apparent whenever two strangers meet and, directly or indirectly, seek to elicit information about each other. Each tries to place the other in some identity at some spot on the social landscape.

Imagine next a society in which every person is completely unique. In this case, every interaction would be different, and there would be no way to learn from one situation how to behave in another similar situation. Each person would need to have an infinite variety of behaviours with which to interact with an infinite number of types of people. We avoid this situation by categorizing people, placing them in groups so that not everyone in our social universe is unique. We group them into categories based on criteria such as gender (female, male, or some other gender); ethnicity (Irish, Italian, Chinese); personal characteristics (short, tall, husky, thin), and so on.

Try to imagine, also, a social landscape in which no person acknowledges any other person or communicates in any way who she or he thinks the other is.

This, too, would represent an impossible situation. People would have no way of acquiring from others confirmation that they occupy the social identities they think they occupy. In reality, our social identities are constructed in large part by others, who, by their behaviour toward us, confirm that we occupy the spot on the landscape we claim to occupy. Put another way, nobody is anybody except in relation to somebody.

Finally, try to imagine a social landscape in which everyone communicates to everyone else that they occupy the wrong spot on the landscape. Every person actively disagrees with every other person about who they are. This situation would be, if not impossible, at least chaotic.

To examine how people in a society determine who they are and communicate who they think they are to others, in this chapter we will explore the ways different societies define the person, the ways individuals are differentiated from others, the ways they find out who they are and convey to others who they are, and the ways they form collective identities. Then in Chapter 6 we will continue our exploration of identity with an in-depth examination of how social identities such as race, gender, and class are constructed.

QUESTIONS

5.1 How is identity, and one's sense of self, learned?

5.2 How does the concept of personhood vary from society to society?

5.3 How do societies distinguish individuals from one another?

5.4 How do societies mark changes in identity?

5.5 How do individuals communicate their identities to one another?

5.6 How do individuals form identities through collective struggles?

QUESTION 5.1: HOW IS IDENTITY, AND ONE'S SENSE OF SELF, LEARNED?

Learning Identities

Hugh Brody begins his book *The Other Side of Eden: Hunters, Farmers, and the Shaping of the World* (2000) with a description of a baby Inuit girl:

> *Imagine the darkness of the far north. Not as something in which the adventurous traveller moves in awe. But as a beginning, for those for whom the Arctic is home. Imagine the inside of a skin tent, or a snowhouse, or a government-regulation low-rental prefab. In this home, an Inuit baby girl wakes in the night. She is held, fed, cuddled—and talked to …*
>
> *In these words, the child is given the sounds of love, and can know that she is safe. Not safe just to feed, to sleep, but safe to do these things as and when she wants. For she is a baby who carries atiq, the spirit and name of her late grandmother. She is the adored baby; she is also her mother's mother, her grandfather's wife. Her grandmother is alive again in the baby. This means the baby is doubly and trebly loved. And she must be treated with respect. (2000, 11–12)*

Is this Inuit baby born with an **identity**? Or is her identity something she must learn? It is certainly very clear to others in her Inuit community that she is the reincarnation of her grandmother, but how long will it take the baby to understand what that means?

---

identity
Learned personal and social types of affiliation, including gender, sexuality, race, class, nationalism, and ethnicity, for example.

Learning to Belong

Hugh Brody suggests that the Inuit baby begins to know that she is an important member of her family almost the moment she is born, and that this knowledge expands daily as she interacts with others. As people tell her stories about her land and its creation, she builds up an image of her world and of her place in it. She learns that she is connected to her land and to all the other creatures that share the land with her.

Stories present people of all ages with ways of knowing about who they are and where they came from. Storytelling is also a way of communicating information from one generation to another (Ridington 1990, 14). No one censors Inuit stories, and children's understanding grows as they grow. Brody describes the Inuit child's experiences with stories told by her grandfather and other adults: "The small child listens for as long as she wishes—she is, after all, also her own grandmother. And she discovers that stories are always a mystery, for they have much that cannot be understood, and much that comes from knowledge and experience beyond understanding" (2000, 13).

As this child grows, she recognizes stories that are told over and over, with the same main characters and events. She also learns that no one understands everything in the stories, and she keeps her sense of wonderment about the world.

Brody's example highlights a key point about identity: we are not born knowing who we are or what our places are on the social landscape; we *learn* to be Canadian or Japanese, husbands or wives, Andrea, Gavin, Homa, Natasha, or Sebastian. We learn how we relate to others as sons, daughters, students, friends, or lovers. Both consciously and unconsciously, individuals form various identities so that they can relate to others and cultivate a space for themselves within their social landscape. At the same time, identities are political and collective, formed around struggles against such threats as colonialism or the state. As we become who we are, we learn how we stand in relation to others.

Identities like gender, sexuality, race, ethnicity, and national identity, to name a few, are not natural or biological. We are not born knowing instinctively what it means to "be Canadian," for instance. Our sense of Canadianness, like any other identity, is cultivated and learned through various agents of **enculturation**. These are sociocultural forces and institutions that teach us, consciously or unconsciously, about what it means to be a Canadian citizen. Agents of enculturation may include the mass media, parents, peers, school, and the government, for instance. Think about the ways in which children are enculturated into the norms of "Canadian identity," for example, in many public school systems across Canada. In elementary school, most children learn how to sing the national anthem, and because provincial governments control the content of the school curriculum, they learn a government-sanctioned version of Canadian history. Students must demonstrate their successful acquisition and knowledge of this history on tests and papers in order to advance to the next grade. Even as they graduate and get older, Canadians continue to learn about Canada through participation in Canada Day parades and other public spectacles, or by watching the national news on Canadian television stations like the CBC (Canadian Broadcasting Corporation). In Canada, the mass media play an important role in shaping ideals of Canadianness through media depictions of sport, for instance. Hockey, in particular, has long been promoted as a component of a distinctive Canadian identity. However, hockey's participants and spectators are mostly white, middle-class, and male (Gruneau and Whitson 1993; Hartman 2009). As such, it is a sport that (perhaps unintentionally) promotes a dominant,

enculturation
The process through which individuals learn an identity. This can encompass parental socialization, the influence of peers, the mass media, government, or other forces.

THE CULTURAL CONSTRUCTION OF IDENTITY   **141**

Canadians playing hockey.

a shared sense of "Canadianness" is created through mediated experiences: watching and listening to stories about the 2010 Vancouver Olympics; attending Canada Day spectacles and ceremonies; following the national news on television, radio, and the Internet or in newspapers; and so on. Because this process of enculturation often begins when we are young, we often fail to see how various cultural forces shape our identities. Thus, we often view our identities as natural, primordial, or biologically based. Think of the many people who are willing to "sacrifice" themselves or die for their country, for instance. Often, an individual is willing to go to such lengths only if they feel that their identification with their nation is somehow instinctual and, by extension, natural.

Over the past century, anthropologists have engaged actively with precisely these sorts of debates. We live in a pop culture that privileges natural explanations for human behaviours. This has been the case since the late 1800s, with the rise of the **"nature versus nurture"** debate in academia. In 1874 the British naturalist Sir Francis Galton, inspired by the principles of Darwinian evolution, coined the term "nature versus nurture." Galton was a eugenicist who felt that some people, by virtue of their class, race, or other factors, were better suited to reproduce as they were more "fit" to survive in society. Galton believed that many human differences, including intelligence, were rooted in biology, or "nature." His ideas spawned wildly inaccurate assumptions and research on the

or normative, ideal of Canadian identity as white, middle-class, and male. This is a problem, given that Canada is officially a diverse, multicultural nation in which no particular gender, sexuality, or ethnic or racial identity should be privileged as "more Canadian" than any other. In this context, hockey's iconic status as a national symbol is ironic, for it excludes a large portion of the nation's multicultural population and promotes hierarchies of Canadianness. To be "truly" Canadian, we learn, is to consume and participate in hockey. In recent years, the sport has been trying to connect with the nation's increasingly multicultural and multilingual population base. Beginning in 2007, for instance, the NHL began broadcasting hockey games in Punjabi.

Despite the problematical nature of hockey as a "Canadian" identity marker, it is important to note that shared experiences, such as sports and other mediated events, are often used to cultivate a sense of **imagined community**. This term, coined by political scientist Benedict Anderson in 1983, suggests that identities, including national ones, are culturally constructed through shared experiences, even in the absence of face-to-face contacts. So, even though a Canadian living in Halifax may never have visited Toronto, Regina, or Whitehorse,

> **imagined community**
> A term coined by Benedict Anderson in 1983. It refers to the fact that even in the absence of face-to-face interactions, a sense of community (e.g., nationalism) is culturally constructed by forces such as the mass media.
>
> **nature versus nurture**
> This phrase, coined by Francis Galton in 1874, references a longstanding scholarly debate concerning whether or not human behaviours and identities are the result of nature (biological and genetic factors) or nurture (learned and cultural factors).

part of academics throughout the late 19th and 20th centuries. At the time, many scholars felt that many of our identities, such as race or class, are acquired, and genetic and thus "natural"—that we are born the way we are.

One of the first anthropologists to engage ethnographically with the nature versus nurture debate was Margaret Mead. In 1926, Mead set out for American Samoa to conduct research that would challenge widespread ideas among scientists that acts of teenage rebellion and experimentation were the result of hormonal or other physical changes brought on by puberty (or "nature"). Such behaviour was commonplace among American teenagers; Mead wondered whether similar behavioural patterns existed in other cultures. Under the direction of her doctoral supervisor, Franz Boas, she travelled to the island of Ta'u to study the behaviour of teenage girls. She observed that their experiences of adolescence were completely different from the experiences of American girls. In Samoa, girls were given a lot of freedom to experiment with their sexuality and did not go through periods of torment with parents. Samoan culture, she argued, did not possess the same Judeo-Christian ideals of sexual morality; this in turn contributed to different behaviours and attitudes toward sexuality. Mead thus argued that the experiences of adolescents varied depending on the culture in which they were raised. She therefore emphasized the role of culture or "nurture" in human behaviour. While Mead's methods and research findings would subsequently be disputed, she continued her ethnographic work on the "nature/nurture" debate in 1935. She visited three tribes along the Sepik river in Papua New Guinea to explore differences in gender roles. She found that in each tribe, men and women took on different responsibilities based on their gender. She was thus able to suggest, once again, that human behavioural differences (in this case, gendered divisions of labour) were the result of culture and not biology.

Research that seeks to link biology with human behaviours and identities is potentially dangerous, for it can provide biological justifications for social inequalities in society. Back in 1968, for instance, Washburn and Lancaster sought to argue that women, for biological and evolutionary reasons, were better "nurturers" of children—an argument that has since been disputed by feminist scholars. But think of the consequences of this type of research. If women can be "proven" to be naturally better "nurturers," then it becomes easy to argue that a woman's place is in the domestic sphere. This information could then inform government policies relating to day care funding, affirmative action, and other social issues.

Anthropological fieldwork in various societies has shed light on the problems associated with viewing all human identities in terms of "nature." Yet the development and widespread valorization of the Human Genome Project continues to link identities with nature. Think of the ways in which scientists are actively searching for specific genes that they believe are the cause of particular behaviours. We live in a society that valorizes the "gene" and that is fascinated by ongoing research on the so-called "gay gene," or the "selfish gene." Such research, however, reduces the diversity of human behaviours to biology, ignores the role of culture in shaping identities like race, gender, and sexuality, and obscures the fact that many individual behaviours, such as "selfishness," may

American anthropologist Margaret Mead in Admiralty Islands.

© Bettmann/CORBIS

THE CULTURAL CONSTRUCTION OF IDENTITY   **143**

Some contemporary Tsimshian children continue to follow tradition by wearing traditional shawls and will change their name upon entering adulthood.

be the result of complex interplays of culture and biology.

Now that we have explored how anthropologists tend to emphasize the learned, culturally constructed nature of our personal and collective identities, in the next section we examine in greater detail how a sense of self or personhood is shaped by various cultural forces.

QUESTION 5.2: HOW DOES THE CONCEPT OF PERSONHOOD VARY FROM SOCIETY TO SOCIETY?

The Importance of Self

Of all the products of our culture, the one we most take for granted is our self.

Personal names in all societies are intimate markers of the person, differentiating individuals from others. Names also can reveal how people conceive of themselves and their relations to others. For many North Americans, they are perhaps the most enduring aspect of the self. Assigned at birth, our names remain with us throughout our lives. Some people may choose to modify them—to shorten Kathleen to Kate, or Phillip to Phil. Whatever form a name takes, it represents the self. How much of the self is revealed by a name varies by culture and situation. University students meeting for the first time exchange personal names, rarely bothering with family names. Theirs is a self independent of any group or past. When North American businesspeople meet, they exchange first names, last names, and business titles. Business people are linked to their organizations. When Moroccans from different towns meet, the names they offer to others include not only the names of their families but the names of the towns they are from. The Moroccan self is embedded in family and place of origin. Among the Tsimshian of British Columbia, the names people use depend on their social position; when they enter adulthood, get married, or assume a higher rank in Tsimshian society, they change their names. The Tsimshian self is inseparable from one's position in society.

Jorge Chimbinda, an anthropology student from Angola, wrote about Umbundu names for his master's thesis at the University of Western Ontario. Among Umbundu people in Angola, there are two ways of naming a child. The most common way is to name a child after a relative who is either alive or dead (an ancestor). The second way is to give a child a new name that refers to some unusual circumstance that was present during the child's birth. For example, a child born during a severe drought will be given a name that refers to the drought and keeps the memory of the suffering alive. The child of a mother who dies in childbirth will be given a name that keeps the memory of his or her mother's suffering and death. The result of this way of naming is that each child has his or her own last name. At the same time, the Umbundu naming system is a historical version of cultural values, such as identity, kinship, geography, folktales, stories, and proverbs. Therefore, beyond an Umbundu name we can find a proverb and beyond this proverb there is a story. As a consequence, when people hear a name, they remember the wise message that is transmitted through this name.

From the Umbundu perspective, names are tools with which people reward the life they have received from their relatives and their world. Names serve to perpetuate the wide kinship web and stress the concept of extended family. Each child represents one of his or her living relatives or ancestors. All relatives and ancestors on both the father's side and the mother's have equal value, because each of them has contributed with his or her life to the existence of the child. These names also inscribe the imprint of lived experiences on children, so that children named after unusual circumstances embody the meaning of the experiences.

Jorge Chimbinda also explores the effects of colonialism on his people. When Angola became a Portuguese colony, the colonial administrators found it too difficult to keep track of Umbundu people because the naming system did not group people in ways that the administrators understood. For the Portuguese, as for most Europeans, last names were shared among members of families and made family identification orderly. Thus, one of the first ways that the Portuguese colonizers tried to destroy Umbundu identity was to force people to discard their Umbundu names and to use Portuguese names instead. The differences in naming practices among different societies reveal the different ways societies conceptualize what a person is and how that person relates to the group. Many North Americans believe that individuals are stable, autonomous entities who exist more or less independently of whatever situations or statuses they occupy. As they move from status to status or place to place—from student to husband or wife, to employee, to father or mother—they believe themselves to be the same persons nevertheless. Otherwise, each time they changed situations or statuses they would in effect become different people and would have to change their names. In this regard North Americans are highly **individualistic.** This does not seem to be the case in other societies, where individuals are not seen as entities distinct from their social position or group. In societies such as the Umbundu, the relationship between the person and the group, or the person and his or her social position, is **holistic**; the person cannot be conceived as existing separately from society or apart from his or her cultural beliefs and values. The holistic view of the self is expressed in Gandhi's metaphor of individuals as drops in the ocean; the drops cannot survive without the ocean, and the ocean loses its identity without the drops.

EXERCISE 5.2

If you were an Umbundu and lived in Angola, which of your ancestors would you choose for the name of your first child? Why would you make this particular choice? In other words, what are the qualities in your ancestors that you would want to transfer to your child? What about your second child and your third?

individualistic
A view of the self in which the individual is primarily responsible for his or her own actions.

holistic
When an individual's sense of self cannot be conceived as existing separately from society or apart from his or her status or role.

THE CULTURAL CONSTRUCTION OF IDENTITY   **145**

The Egocentric and Sociocentric Self

These differences between the individualistic and holistic conceptions of the self led Richard A. Shweder and Edmund J. Bourne to delineate two distinct ways in which the person is conceived in different societies: the **egocentric** and the **sociocentric** views of self. Note that these terms are generalizations about the nature of self in different societies. There will, of course, be exceptions to these patterns, especially given the increasing influence of globalization in constructing our identities. For example, over the past 40 years or so, individuals have become increasingly mobile, travelling in search of work, for immigration, as tourists, or as refugees. Many people's sense of self is also shaped by relationships and experiences with mediated technologies, such as the Internet, which disseminate new ideas within various societies. So it is important to recognize that there exist multiple definitions and interpretations of self, even within the generalized contexts of the societies described below.

In the *egocentric* view, typified in many ways by the Western view adopted by North American societies, each person is a replica of all humanity, the locus of motivations and drives, capable of acting independently from others. For Westerners, the individual is the centre of awareness, a distinct whole set against other wholes. Social relations are regarded as contracts between autonomous, free-acting beings. Individuals are free to negotiate their places in society, and the dominant idea is that each individual is responsible for what and who he or she is. Moreover, individuals possess intrinsic qualities such as generosity, integrity, or beauty. The egocentric view of the person places a high value on individualism and self-reliance.

Keeping in mind that factors such as poverty and ethnicity may make individualism and self-reliance difficult to achieve, it is worthwhile to explore the beliefs associated with this view of the individual. Robert Bellah and his co-authors of *Habits of the Heart* (1984) examined ideas of the individual in the United States that seem to apply equally to Canada. The self in the United States, they say, seeks to work out its own life plot by individually pursuing happiness and satisfying its wants. Unlike individuals in some other societies, many Americans seek to cut themselves off from the past, especially from their parents. Each wishes to become his or her own person, to find his or her own self. Americans seem to want to give birth to themselves. Young men and women need to demonstrate that they can stand on their own two feet and be self-supporting. This belief in a self-reliant, independent self underpins the belief Americans hold that success is the outcome of free and fair competition among individuals in an open market. Most successful Americans, say Bellah and his associates, claim that they achieved success through their own hard work, seldom acknowledging the contributions made by their families, their schooling, or their position as a member of the upwardly mobile middle class. The only way they can say they deserve what they have achieved is by succeeding through their own efforts.

Because of this dominant perspective of self, many people who were raised within Western, industrialized societies are inclined to view those afflicted with, for instance, eating disorders such as anorexia nervosa or bulimia, as suffering from an individual pathology. It's as if eating disorders were the result of an individual's "problem." Helen Gremillion (2003) conducted fourteen months of ethnographic research at a small inpatient

---

egocentric
A view of the self that defines each person as a replica of all humanity, as the location of motivations and drives, and as capable of acting independently from others.

sociocentric
A context-dependent view of self. The self exists as an entity only within the concrete situations or roles occupied by the person.

eating disorder clinic in the United States. She discovered there that the various cultural forces that have contributed to increases in diagnoses of eating disorders are being ignored in favour of "individualistic" explanations. For example, Gremillion and others often point out that mass media advertising plays a role in constructing normative expectations of an impossibly ideal femininity. Increasingly, the feminine ideal is being defined by physical appearance—in particular, by representations of predominantly white, youthful, slender, "beautiful" women. In this way, advertising on television and the Internet, in magazines, and on billboards is playing a powerful role in shaping Westerners' sense of self. Advertising provides a blueprint, or a measuring stick, for comparing our bodies with others. Yet its images of ideal femininity have themselves been constructed and manipulated by computer technologies, which remove wrinkles or fine lines, minimize fat, and reshape facial features. Gremillion argues that because they fail to recognize the role of culture in shaping the self, many eating disorder treatments replicate Western notions of individualism within their treatment plans, which include the careful daily monitoring of weight and patient "progress." These principles of egocentrism, of the individual monitoring of the body—and, by extension, the self—have led to a proliferation of eating disorders.

In contrast to the egocentric view, the *sociocentric* view of the self is context-dependent. The self exists as an entity only within the concrete situations or roles occupied by the person in much the same way that Tsimshian names are linked to a position in society and not to some autonomous, separate self. From a sociocentric perspective, there is no intrinsic self that can possess enduring qualities such as generosity, integrity, or beauty. These qualities can apply only to concrete social situations. Instead of saying that a man is generous, a sociocentric perspective would be that "he gives money to his friends." Instead of saying that a woman is principled, the perspective would be that "she does not give away secrets."

Personhood in Japan and North America

Some anthropologists attribute a sociocentric view of the self to people in Japan. Anthropologist Christie Kiefer (1976) explained that the Japanese are more likely to include within the boundaries of the self the social groups of which the person is a member. Contrast this with the North American self-concept, which does not extend beyond the physical body. Japanese children are not trained to rely solely on the self, as many North American children are. They are taught that interdependence between the person and the family or group is more important than independence.

Robert Smith (1983) noted that the Japanese view of the self is expressed in their language. For example, Japanese language does not include anything resembling English personal pronouns. In English, children quickly learn to use the two personal referents, I and you; Japanese boys, on the

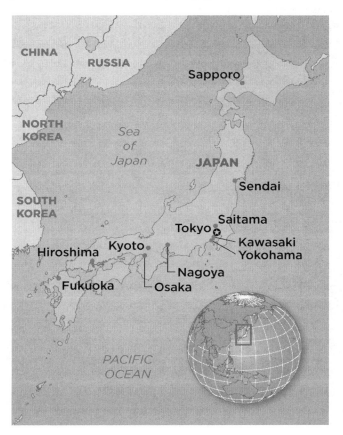

THE CULTURAL CONSTRUCTION OF IDENTITY 147

other hand, must learn six, and girls must learn five. The personal referent used in Japan depends on the speaker's relationship to the listener. It expresses how the self is defined relative to a specific social interaction.

In addition, wrote Smith, the Japanese language contains vocabulary that is very conscious of status. It is characterized by what the Japanese call *keigo*, or "polite speech." *Keigo* has the effect of establishing at the outset of a conversation the relative social standing and degree of intimacy of speaker and listener. Japanese speakers use different forms of address depending on their social position relative to the person to whom they are speaking. Since the Japanese language is status based, people must be careful of the linguistic forms they use in conversations. When conversing with someone in a superior social position, a speaker must linguistically acknowledge the social difference between speaker and listener. Japanese advertisers have a problem with *keigo* because actors should not give imperative commands (e.g., "Drink Coke") for fear of offending people. They solve the problem by using low-status people who are nonthreatening (e.g., clowns, coquettish women, or children) to issue the commands.

The sociocentric Japanese differ also in their approach to social interactions. Most North Americans believe it is desirable to assert themselves;

some even take assertiveness training. They believe that it is desirable for people to stand out, to take charge. The Japanese believe that social interactions should be characterized by restraint or reserve, traits they identify as *enryo*. With *enryo*, giving opinions is avoided; this attitude is summarized by the Japanese proverb "the nail that sticks up shall be hammered down."

Yet the Japanese *do* conceive of themselves as separate entities. They are as attached to their personal names as North Americans are, if not more so. Moreover, they believe in self-development. But for them, the autonomy of the individual is established, not in social situations where they actively distinguish themselves from others, but *away from* society, where self-reflection and introspection are legitimate. It is through introspection that the Japanese find their true heart (*kokoro*) and are put in touch with their true nature—their *hara* ("belly") and *jibub* ("self").

In the remainder of this chapter, we will be looking at the self less from an egocentric perspective and more from a sociocentric perspective, as something contingent and relative to the situation. Our focus will be on that part of the self that is defined by social relations and social processes and that is subject to change and redefinition.

QUESTION 5.3: HOW DO SOCIETIES DISTINGUISH INDIVIDUALS FROM ONE ANOTHER?

Differences and similarities among persons are the materials from which we construct our social landscapes. Those materials are what allow us to distinguish individuals from one another or assign them to one group or another. From these similarities and differences we construct our social identities. However, all societies do not use the same similarities and differences to construct a social code,

EXERCISE 5.3

Young people begin to learn in early childhood what their culture expects of them with regard to appropriate behaviour. Schools in North America are significant environments for learning about self and others. How does the school environment function to help shape the identity of individuals and groups? Are there ways in which individualism is submerged? Might school settings differ in the extent to which the egocentric, as opposed to the sociocentric, self is developed?

nor do they use these similarities and differences in the same way. Some characteristics of persons—some tools in the "identity toolbox," so to speak—are used almost universally to differentiate people or to group them together. For example, most societies use family membership, gender, and age as categories within a social code. But there are other characteristics that figure prominently only in some societies—ethnic group membership, skin colour, and wealth, for example.

In many societies, the most important characteristics for defining the self are related to kinship and family membership. In these societies, kinship is the central organizing principle—the main determinant of a person's social identity. Anthropologists working with these societies are often "adopted" by a family. This act is a signal of acceptance; but it also serves the practical purpose of assigning an outsider a social identity through which she or he can be approached by others. To have no kinship label or designation in such societies is to have no meaningful place on the social landscape.

Language is another important identity marker, one that is sometimes viewed as essential for the maintenance of group identity. Language is often tied strongly to a national identity, and many countries have established institutions to oversee the "purity" of the national language. The Académie Française has for centuries been charged with keeping the French language free of foreign borrowings, such as "le hot dog" or "le weekend." In some countries, conflicts between groups focus on language issues. In Quebec, for example, efforts of one group to preserve French as the official language of the province, and thus protect what it sees as essential to group identity, have led to a movement for independence from the English-speaking remainder of Canada.

The Québécois, however, argue that Quebec identity is not based solely on language. As they see it, their history in Canada is one of "slights, assaults, yet survival" (Eller 1999, 297). The conflict between anglophones and francophones in Canada has been ongoing since both arrived on North American shores. In 1759, the English drove the French "Acadians" out of eastern Canada; and after the Battle of the Plains of Abraham, outside the walls of Quebec City, the Treaty of Paris gave Canada to the English. In 1791, two separate societies were formed: Lower Canada was French and Upper Canada was English, and each had its own culture, religion, stories, political views, and language. Then in 1841, the Act of Union joined the two societies together, but this was an uneasy union: Canada East was still French, Canada West still English. Canadian Confederation, set out in the British North America Act of 1867, created two provinces: Quebec for the French and Ontario for the English. Even so, the two were part of a single entity, Canada, and that entity was ruled by the English.

In the 1960s, during what is often referred to as the Quiet Revolution, Quebec began building its own sense of nationalism, which saw Quebec as a "homeland" in which the French were "masters in their own house" (Eller 1999, 327). That "house" was no longer inhabited by French Canadians or francophones; rather, it was the house of the Québécois—people who were ready to take control of their own lives and separate from the rest of Canada, if necessary.

© Alain Nogues/Sygma/Corbis

Continuing his support of Quebec's Quiet Revolution, French president Charles de Gaulle declared, "Vive le Québec libre!" in his historic 1967 speech at Montreal's town hall.

QUESTION 5.4: HOW DO SOCIETIES MARK CHANGES IN IDENTITY?

Identities are not static, and people are constantly changing their identities as they move through the life cycle. These changes in identity are announced in myriad ways. Many societies have particular ceremonies or rituals that mark a change in a person's status or role in society. Most societies hold religious and/or secular events such as baptisms, confirmations, bat/bar mitzvahs, birthdays, funerals, and graduations to mark significant changes in an individual's status in society. In this section we explore cross-cultural examples of these phenomena.

The Transition to Adulthood

In a 1908 book now considered a classic of anthropology, Arnold van Gennep introduced the concept of **rites of passage**. These rituals mark a person's passage from one identity to another, in the same way that a person's progress through a house might be marked by entering one room after another. Van Gennep identified three phases in rites of passage: separation, liminality, and reincorporation. First, the ritual separates the person from an existing identity; next, the person enters a transition phase; finally, the changes are incorporated into a new identity. These phases of rites of passage are not equally elaborated in all ceremonies. The separation phase, for example, is a major part of funeral ceremonies designed to help the living let go of the deceased; transition is a major part of initiation ceremonies marking the passage of a person from, say, childhood to adulthood; and incorporation is emphasized in marriage ceremonies, which in most societies mark the transfer of a person from one social group to another.

Rites of passage are visible in Canadian society. For instance, a young man or woman who joins the military is required to undergo "boot camp." Geographically and spatially sequestered from mainstream society, the new recruit lives with other recruits in a dormitory. He or she marks this sense of separation by undergoing physical changes, such as cutting one's hair and wearing a uniform. These acts standardize physical appearances and visually mark an individual as a newcomer/initiate. Recruits then undergo a period of transition or liminality, where they are expected to perform physically and emotionally draining tasks, such as running long distances when sleep deprived, or enduring verbal insults. Finally, a recruit who is able to endure the stresses of boot camp re-enters mainstream society with a new status—soldier. This period of reincorporation is marked by a new uniform and by a ceremony where the initiate is reintroduced to family and friends with a new status.

Prominent in most societies around the world are ceremonies that mark the transition of a male from boyhood to manhood. Most such ceremonies involve a test of courage. According to anthropologist David Gilmore (1990), one reason why so many societies incorporate tests of masculinity and tortuous initiation rituals for males is that the male identity is more problematical than the female identity. For every individual, there is at the beginning of life a subliminal identification with the mother, and men must make greater efforts to differentiate themselves from their mothers. Consequently, societies incorporate rituals that symbolically separate the boy from his mother, while at the same time incorporating him into manhood.

Victor Turner (1967) used van Gennep's model of rites of passage to describe the move from boyhood to manhood among the Ndembu of Zambia. When Ndembu boys reach puberty, they are taken, as a group of age mates, away from their mothers and

> **rites of passage**
> This term, coined in 1908 by Arnold Van Gennep, refers to rituals that accompany changes in status, such as the transition from boyhood to manhood, living to dead, or student to graduate.

out of the village (separation), to live in the forest (transition). There the boys shave their heads and remove anything from their bodies that might identify them as individuals. While in the forest, the young Ndembu are circumcised and taught all of the special knowledge that Ndembu men know. But in the forest, they have no identity; they are no longer boys, but they are not yet men. In Turner's words, they are "betwixt and between." Once their circumcisions heal and the lessons are completed, the young men return to the village (reintegration) as new persons with new identities. These men, who made the transition to manhood together, will remain in close association throughout their lives as age mates, a category that cuts across kinship groups and that has special tasks in many societies, such as herding animals among pastoralists.

QUESTION 5.5: HOW DO INDIVIDUALS COMMUNICATE THEIR IDENTITIES TO ONE ANOTHER?

Both consciously and unconsciously, we make statements about our identity—who we think we are, or who we want to be—with objects and material things. The clothes we wear and the things we possess are used to display an identity that we desire or that we think we have. In North America, think about how designer clothing, shoes, and bags are coveted by some women as markers of class and status. Similarly, we use language, or the way we speak, to communicate our identities. In many societies, for instance, one's accent is a marker of class status, gender, geography, or other phenomena. Think about how accents in Britain are based not only on where an individual lives—Londoners have a different accent from Liverpudlians—but also on class.

Similarly, clothing can express class as well as gender, sexuality, ethnicity, or religious affiliation. In some cases, clothing marks some individuals as

"Other" even within their own society. Women who wear the Muslim veil in North America, for instance, have often been identified as "the enemy within," especially since 9/11. Some Muslims in Canada have dealt with this by changing their names and creating fictitious origins. Others have removed visible signs of their Muslimness, particularly with regard to their dress. Still others have tried to show Canadians that the stereotype that all Muslims are terrorists is not only wrong but completely illogical.

In a study conducted by Homa Hoodfar (2003), young Muslim women in Canada reported that wearing the veil was not something their parents forced them to do. In fact, most of the women Hoodfar talked to said they had had to fight with their parents in order to wear it. This contradicts the claims made by some North American feminists that banning the veil will free women from Islamic patriarchal oppression (2003, 15). When Hoodfar and her research assistants asked young women why they wear the veil, one woman said that doing so "allowed her to be a 'person' rather than an object of male scrutiny" (2003, 17–18). Other women explained that they took up the veil when they started university because wearing it communicated certain values. In Hoodfar's words, "By taking up the veil, they symbolically but clearly announce to their parents and their community that, despite their unconventional activities and involvement with non-Muslims, they retain their Islamic mores and values. They are modern Muslim women who want to be educated and publicly active, but not at the cost of their moral principles" (2003, 21). In the same sense that "a picture is worth a thousand words," they believed that wearing the veil communicated identity in a way that saved them from having to explain why they behaved in certain ways.

While some Muslim women in Canada choose to wear "Islamic dress"[1] to emphasize their modesty

[1] There are different interpretations as to what constitutes an "Islamic dress." For example, some women wear a head scarf and a long dress over their clothes to cover the body completely, and sometimes conceal part of the face; others believe that a head scarf suffices to fulfill the requirements of their faith.

and to divert attention from the contours of their bodies and their sexual appeal, people in some societies may want to *highlight* their sexuality so that it is immediately visible to others. Men in some groups in New Guinea, for example, wear penis gourds. And in 17th-century Europe, men wore codpieces to emphasize their male anatomy.

Sexual identification is an important identity marker, but there are other signals that people use to display their identity. In some parts of Africa, people from different villages have different hairstyles; in North America, teenagers encode their schools or teams by the jackets they wear. People signal their connectedness to others by holding hands, by wearing rings, or by feasting and drinking together.

Rituals of Gift Giving and Hospitality

One of the most influential works in the history of anthropology is *The Gift* (1925), by Marcel Mauss. In it, Mauss identifies what he calls the **principle of reciprocity**: the giving and receiving of gifts. His main point is that gifts, which in theory are voluntary, disinterested, and spontaneous, are in fact obligatory. The giving of the gift creates a tie with the person who receives it and who, on some future occasion, is obliged to reciprocate. To Mauss, what is important is not what is given but the relationship that is maintained or established by the gift. The types of things given and received signal the identities of the participants in the exchange and the kind of relationship that exists between them. If the gifts are roughly of equal value, the relationship is one of equality. But if the gifts are unequal in value, the person who gives the more valuable gift is generally of higher status than the receiver.

A well-known example of gift giving in the anthropological literature is the ***kula* ring** of the Trobriand Islanders. The seagoing Trobrianders leave their homes on islands off the eastern coast of New Guinea and travel from island to island, visiting and trading. Noteworthy in their travels is their pattern of gift giving. Each man has trading partners on the islands he visits, and these partnerships are signalled with gifts of red shell necklaces or white shell armbands. As a man travels and trades objects, he gives and receives necklaces and receives armbands. A man who receives either an armband or a necklace does not keep it but passes it along to another trading partner. There is a set pattern to the exchange: necklaces travel from island to island in a clockwise direction, while armbands move counterclockwise. The time between exchanges and the distances between the islands are so great that it may take two to ten years before the necklaces and armbands make a complete circle.

The *kula* ring serves as a concrete representation of ties among individuals. Any change in the pattern of gift giving reflects a change in the nature of the social ties. Special gifts that are individually owned are also circulated, and the owner's status and

EXERCISE 5.4

Suppose you were to travel to an island where no one knows anything about you or the society you came from. Also suppose you could only communicate to people on the island using objects that you carried with you, and you could only take five things to tell people about yourself. What would they be?

principle of reciprocity
According to Marcel Mauss, gift giving involves reciprocity. The idea is that the exchange of gifts creates a feeling of obligation, in that the gift must be repaid.

***kula* ring**
A system of inter-island gift exchange documented by anthropologist Bronislaw Malinowski in the Trobriand Islands. It involves the exchange of shell necklaces and armbands. According to Malinowski, the kula ring serves, among other things, to create alliances and social ties among individuals living on different islands.

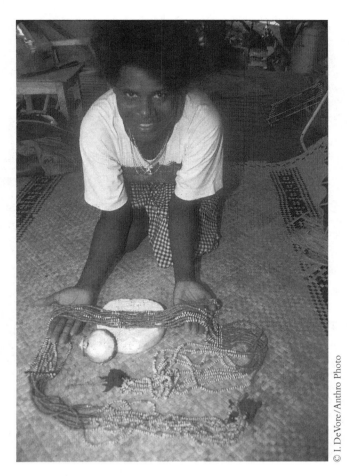

Trobriand Islanders define and maintain their social identities by participating in the *kula* ring, a ritualized pattern of gift giving involving the exchange of necklaces and armbands.

© I. DeVore/Anthro Photo

renown grow as the goods he owns circulate along predetermined paths. A successful *kula* operator participates in many such exchanges and can profit from them by keeping items for as long as he can before passing them along. Of course, if he keeps them too long, others will be reluctant to exchange, so a good deal of social skill is required to *kula* successfully.

Anthropologist Margaret Anderson has devoted many years to studying another famous example of gift giving: the **potlatch** ceremony of the people of the Northwest Coast of British Columbia. Among the Tsimshian, the potlatch is typically a feast that legitimates a change in social relations, such as a funeral. Someone who dies is vacating a spot on the social landscape—or, more specifically, leaving a name empty. The Tsimshian are organized into matrilineal clans or houses. Each house has associated with it a fixed number of personal names, and each name has associated with it specific spiritual powers, honours, and objects of wealth. The man with the highest ranking name is recognized as the owner of the house. The name a Tsimshian holds when he dies is vacated until it is claimed by or given to someone else. If the name vacated belongs to a chief, the feasting will begin with his death and end with the acceptance of a new chief, who is usually the eldest son of the deceased chief's eldest sister. A person who disgraces his name by doing something wrong (such as having an automobile accident or being put in jail) must give a feast to "clean the name."

The potlatch feast, however, does more than allow a Tsimshian to obtain a new name and identity. It also serves to symbolically reorder and validate the names, and hence the social positions, of everyone at the feast through the distribution of gifts. Members of the house of the deceased generally serve as hosts to members of the deceased's father's house. The guests are feasted for the services they have performed (preparing the corpse, carving a pole) and as repayment for the gifts they formerly gave the deceased to help him acquire his name. When the guests are seated, the hosts announce the gifts they are giving to the guests, along with the name of the person from the host group who has contributed the gift. Higher ranking guests receive more gifts at a potlatch than lower ranking guests. Consequently, the seating arrangements and the value of the gifts given to guests at the feast serve to announce or publicly notarize the social position or identity of each guest.

potlach
A celebration, usually involving elaborate feasting and the redistribution of gifts, found among many indigenous Northwest Coast groups, such as the Tsimshian. The potlatch is a means of creating a new identity or of reinforcing social status within a group.

THE CULTURAL CONSTRUCTION OF IDENTITY 153

Anderson argues that although the potlatch has changed since Christianity was introduced in 1857 (when William Duncan of the Church Missionary Society came to Fort Simpson), its meaning and symbolic value have remained, in part because as long as the feasts began with a prayer, Duncan considered them respectable.

Exchanges that convey recognition of identities need not be limited to material goods. The exchanges also may consist of emotion and sentiment. Hawaiians, for example, define a desired identity in part by expressions of gregariousness and hospitality. The emotional qualities of a person's relationships are one criterion by which others judge, interact with, and respond to that person. For example, if you accept an offer of hospitality in Hawai'i, it is a signal that you recognize the generous nature of the offer and that you wish to maintain the social link. If you reject the offer of hospitality, it is seen as a hurtful sign that you do not recognize the generous nature of the person making the offer and do not wish to maintain the relationship. Hawaiians attempt to keep social pathways open through altruistic exchanges of love (*aloha*), sincerity, feeling (with heart, *na'au*), and warmth (*pumehana*).

Gifts and Commodities

An important characteristic of traditional *kula* and potlatch goods is that they have histories. A Trobriander who receives a necklace or armband can probably recite the history of the object, sometimes from its creation through all the persons who possessed it at one time or another. These goods are similar to heirlooms in our own society, whether it is the family wedding ring that has been worn by brides for three generations, the watch that was owned by a great-grandfather, or the quilt that was made by a great-aunt. The histories of these objects, especially when they are given as gifts, are vital to the identity of the person who gives them. They say something special about the relationship between the giver and the receiver of the gift. The same is true to a lesser extent of gifts that are

produced by the giver: these carry a special meaning apart from the object itself. A lamp made and given as a gift is often far more meaningful than a lamp purchased at a department store. However, we often must choose the gifts that we give from among thousands of mass-produced, largely impersonal goods available in department and chain stores. Herein lies a dilemma.

James Carrier, in his book *Gifts and Commodities: Exchange and Western Capitalism Since 1700* (1995), argues that since the 16th and 17th centuries, the production and distribution of goods has become impersonal, and that the spread of industrial and commercial capitalism has meant the spread of alienated objects and relations. In earlier times, commodities were personalized in various ways. The relationship between the producer and the seller of goods was a personal one between relatives or friends; the buyer knew who made and sold the object purchased. Even when stores replaced home trade and markets, the buyer knew the store owner, who further personalized the goods by buying them in bulk and individually packaging and displaying them. The buyer–seller relationship was further personalized by the extension of credit from seller to buyer and by the customer loyalty expressed by the buyer to the seller. Today the buyer knows neither the producer nor the seller, and if the item is bought on credit, it is through a credit card issued by some distant bank based on the filing of an impersonal application, with the transaction accomplished completely by mail. Eyes never meet.

Carrier labels goods that carry no special meaning **commodities**, to distinguish them from what he calls possessions. Gifts, says Carrier, must be possessions before they can carry meaning in an

> **commodity**
> Traditionally, commodities are items that involve a transfer of value and a counter-transfer: A sells something to B, and the transaction is finished. A longstanding personal relationship between buyer and seller is not established. This is typical of capitalist market-exchange systems.

exchange. Commodities involve a transfer of value and a counter-transfer: A sells something to B, and the transaction is finished. But in a gift exchange, a more or less permanent link is established between giver and receiver. Gifts are inalienable, that is, they are bound to people after the presentation; commodities are independent of their sellers (or producers). It is easy to return, destroy, or give away a commodity; it is a dilemma to do any of those with a gift. Ralph Waldo Emerson vividly expressed the difference between gifts and commodities when he wrote that "the only gift is a portion of thyself. Thou must bleed for me. Therefore the poet brings his poem; the shepherd, his lamb; the farmer, corn; the miner, a gem; the sailor, coral and shells; the painter, his picture; the girl, a handkerchief or her own sewing. This is right and pleasing … when a man's biography is conveyed in a gift" (in Carrier 1993, 56). Or, as Emerson said again, "It is a cold, lifeless business when you go to the shops to buy me something that does not represent your life and talent" (in Carrier 1993, 56).

As noted, for North Americans the contrast between commodities and gifts poses a special problem. Most of the items we give as gifts are store-bought commodities, often mass produced. Their history is brief and undistinguished: an item of clothing was probably assembled in some factory in Mexico or Indonesia by a young woman earning perhaps a dollar an hour; a sports item was probably assembled in some factory in South America, shipped to a warehouse in Toronto or Chicago, and sold through a mass-produced catalogue; a radio, iPod, or CD player, assembled in Korea, distributed by a Japanese company, was probably sold in a North American chain store. These are commodities, not gifts. Their meaning is contained in their worth or utility, in their materiality. The meaning of a gift is different: the perfect gift is priceless, its materiality is immaterial.

For Carrier the problem is how, in a world filled with impersonal, alienated commodities—goods without history, so to speak—we can turn these things into personal items with meaning and history, into possessions that carry something of the buyer's identity. In gift giving, how do we turn commodities into items that say something about the relationship between the giver and receiver? How do we make commodities meaningful?

We convert commodities into possessions and gifts, says Carrier, through a process of appropriation. For example, when a person takes an impersonal space—a dorm room, say, or a rented apartment—and decorates and modifies it, he or she has appropriated it and given it meaning. When we buy food at the supermarket, we appropriate it by preparing or cooking it. When a person buys an automobile, one that is virtually identical to thousands of others of the same make, model, year, and colour, and comes to think of it as unique, as an expression of his or her identity, that person has appropriated an object and made it a possession. Shopping itself, says Carrier, is a way of appropriating commodities; the "wise shopper" chooses what is "right" for them or what is "right" for the recipient of the gift.

Manufacturers and sellers, of course, try to aid the process of converting a commodity into a possession by themselves stamping their products with a distinct identity. A good example is Harris tweed, which most buyers associate with some Harris Islander weaving on a loom in his shed, creating the item as his ancestors have done for centuries, and even giving each item its own serial number. In fact, the yarn that is used is spun in textile mills and then woven on looms given to the weaver with the frames already warped so that no special skill is necessary to weave the cloth. In actuality, other than the fact that they are narrower, the only difference between the looms they use and the ones used in factories is that the Harris Island weaver supplies the power with a foot treadle rather than a machine.

Endorsements from sports or movie celebrities help consumers transform a commodity into a possession. Also, displaying goods in catalogues in ways that help the buyer appropriate commodities has become a fine art. For example, when Wayne

THE CULTURAL CONSTRUCTION OF IDENTITY   **155**

Gretzky endorses a product, it takes on a Canadian flavour, regardless of where it was manufactured.

Gift Giving and the Christian Celebration of Christmas in North America

The dilemma of converting commodities into gifts is especially acute during the Christian Christmas holiday season, when most gift giving takes place in North America. Christmas as Christians know it did not really emerge until the height of the Industrial Revolution. Its precursors included the traditional end-of-year festivities that took place in England, where gifts consisted of food or feasts given by superiors to their dependants. In the 1770s in New York City, people began celebrating 6 December, the day of St. Nicholas, instead of the New Year. This was actually something of an anti-Christmas celebration; St. Nicholas was Dutch, and the colonists were celebrating things Dutch to protest British rule over what had been New Amsterdam before British colonization. It wasn't until 1809 that the holiday began to spread and that St. Nicholas turned into Santa Claus giving gifts of candy to children. The appearance of Clement Moore's *A Visit from St. Nicholas* in 1823 (or *'Twas the Night Before Christmas*, as it later became known) marked the movement of the holiday to the end of the year. At this point children began to get toys rather than food. Even then, Christmas was celebrated largely on New Year's Day and in the industrial northeast.

The next major step in the evolution of Christmas was the appearance of Charles Dickens's *A Christmas Carol* in 1843. It was an immediate sensation, especially with its victory of Bob Cratchit and Tiny Tim and their world of the home over Scrooge and the cold, impersonal world of work. By 1865, Christmas had been declared a national holiday, and in 1862, the Thomas Nast image of Santa Claus began appearing in *Harper's Weekly*, completing his construction as a fat, jolly,

old man dressed in fur-trimmed robes (inspired, Nast later admitted, by the fur-trimmed clothing of the wealthy Astor family). By the 1880s, writers were beginning to complain about the commercialization of Christmas.

Most social scientists who have written about the Christian celebration of Christmas agree that it is largely a celebration of the family, serving especially to distinguish the world of the family from the outside world of work. Christmas serves to affirm the identity of Christians all over the world as members of specific family groups, and the circle of kin with whom gifts are exchanged defines the boundaries of the family. In one study conducted in a midwestern American city, 90 percent of all

© Monika Graff/The Image Works

In North American societies, the yearly Christian ritual of Christmas shopping provides a means of converting impersonal commodities into personalized gifts that show one's love for family members and close friends.

gifts exchanged at Christmas were exchanged with family members. Christmas heightens a person's sense of family identity, expressing how warm the family is and how cold the world outside may be.

Thus, it is within the family that the Christmas gift is most important. Furthermore, the gift must contain something of the biography of the giver and the history of the relationship—that is, it must be a possession rather than a commodity. The question is how to resolve the problem of using commodities as family gifts, how to transform commodities to make them suitable as statements of the special role that family and family relations play in defining our identity. This problem, apparently, is not a new one. The dilemma of giving gifts that are manufactured and sold in stores apparently existed as early as the mid-19th century, when department stores tried to convince buyers to purchase their gifts in stores by advertising them as "special Christmas stock." Even today, through Christmas decorations, music, and special attractions, such as the ever-present Santa Claus, retailers try to inject the spirit of Christmas into their stock of goods.

But there are other ways that consumers try to appropriate commodities and turn them into Christmas gifts. First, we may simply say that the nature of the gift itself is immaterial, that "it's the thought that counts." A second way is to purchase things that aren't very useful, giving frivolous or luxurious gifts, or items that are Christmas-specific, such as Christmas tree decorations or clothing with Christmas decorations on it. Third, and very important, there is the wrapping rule: Christmas gifts must be wrapped. The wrapping itself converts the commodity into a gift. Difficult-to-wrap presents (a piano, a horse, a bicycle, etc.) must be decorated with a bow. The only categories of things that needn't be wrapped are items made by the giver, such as breads or jams. These items need only a bow and a card.

Finally, says Carrier, there is the shopping itself, the time we spend getting the "right" gift for the "right" person. Why, he asks, do we go through all of this? It is onerous, it is stressful, and it is expensive. Yet one-third of all retail sales are made in November and December, most of them accounted for by Christmas shopping. One-sixth of all retail sales are related to Christmas. People complain about the materialism of Christmas and Christmas shopping. Yet people shop intensely for Christmas.

In the face of this bother and complaint, why do North Americans, even devout Christians, spend so much effort in Christmas shopping? Why not give homemade gifts? Indeed, why give presents at all? Why not give a Christmas card instead? It is true that the giving of purchased gifts reflects a number of motives, ranging from displays of affluence to a desire to shower a loved one with lovely things. However, these more commonly recognized motives do "not explain the intensity of Christmas shopping and people's ambivalence towards it" (Carrier 1993, 62).

Carrier suggests that the answer to this riddle lies in the fact that shopping in itself is a method of appropriation, of converting a commodity into a gift: we exercise a choice from among the mass of commodities presented to us. As Carrier puts it, "Christmas shopping is an annual ritual through which we convert commodities into gifts. Performing this ritual indicates that we can celebrate and recreate personal relations with the anonymous objects available to us, just as it strengthens and reassures us as we undertake the more mundane appropriations of everyday life during the rest of the year" (1993, 63).

Christmas shopping also demonstrates to people, says Carrier, that they can create a world

EXERCISE 5.5

These days, gift cards for stores, restaurants, spas, or other goods and services are popular holiday gift items. After reading Carrier's work, discuss how gift cards might fit into his discussion of commodities and gifts. How can gift cards, as commodities, be turned into gifts? Or can they be?

THE CULTURAL CONSTRUCTION OF IDENTITY

of family, a world of love, out of the impersonal commodities that flood the world "out there." The Christian celebration of Christmas is a time when North Americans make a world of money into a world of family, a time of contrast between the impersonal world of commodities and the personal world of possessions and gifts.

THE CULTURAL CONSTRUCTION OF SOCIAL HIERARCHY

This painting of construction workers by the famous French artist Fernand Léger depicts a scene of reconstruction in post–Second World War France. In many ways, it represents the struggles of the working classes; it also serves as a metaphor for the formation of various social hierarchies in conjunction with the rise of capitalism and industrialization in the West. Racism, caste, and gender will also be discussed in this chapter as social hierarchies. As we see in the epigraph, racism operates in a particular way in Canada.

Although it may never be possible to quantify the degree of racism that exists in a given society, the evidence unmistakably reveals that racism widely distorts the attitudes of white Canadians toward Aboriginal peoples. Whether blatantly or covertly, many Canadians still believe that Aboriginal people are inferior; as a result, these people believe that there is a sound, rational basis for discriminating against Aboriginal persons at both the individual and institutional level.

James S. Frideres and Rene R. Gadacz

PROBLEM 6

Why are modern societies characterized by social, political, and economic inequalities? How are certain gender, class, racial, and other identities privileged or marginalized in various social contexts?

INTRODUCTION

The Rationale for Social Inequality

The maldistribution of wealth, status, power, and privilege is a significant problem throughout the modern world. To North Americans it is visible in the starving faces that stare out from our television screens in documentaries and on the evening news, interspersed with advertisements for luxuries such as automobiles, cosmetics, and household appliances. Some people can purchase the finest amenities, while others lack the basic necessities of life, such as food, shelter, and health care. There are few, if any, modern nations in which one portion of the population does not in some way enjoy privileges that other portions do not share.

Anthropologists use the interchangeable terms **social stratification** and **social hierarchy** to refer to the ordering and ranking of individuals within a society. This ranking is normally based on pervasive systems of inequality that privilege particular classes, castes, races, or genders over others.

Social hierarchy is not an inevitable feature of human societies. For example, groups such as the Ju/'hoansi and the Inuit are not totally egalitarian, but people go out of their way not to

> **social stratification/hierarchy**
> The ordering and ranking of individuals within society. Those at the top of the hierarchy are generally afforded more power, wealth, prestige, or privileges in a society. Hierarchies can be based on race, gender, class, caste, ethnicity, national affiliation, or other factors.

appear better than others. Moreover, there does not seem to be a universal inclination to rank people by one criterion or another; in some societies, skin colour makes a difference, while in others it does not. In some societies, men are accorded far greater status than women; in others, there is little if any difference in gender rank. Even the use of age as a criterion of rank varies from society to society. The only general rule seems be that as societies become more complex and more populous, their propensity for social stratification increases.

Some people contend that the hierarchical ordering of people and groups is unavoidable. In their view, scarce resources, occupational specialization, and the power of an elite group to control the behaviour of others inevitably result in some form of social stratification. Others maintain that stratification is not only avoidable but also counter to human nature. According to anthropologist Thomas Belmonte, "since the emergence of stratification, man's history (his changing ways of relating to nature and other men) has stood opposed to his humanity. The emergence of power-wielding elites … laid the basis for a new kind of anti-collective society whose vastly accelerated growth was founded, not on the reconciliation of antagonisms between men, but on their origination and amplification in slavery, caste, and class" (Belmonte 1989, 137).

Those who support Belmonte's view note that in societies such as those of Ju/'hoansi and Inuit, there are no "poor," "rich," "inferior," or "superior" people. This is not to say that these societies are totally egalitarian, or equal; even in small-scale societies, valued statuses are not available to some members. Rather, the question at hand is why modern societies are characterized by extremes of poverty and wealth. It is worth noting here that poverty is not random; indigenous populations, ethnic minorities, and women are the social categories of people most at risk for poverty. In Mexico, for example, over 80 percent of the indigenous population lived in poverty in the early 1990s, compared to 18 percent of the non-indigenous population (Psacharopoulos and Patrinos 1994, 4). In Canada, Frideres and Gadacz found that the average Aboriginal income in 2001 was $17,000; among all Canadians it was $24,000 (2001, 91). Also in Canada, Kazemipur and Halli examined the 1991 and 1996 census data and found that "immigrants were consistently over-represented among the poor, and that this over-representation had a clear ethnic and racial colour, with visible minority immigrants experiencing the most severe conditions" (2001, 217). Finally, in the United States in 1997, women living in poverty outnumbered men by a ratio of 4:3. Furthermore, because women are most often the primary caregivers, children pay an even greater price than women do. In the United States, child poverty rates fluctuated between 18 and 21 percent between 1995 and 2000, but only 5.7 percent of French children and 7.3 percent of British children were considered poor. As Valdas Anelauskas (1999) has pointed out, children in the United States are twice as likely to be poor as Canadian children, three times more likely to be poor than British children, four times more likely to be poor than French children, and seven to thirteen times more likely to be poorer than German, Dutch, and Swedish children. How do we explain the distribution of poverty, power, prestige, status and wealth based on **race**, indigenous status, and gender, among other factors?

In this chapter we examine how societies construct social hierarchies and why some groups erect social edifices based on social dominance and submission, high and low status, and oppressors and oppressed. We examine why most people in stratified societies—both those at the top and those

> **race**
> A culturally constructed form of identity and social hierarchy, race refers to the presumed hereditary, phenotypic characteristics of a group of people. These physical or phenotypic differences are often erroneously correlated with behavioural attributes.

6.1 How do societies rank people in social hierarchies? Class and Caste.

6.2 How do people come to accept social hierarchies as natural?

6.3 How is gender a form of social hierarchy?

6.4 How do people living in poverty adapt to their condition?

6.5 Can a non-stratified community exist within a large society?

6.6 How can anthropology be applied to alleviate the effects of inequality?

at the bottom—consider social ranks to be "the nature of things." We ask how people at the bottom levels of the hierarchy—those who live in poverty, for example—adapt to their conditions, and we explore whether a nonstratified community can exist within a large-scale society. Finally, we explore how an anthropological perspective can be applied to alleviate the effects of inequality.

QUESTION 6.1: HOW DO SOCIETIES RANK PEOPLE IN SOCIAL HIERARCHIES? CLASS AND CASTE

Social hierarchies in different societies vary along several dimensions: the criteria used to differentiate people into one level of society or another; the number of levels that exist; the kinds of privileges and rights that attach to people at different levels; and the strength of the social boundaries that separate the different levels. In Canada and the United States, for example, people are stratified by income and personal possessions into social **classes** (e.g., lower class, middle class,

and upper class). They are classified by cultural or family background into ethnic groups (e.g., Italian, Jewish, Hispanic, or white Anglo-Saxon Protestant), or by physical appearance or skin colour into racial categories or visible minorities (e.g., black or white). They are also classified by gender and age, as well as by standards such as education. People in Canada and the United States may move from class to class, and they may choose to emphasize or de-emphasize their ethnic group membership, but generally, their racial category and gender are perceived as fixed.

EXERCISE 6.1

Remember that social hierarchies are based on people's perceptions of others. Below is a list of personal attributes. Your task is to rank them by number from most to least important to you in judging a person's social or personal worth. No ties are allowed. If there is an attribute not included in the list that you wish to add, do so. What are some of your reasons for your rankings? Why are some attributes more important to you than others? What do your rankings tell us about our society?

Rank

____ Personal appearance

____ Income

____ Gender

____ Age

____ Religion

____ Ethnic or community origin

____ Family background

____ Intelligence (as indicated by school performance)

____ Athletic ability

____ Personal possessions (clothes, car, etc.)

____ Personality (fill in your description of type of personality)

class
A form of identity informed by perceptions of an individual's economic worth or status. It is also a form of social hierarchy.

Class as a Form of Social Hierarchy

Social class refers to perceptions of an individual's standing or status in society, normally based on economic criteria, status, or other factors, which may vary from society to society. Max Weber argued that social class can be based on economic wealth and/ or "status class": prestige, honour, educational or occupational achievements, or religious or spiritual affiliation. In North American societies, for instance, we tend to place particular value on some occupations that require years of post-secondary schooling over more "hands on" professions such as construction work and trades. While many tradespeople earn sizable incomes, their professions lack the "status" associated with medicine or law. Also, we live in a commodified, consumer-driven society in which material possessions such as cars, houses, clothing brands, and other objects are often perceived as markers of an individual's class background and, by extension, his or her access to wealth, power, and prestige. Unlike social identities, such as race, which is normally perceived as an ascribed (fixed, unchanging) status, class in North American society has long been viewed as a more fluid social identity. In other words, it can be either an **ascribed status** or an **achieved status**. An individual may be born into a life of wealth, power, and high status as a Rockefeller or a Massey; or alternatively, he or she may, through hard work and determination, overcome the odds and achieve a higher class status for themselves. This popular myth that class is an achieved category is enshrined in American fiction (F. Scott Fitzgerald's *The Great Gatsby*) and in real life (Barack Obama). However, these stories overshadow the ways in which class intersects with other identities, such as gender and race. In many ways, stories of opportunity, available for all, privilege a white male perspective. As discussed earlier, ethnic minorities and women, for instance, are often positioned at the bottom of many social hierarchies, making it difficult for them to have the same opportunities or access to tools—such post-secondary education, training, or other resources—that are needed to "achieve" a higher class status.

Caste as a Form of Social Stratification

In India, the population is stratified into hundreds of different **castes**. In a caste system, individuals are assigned at birth to the ranked social and occupational groups of their parents. A person's place in the social order is fixed; there is no mobility from one caste to another. This is one feature that distinguishes the notion of caste from class. Castes are also separated by strict rules that forbid intermarriage and other forms of interaction, such as eating together, speaking to one another, or working together.

In any stratified society, people's access to jobs, wealth, and privilege is determined largely by their position in the hierarchy. Castes in India are based on traditional roles, for example. The Brahmins, priests whose lives were devoted to worship and teaching, occupied the top of the caste hierarchy. Directly under them were the Kshattriya castes, whose members comprised the soldiers, politicians, and administrators. Next were the Vaisya castes, made up of farmers and merchants. At the bottom of the hierarchy were the Sudra castes, which were devoted to the service of other castes. Beneath the religious hierarchy were the Harijans, "untouchable" or "unclean" persons whose occupations were believed to be polluting to others. Members of the Harijans caste have recently changed their name to *dalit*, which means "oppressed" or "ground down." *Dalit* included washermen, tanners, shoemakers, and sweepers, people whose occupations

ascribed status
An identity that is perceived as fixed and unchanging because a person is believed to be born with it. In Canadian society, race is often assumed to be ascribed at birth.

achieved status
An identity that is believed to be in flux and that is dependent upon the actions and achievements of an individual.

caste
A form of social stratification and identity in India where individuals are assigned at birth to the ranked social and occupational groups of their parents.

required them to come into contact with animal or human wastes. The Indian government has outlawed discrimination against *dalit* based on caste membership, but it persists nevertheless.

QUESTION 6.2: HOW DO PEOPLE COME TO ACCEPT SOCIAL HIERARCHIES AS NATURAL?

Race as a Form of Social Stratification

Sociocultural anthropology is about seeing behind the façade of everyday appearances to what lies behind those appearances. Understanding how societies construct rationales to justify and legitimize social discrimination is one of the most important and, to some extent, the most difficult tasks in anthropology. Franz Boas, a founder of anthropology, was among the first social scientists to discredit racist and sexist theories and ideologies that sought to legitimize the marginalization of people based on race, religion, gender, and ethnicity. Part of the problem is that racist and sexist theories exist not only in popular culture but also in science. It will be useful, then, to examine how such theories are constructed and often taken for granted, and how they are used to justify the ranking of people within the social hierarchy.

Constructing the Ideology of Racism

As discussed earlier, in Canada and the United States the ideology of class is based on the assumption that a person's position in the class hierarchy is determined largely by achievement or individual effort; that is, individuals who work hard and dedicate themselves to their work will succeed. Yet

Franz Boas (1858–1942), was one of the founders of anthropology and one of the first anthropologists to challenge racism and sexism in popular culture.

there is also the attempt to justify social position by a person's innate, biological makeup—largely by race, innate mental ability (intelligence), and other factors. This hierarchical ordering of society is seen as an expression of a natural law that some people are born more fit to lead and succeed.

The term *race* is used here to refer to the presumed genetic, natural, heritable characteristics of a group of people, normally based on physical attributes like skin colour, eye colour, or hair type. We live in a society that views race as a natural, ascribed category; it is something we believe we are born with. Unlike class, then, race in many industrialized societies (such as Canada) is seen as a fixed, unchanging form of identity.

Anthropologists and other scholars, however, maintain that there is no scientific basis for positioning different groups of people into discreet "races" on the basis of physical features. This is because there is no population of individuals anywhere in the world that is morphologically distinct. In other words, for a "race" to scientifically exist, a certain physical feature (e.g., skin colour) would have to be demonstrated as occurring consistently and uniformly within a particular population. But there is no group of people, anywhere in the world, that fits this criterion. Simply put, there is too much physical diversity within specific populations. The Executive Board of the American Anthropological Association, the largest professional association of anthropologists in the world, sums up this argument:

Both scholars and the general public have been conditioned to viewing human races as natural and separate divisions within the human species based on visible physical differences. With the vast expansion of scientific knowledge in this century, however, it has become clear that human populations are not unambiguous, clearly demarcated, biologically distinct groups. Evidence from the analysis of genetics (e.g., DNA) indicates that most physical variation, about 94%, lies within so-called racial groups. Conventional geographic "racial" groupings differ from one another only in about 6% of their genes. This means that there is greater variation within "racial" groups than between them. In neighbouring populations there is much overlapping of genes and their phenotypic (physical) expressions. Throughout history whenever different groups have come into contact, they have interbred. The continued sharing of genetic materials has maintained all of humankind as a single species. (American Anthropological Association 1998; http://www.aaanet.org/stmts/racepp.htm)

These days, most academics view race as a culturally constructed form of identity. In other words, they view race as a byproduct of cultural beliefs, not biology. Race may not exist from a strictly scientific perspective, but that does not mean it is not an important topic for anthropologists to explore. In Canada, we live in a society in which the myth prevails that race is a natural category (i.e., as a biological, ascribed category). Because of this, race has had a variety of social consequences. Over the years, for instance, race has been conflated with behavioural characteristics, resulting in **racism**, or systems of prejudice based on the stratification of physical differences, which are erroneously thought to correlate with behavioural, physical, or intellectual differences in certain populations. The book *The Bell Curve*, discussed below, is a problematical example of how science is often used in an uncritical manner to foster racism, classism, and social stratification.

For centuries, European and North American societies have been characterized by racial stratification. In these societies, membership in certain racial or ethnic groups has been enough to place people in particular positions in a hierarchy that defines their social, political, and economic worth. In the United States, for example, one's position in the racial hierarchy has often determined whether a person can vote, hold political office, pursue a particular occupation, live in a certain area, use certain public facilities, attend certain schools, or marry a particular person.

Although most Canadians consider themselves to be far less racist than their southern neighbours, racism has a long history in Canada, and groups have been formed on the basis of white supremacy in both countries. The Ku Klux Klan, for instance, was founded in Tennessee in 1865 to terrorize newly freed slaves who questioned white supremacy. By the 1920s, the Klan was well established in Canada. When it arrived from the United States, it added French Canadians and Catholics to its list of inferior

racism
Refers to the discrimination and mistreatment of particular "racial" groups.

peoples. In the 1960s, the Canadian Nazi Party and the Edmund Burke Society, the forerunner of the Western Guard, openly supported racism. Ten years later, the Nationalist Party and the Aryan Nations took their place among the radical right. The common belief shared by these groups was that the "white race" was superior and that it was on the verge of being "wiped out" by the "dark-skinned races." As Stanley Barrett put it, "according to white supremacists, interracial mixing, or as they preferred, mongrelization, was more dangerous to humankind than the atomic bomb, because without the genetic purity of 'the master race' the world could not survive" (2002, 92).

African Canadians are not the only ones to experience racism in Canada. Racist beliefs about Aboriginal peoples are deeply rooted in Canadian history. James Frideres and Rene Gadacz call this structural racism (as opposed to prejudice and discrimination by individuals), because it is embedded in Canadian social institutions. Frideres and Gadacz argue that the Indian reserve is "an internal colony" in which "Canadians are seen as the colonizing people, while Aboriginal persons are considered the colonized people" (2001, 4).

Stratification by race has existed for a number of reasons. It was certainly economically profitable to people who could buy black slaves or obtain workers

Canadians assisted fugitive slaves, as depicted in the Charles T. Webber painting *The Underground Railroad.*

from among groups legally or socially barred from anything but low-paying jobs. It was advantageous, also, to those who did not have to compete for jobs with people who were socially or legally barred from them. However, stratified societies often claim that the ranking of people by race and ethnicity is natural and that social hierarchies are not socially constructed. In the case of racial stratification, some proponents claimed that it was the Christian God's will that some persons were inferior to others; others claimed that God created different races as He created different species of animals, and, furthermore, that the Christian Bible says the species are to be kept apart. Others claimed that members of one race or another were intellectually or morally superior to members of other races. Generally, of course, it was the race of the person making reference to the Christian God or the Bible that was somehow superior.

Most people had little trouble constructing an ideology to justify racial stratification, especially since it was reinforced by state and religious authorities. Even the supposedly objective findings of scientists assisted in building a racist ideology. In the 19th century, reputable scientists devoted much time and energy to proving that the racial stratification of society was "in the nature of things." Indeed, many contemporary forms of racism emerged out of 19th-century scientific studies of race. Both misguided and ethnocentric by today's standards, they functioned to maintain what Peggy McIntosh refers to as **white privilege**—the positioning of "white" individuals at the top of racial hierarchies. Science thus became a tool for naturalizing the power, authority, and privileges afforded to individuals with white skin. Their research findings supposedly proved that members of one race (usually whites or Europeans) were intellectually superior to members of another race (usually blacks or Asians).

white privilege
Refers to the fact that in many societies, "white" people have access to greater power, authority, and privileges than non-white people.

Samuel George Morton was a respected scientist and physician who began in the 1820s to collect and measure skulls from all over the world. When he died in 1851, he left a collection of some 6,000 skulls. Like many in the 19th century, Morton believed that a person's intelligence was related to the size of his or her brain; the larger the brain, the more intelligent the person. Since the size of the brain could be determined by the size of the skull, he believed that a ranking of the races could be objectively achieved by a ranking of skull size.

Morton first measured the size—more specifically, the cranial capacity—of skulls by filling them with mustard seed and then pouring the seed into a container to measure the skull's volume in cubic inches. Dissatisfied with the inconsistency of measurements obtained with mustard seed, he later used 1/8-inch-diameter lead shot. He concluded from his measurements that "white" skulls had a mean value of 92 cubic inches, "American Indian" skulls 79 cubic inches, and "black" skulls from America, Africa, and Australia 83 cubic inches. Among "white" skulls, the largest were those of Germans and English people; in the middle were those of Jews; and at bottom were those of Hindus. Thus, the social hierarchy of whites at the top, with the English and Germans at the top of the top and blacks on the bottom, was said to be supported by the evidence of brain size and intelligence.

Morton concluded from all this that "whites" (specifically, northern European "whites") were not only socially superior but also biologically superior. He believed he had provided objective evidence that the distribution of status and power in 19th-century North America accurately reflected not merely social but biological merit.

When Stephen Jay Gould, a Harvard paleontologist, re-examined Morton's published data in 1977, he concluded that Morton's summaries were a "patchwork of fudging and finagling" to reach conclusions that supported the socially constructed hierarchy. Gould found no evidence of conscious fraud. He concluded that Morton had simply selected or rejected certain data to ensure that the results confirmed what he and most other Americans "knew": that whites were naturally more intelligent than the people they called Indian or black.

Working with the same skulls Morton had used more than 150 years earlier, Gould discovered that the sample of 144 Native American skulls included proportionally more small-brained Inca skulls from Peru and fewer large-brained Iroquois skulls. This naturally produced a lower mean cranial capacity for indigenous Americans than would have occurred had Morton correctly adjusted for this discrepancy. Moreover, Gould discovered that Morton's failure to include the small-brained Hindu skulls with his "white" skulls had produced a higher average cranial capacity for white skulls. When Gould corrected for Morton's sample biases, he discovered that there was no difference between

Source: From Nott and Glidden, *Indigenous Races of the Earth*, 1869, taken from *The Mismeasure of Man*, by Stephen Jay Gould

Nineteenth-century scientists attempted to "prove" that whites were naturally superior to other races. In this illustration from an 1868 racist tract, the proportions of the skulls were distorted, giving the impression that blacks might even rank lower than the apes.

Euro-American and indigenous American cranial capacity. As for comparisons between "white" and "black" skulls, Gould discovered that Morton had ignored the facts that brain size is related to body size and that male skulls are larger than female skulls. Examination of Morton's black skulls indicated that the group included proportionally more female skulls and fewer male skulls. When Gould remeasured the "black" and "white" skulls, he discovered that the mean cranial capacity of black males was slightly higher than the mean for white males, while the mean for white females was slightly higher than that for black females.

Gould did not believe that Morton consciously manipulated his skull measurements to prove that whites were intellectually superior to Native Americans or blacks. Rather, he thought that Morton had simply assumed that this is what his measurements would prove and that he set about achieving the results he expected. For example, Gould observed that when Morton used mustard seed to measure cranial capacity, he obtained even greater differences between his "white" and "black" skulls than he had obtained using lead shot. Gould concluded that because mustard seeds are smaller and lighter than lead shot, Morton, probably unconsciously, packed more mustard seed into "white" skulls to obtain a greater difference in cranial capacity between "blacks" and "whites." Unfortunately, while Morton's measurements were obviously in error, as was his assumption that cranial capacity reveals intelligence, and though his conclusions were dictated by the socially constructed hierarchy of his day, they were used well into the 20th century to support the ideology that the racial ranking of persons in society could be justified on natural rather than social grounds.

Class, Race, and the Social Construction of "Intelligence"

Morton's experiments were just one example of the efforts in North America and Europe to show that people somehow deserve their ranking in society,

that it is not the result of chance or family privilege but, rather, the result of innate attributes. To believe otherwise would threaten a key assertion of North American ideology: that everyone in Canada and the United States enjoys an equal opportunity for success. Moreover, there are serious political and economic consequences to believing otherwise. If poverty and a low ranking in society are not the fault of the poor, then they must be the result of some failure of society. Such an admission provides a strong reason for governments to enact social and economic policies (such as affirmative action, programs of economic redistribution, and laws barring racial and other forms of discrimination). However, such changes might lead to a loss of privilege for those who benefit from present policies, so there is strong motivation to find some concept that legitimizes inherited privilege while still placing the blame for poverty or lack of success on the poor themselves.

The concept of intelligence neatly solves this problem; if people accept the idea that intelligence can explain how well people do, then the fiction that people's rank in society depends solely on their own innate ability can be maintained. Moreover, if it can be shown that intelligence is inherited, then we can explain why it is that the children of successful people tend to be successful, and why certain groups, notably people of colour and certain immigrant groups, are disproportionately poor.

The failure of the thesis that cranial capacity, and hence brain size, reveals intelligence did not end all attempts to link intelligence to success and to race and ethnic class membership. There has been, instead, a continuing effort on the part of some members of the scientific establishment to marshal evidence that intelligence is inherited and that it varies among racial groups. These efforts have included the work of Arthur Jensen in the 1960s and 1970s and, more recently, the publication in 1994 of *The Bell Curve* by Richard J. Herrnstein and Charles Murray. Missing from most of these accounts is any acknowledgment that intelligence itself is a social construct, an invented idea. We need,

THE CULTURAL CONSTRUCTION OF SOCIAL HIERARCHY

then, to look closely at our concept of intelligence. How did it evolve?

To begin, anthropologist Allan Hanson notes that the concept of intelligence contains a number of questionable assumptions. First, intelligence is assumed to be a single entity. Second, it is assumed to be measurable and unequally distributed in the population. Third, the amount people have is assumed to be relatively fixed throughout life. Fourth, the amount people have is assumed to largely explain their degree of success in life. Finally, it is assumed to be largely inherited.

Each of these assumptions is critical to the intelligence construct as most people think of it, and each has been the subject of enormous scientific attention and criticism. The first assumption requires that we accept the idea that if someone is intelligent in one way, they will be intelligent in other ways, rather than believing that some people can be intelligent in some ways but not in others. The second assumption implies that we can somehow measure innate intelligence, as opposed to achievement, and the third presumes that we can show that whatever is measured does not vary throughout a person's life. The fourth is built on the idea that people who have more measurable intelligence are more likely to be successful, while the fifth assumption requires us to show that the children of people with high measurable intelligence also have high measurable intelligence.

In spite of the number of assumptions that lie behind the notion of intelligence, and in spite of the studies that illustrate how questionable each of these assumptions really is, most North Americans take the notion for granted. Yet it is an almost unique idea, one that is not shared by many other societies. Indigenous maritime navigators of the South Pacific, for example, learned to read wave patterns, wind direction, celestial constellations, and other signs and find their way thousands of miles from one island to another. Yet others in the same society who are unable to duplicate this feat did not view the navigators as somehow being smarter; they saw them as people who could navigate. The Japanese view what we call intelligence in much the same way as we view health—except in certain (and generally temporary) circumstances, we all have enough of it.

This book is not the place to summarize all those works that call the concept of intelligence into question. Nevertheless, we might learn something about the social construction of ideologies of class by looking briefly at the early history of the intelligence construct and by reviewing how reputable scientists proceeded to develop it. Three pioneers—Francis Galton, Karl Pearson, and Charles Spearman—supplied the basic ideas and experimental proofs for the classic concept of intelligence as a fixed, "mental" entity that is differentially distributed in the population, is measurable, largely explains a person's educational and occupational success, and is inherited.

Francis Galton was one of the leading intellectual figures of the late 19th century. He was the founder of modern statistics as well as the founder of eugenics, which is the attempt to identify the most desirable human traits, specify the individuals who possess them, and, through selective reproduction, enhance the number of people possessing those desired characteristics. In his best-known work, *Hereditary Genius* (1867), he sought to demonstrate that the "genius" of selected eminent men was linked to the fact that they had eminent parents and, it followed, that their "genius" was largely inherited. In his sample of 997 eminent British men, he found that 31 percent had eminent fathers, that 48 percent had eminent sons, and that 41 percent had eminent brothers—far higher percentages than one would expect by chance. For Galton, this illustrated the power of heredity in the distribution of "genius." He was, of course, rightly criticized for ignoring the impact of environment. But he did something else that was more interesting, something that went largely unchallenged: he selected the eminent men from the British upper and upper middle classes, ignoring the "captains of industry and finance" and, of course, women. That is, for him, eminence was eminence only within a select range of activities and occupations. Galton, a nephew of Charles Darwin and of upper-middle-class background, was faithfully reproducing the judgments of his own status as to what constituted intelligence.

Much of Galton's later research was devoted to arguing that what he called "genius," "mediocrity," and "imbecility" were analogous in their statistical distribution within a society to certain physical characteristics. He developed a number of tests for cranial capacity and for sensory capacities—the ability to discriminate between colours or smells, for example. He was not the only one trying to do this; in Germany, the United States, and England, other researchers were trying to measure intelligence, largely by measuring sensory and reflex activities, such as reading aloud rapidly, rapidly giving the colours of named objects, naming and classifying plants, animals, and minerals, and other tests of memory and spatial judgment. Around 1900, however, there was a move away from these kinds of measures, because they weren't showing any correlations with one another and, more important, because they showed only a low correlation with teachers' estimates of the mental capability of their students. Regardless, by 1900 the classic intelligence construct had been laid out, although its proof was somewhat wanting.

The next figure in our story is Karl Pearson, one of the most fascinating figures of the late 19th and early 20th centuries, whose published works included more than 400 articles on mathematical physics, statistics, and biology, as well as poetry, a passion play, art history, studies of the Reformation and Medieval Germany, and political essays. In 1901, Pearson published a study in the *Proceedings of the Royal Society* of London in which he concluded that "the mental characteristics in man are inherited in precisely the same manner as the physical. Our mental and moral nature is quite as much as our physical nature, the outcome of hereditary factors" (Pearson 1901, 155).

It is instructive to look at how Pearson reached this conclusion. He took pairs of brothers and measured specific physical characteristics, such as stature, forearm length, hair colour, eye colour, and cephalic index. He found, not surprisingly, that there were high correlations among brothers for these traits, as well as a mean correlation of .5171. He then asked teachers, using a separate sample, to rank brother-pairs on seven "mental characteristics": intelligence, vivacity, conscientiousness, popularity, temper, self-consciousness, and shyness. Thus, under "conscientiousness" teachers were asked to rate each child as "keen" or "dull" and to choose among six subdivisions of intelligence. When the teachers' evaluations of brother-pairs were tabulated, Pearson found a strong correlation between brother ratings, and a mean correlation of .5214, thereby proving the power of inheritance.

Much about this study is questionable, but of particular note is the role of teachers' judgments. Clearly, teachers were evaluating selected behaviour patterns and personal characteristics— patterns and characteristics that they judged to be evidence of various "mental characteristics." In other words, the teachers' judgments were highly subjective and, at best, questionable. But Pearson's work marked an important development in the construction of our concept of intelligence: he claimed to be showing that whatever intelligence was, it was obviously inherited at least as much as physical characteristics.

Let's move forward a couple of years to the next important stage in the construction of the intelligence construct: Charles Spearman and "general intelligence." Spearman's research, published in the *American Journal of Psychology* in 1904, was designed to prove that there were different degrees of correspondence between an individual's performance on different types of tests. Thus, one would expect a high correspondence between one's performance on geometrical tests and tests of spatial perception, and a low degree of correspondence between one's performance on, say, tests of musical ability and tests of weight discrimination.

If there were some degree of correlation between all the test results, this would point to some general factor, "g," that affected performance on all tests. Thus, tests that resulted in a high correlation (e.g., geometrical ability and spatial perception) would be heavily saturated with g, while tests with little correlation would not be. For example, to use an athletic analogy, if someone hits both a baseball and a golf ball a long way, we might assume that there exists some general factor for athletic ability accounting for both skills.

Spearman was suggesting that the g factor underlay all mental operations and that if it could be found, it would approximate true intelligence. This was a major claim, for if the existence of g could be proved, it would dismiss the idea—widely held at that time—that different people can be intelligent in different ways and that each person has a unique contribution to make. With g, people would be intellectually different in only one way, and people with lots of g would have more to contribute than people with only a little g.

To experimentally prove the existence of general intelligence, Spearman isolated four kinds of intelligence that, he claimed, when correlated would show a high degree of correspondence: "present efficiency," "native capacity," "general impression produced upon other people," and "common sense." "Present efficiency" referred to the "ordinary classification according to school order" in subjects such as Greek, Latin, and mathematics. "Native capacity" was arrived at by taking the difference between a child's rank in school and his age, while "general impression produced on other people" was obtained by asking the teacher of a class who was the brightest pupil, the next brightest, and so on. "Common sense" was arrived at by asking the oldest child in a class to rank her school fellows on the basis of "sharpness and common sense out of school." As Spearman said, she seemed "to have no great difficulty in forming her judgments concerning the others, having indeed known them all her life." As a check on the reliability of judgments, he

also asked the rector's wife to rank the children, although as Spearman notes regretfully, she did not know some of them. Spearman, not surprisingly, found that children who ranked high on one kind of intelligence tended to rank high on others, thereby validating the existence of g.

Obviously, the methodology of these classic studies was seriously flawed, relying as it did on subjective judgments as to who was intelligent and who was not—judgments that were bound to be biased by such factors as the social class of teachers and students. From Galton's first major work on hereditary genius through Spearman's work on general intelligence, members of the professional middle class were selecting as intelligent those people whose behaviour patterns and appearance most conformed to their own. Moreover, little effort was made to conceal the fact: subjective judgments of members of the professional class were the principal means for defining intelligence. Regardless, the intelligence construct as we know it was generally complete and was perceived by reputable scientists as having been validated experimentally: intelligence was a singular trait, represented by "g," that was inherited and that was differentially distributed in the population.

Much more was to come, of course, in the social construction of intelligence. Most notable in this regard was the development of the Stanford-Binet IQ test, and later the Scholastic Aptitude Test (SAT; recently renamed the Scholastic Assessment Test). Additional and more sophisticated experiments were performed that some claimed supported the conclusions of Galton, Pearson, Spearman, and other early researchers. But the most interesting feature was the continued part played by the social judgments of people—largely teachers, psychologists, and school administrators—in determining what did or did not constitute intelligence. As late as the 1960s, intelligence test results were still being cross-checked with teachers' judgments and students' ranks in class; if the test scores failed to correlate with the teachers' judgments, the tests were changed.

Race, Class, and Social Hierarchies in Brazil

Despite the efforts of some scientists to find a biological basis for racial hierarchies, it should now be clear that race is culturally constructed, as is class. We can now turn our attention to an ethnographic example of how categories like race and class are negotiated in Brazil. Anthropologist Alexander Edmonds has explored the ways in which race and class converge in Brazil to form social hierarchies. While conducting his doctoral dissertation fieldwork in Rio de Janeiro, Edmonds noticed that plastic surgery clinics proliferated in urban areas of Brazil. Furthermore, while access to plastic surgery had once been a marker of middle- or upper-class status (due to the high cost of such surgeries), the attainment of physical "beauty" was regarded as a necessary means of achieving social mobility. In Brazil, plastic surgery rates are among the highest in the world, and the government subsidizes plastic surgeries for the working classes. There are even plastic surgeons who practise "charity" surgeries on behalf of the urban poor. "Beauty" is thus a marker of class status, and is increasingly viewed as a "right" that should be available for everyone.

Plastic surgery, however, is also a means by which non-white Brazilians can seek to "whiten" their appearance by correcting what some of Edmonds's informants viewed as an undesirable—a "Negroid" nose, for instance. In Brazilian society, race exists along a continuum, and white skin and stereotypically "white" facial features are associated with power, privilege, and prestige. Indeed, many of Edmonds's informants, especially young women, did improve their employment prospects, and ultimately their class status, by undergoing plastic surgery. In this context, plastic surgery represents a means by which some Brazilians can "whiten" their bodies and, by extension, improve their social standing in Brazilian society. Interestingly, Brazil has been mythologized as a multicultural nation, and while its citizens are encouraged to celebrate diversity, there exists enormous social pressure to emulate the powerful (i.e., white, upper class) in Brazilian society. Racial identity is also understood to be malleable, and linked to one's social class— according to a popular Brazilian adage, "money whitens." Ultimately, this ethnographic example highlights the fluid and interconnected nature of social hierarchies such as class and race, as well as the ways in which the conscious manipulation of

EXERCISE 6.2

In Canada, we tend to pride ourselves on being an accepting, multicultural nation. However, there are many examples of embedded/institutionalized racism in our society. Select a recent (published within the past two years) Canadian newspaper or magazine article that offers an example of embedded racism. Provide a brief overview of the article and outline how institutionalized racism is at work.

features like "attractiveness" are viewed as a means of achieving a sense of individual fulfillment, well-being, and status.

QUESTION 6.3: HOW IS GENDER A FORM OF SOCIAL HIERARCHY?

Constructing Male and Female

We often assume that gender, like race, is biological. But there is an academic distinction between the terms "**sex**" and "**gender**." Sex refers to biological, hormonal, and chromosomal differences between males and females; gender, by contrast, is cultural. In other words, gender is the cultural interpretation of sex. Cross-culturally, different standards apply to being male, female, and (in some societies) a **third gender**. As such, there is no cross-cultural, universal understanding of what is considered to be "appropriate" dress, demeanour, behaviours, occupations, or roles for men or women; rather, these understandings must be learned in their respective cultural contexts.

In North America, this process of gendered learning begins at birth with the announcement: "It's a girl" or "It's a boy." However, these commonsense proclamations conveniently ignore the 4 percent of births in which the infant has various combinations of male and female characteristics (e.g., an infant with one testis and one ovary, an infant with one testis and aspects of the female genitalia, or an infant with ovaries and some aspect of male genitalia). Once the announcement of gender is made (or after a surgical procedure in which the infant is "corrected" to fit into either the male or female category), the infant is given a gender-appropriate name, dressed in properly designed and coloured clothing, and spoken to in gender-appropriate language. Parents and other caregivers then teach male children that it is manly to endure pain, to be strong and tough. Male children are discouraged from expressing discomfort and encouraged when they can withstand it. Female children, on the other hand, are comforted when they hurt themselves. Although gender stereotypes are changing, many North American male children are still encouraged to be aggressive and competitive; they learn to compete in games and play with toys that require aggressive behaviour. Females are still taught to be caring and helpful; they are given toys such as dolls that encourage "feminine" behaviour.

Also, societies vary in the number of gender categories they recognize. For example, many Native American societies recognize a third gender, such as that of the *two-spirit* among the Cheyenne and Lakota. The *two-spirit* is a biological male who does not fill a standard male role. Such individuals are not seen as men, nor are they defined as women. They occupy a third role, one that is culturally defined, accepted, and in some cases revered. Male children among the Lakota and Cheyenne thus can choose from two gender categories, rather than learning that gender roles are defined by physiology. Among the Lakota, male children learn that if they desire, they can adopt the dress and work roles of women and have sex with men, although the *two-spirit* role does not necessarily involve sexual behaviour. The *two-spirits* do not play only women's roles, however; some are noted for their hunting skills and exploits in war. In North American societies, in contrast, individuals who do not assume the gender roles associated with their anatomy are most often

sex
Hormonal, chronosomonal, or physical differences between men and women.

gender
Culturally constructed ideals of behaviour, dress, occupations, roles, and comportment for particular sexes.

third gender
A gender role given to someone who does not fit within strictly masculine or feminine gender roles in a given society.

defined as deviant, abnormal, or nonconformist, unless the reversal of gender roles is framed as play.

One way to learn about how a society constructs gender differences and relationships is to explore theatrical and ritual transvestism, as Michael Taft did on the Canadian Prairies when he studied mock weddings. The principal feature of a mock wedding is role reversal: men dress and act like women and sometimes women dress and behave like men. These mock figures are often as much caricatures as stereotypes, reflecting some feature of the identities of the actual wedding pair.

Taft's study focused on men who dressed as women in these rituals of reversal, which were filled with ludic (i.e., playful) behaviour. He repeatedly asked men why they did this, and the most frequent answer he received was that they were just being "good sports." As good sports, men do not attempt to become women in their role in the mock wedding. In Taft's words, "they play clownish and distorted women. They exaggerate the female physique with over-large breasts and behinds. They mince and wiggle in mockery of femininity" (1997, 135).

Thus, these men are expressing their views of women to one another. Taft suggests that one

reason men do this may have something to do with the economic conditions of farming on the Prairies. Although farmers or ranchers may *seem* to be independent, in reality they are dangerously dependent on government bureaucrats, subsidies, and the world market. In contrast, women have considerable power on farms and often do the same work as men, besides working part-time off the farm in order to pay the bills. By making fun of women, men may be reasserting their own importance. Whatever the men's motives, Taft argues that "wherever it is found, theatrical transvestism acts as a sounding board for commentaries on gender relations" (1997, 137).

Constructing Stratification by Gender

As discussed earlier, the biases that falsely linked race to biology and intelligence to class also led to the belief in the "natural" (as opposed to socially constructed) superiority of men over women. Many people believed that women's bodies defined both their social position and their function, which was to reproduce, in the same way that men's bodies dictated that they manage, control, and defend.

The view that the biology of females makes them lesser persons than males is embedded in North American cultures, sometimes in very subtle ways. An example is the language used by professionals to describe women's bodily processes of menstruation and menopause. Anthropologist Emily Martin says that during the 19th century, Americans regarded the female body as if it were a factory whose job was to "labour" to produce children. Menopause was viewed negatively because it marked the end of productive usefulness, and menstruation was described as a sign of the failure of the implantation of a fertilized egg. Medical writers of the time such as Walter Heape, a Cambridge zoologist and militant antisuffragist, described how in menstruation the entire epithelium (cellular tissue) is torn away, "leaving behind a ragged wreck of tissue, torn

In this photograph of a mock wedding ritual on the Canadian Prairies, transvestism represents a form of gendered social commentary on notions of power, equality, and the position of women in this community.

Courtesy of Saskatchewan Archives Board

glands, ruptured vessels, jagged edges of stroma, and masses of blood corpuscles, which it would seem hardly possible to heal satisfactorily without the aid of surgical instruments."

According to Martin, the same attitudes toward female reproductive functions that existed in the 19th century persist today, encoded in contemporary medical and biology textbooks. Menstruation is likewise described even today as a breakdown in the reproductive process. When an egg is not implanted, the process is described in negative terms as a disintegration or shedding. Here is one example Martin found:

The fall in blood progesterone and estrogen "deprives" the "highly developed endometrial lining of its hormonal support," constriction of blood vessels leads to a "diminished" supply of oxygen and nutrients, and finally "disintegration starts, the entire lining begins to slough, and the menstrual flow begins." Blood vessels in the endometrium "hemorrhage" and "the menstrual flow consists of this blood mixed with endometrial debris." The "loss" of hormonal stimulation causes "necrosis" (death of tissue). (in Martin 1987, 45)

Another otherwise objective text states that "when fertilization fails to occur, the endometrium is shed, and a new cycle starts. This is why it used to be taught that 'menstruation is the uterus crying for lack of a baby.'"

In yet another textbook, menstruation is depicted as a sign of an idle factory, a failed production system, a system producing "scrap" or "waste." However, Martin notes that very different language is used in the same textbooks to describe male reproductive functions. For example, the textbook from which the above description of menstruation is taken describes the production of sperm as follows: "The mechanisms which guide the remarkable cellular transformation from spermatid to mature sperm remain uncertain. Perhaps the most amazing characteristic of spermatogenesis is its sheer magnitude: the normal human male may manufacture several hundred million sperm per day" (in Martin 1987, 48).

This text, which describes menstruation as "failed production," fails to mention that only about one of every 100 billion sperm ever makes it far enough to fertilize an egg. Moreover, other bodily processes that are similar to menstruation are not spoken of in terms of breakdown and deterioration. Seminal fluid picks up shredded cellular material as it passes through the male ducts, and the stomach lining is shed periodically. Why are these processes not also described in the same negative terms as menstruation? Martin says the reason is that both men and women have stomachs, but only women have uteruses. The stomach falls on the positive side, the uterus on the negative.

Rather than describing menstruation as failed production, Martin suggests that it might be more accurate to describe it as the successful avoidance of an egg implant. If a couple has done anything to avoid the implantation of an egg, is it still appropriate to talk of the reproductive cycle in terms of production?

Emily Martin's analysis reveals that in contemporary North American societies, the ideology of gender stratification remains embedded in our language and in our ideas about the bodily functions of males and females. Describing the bodily processes of women in negative terms makes women seem to be lesser human beings. Moreover, describing menstruation and menopause in negative terms leads women themselves to believe that their bodily functions are less clean and less worthy than those of men.

Gender Stratification and the Privileging of Hegemonic Masculinities

All societies have particular images and stereotypes of masculinity and femininity that are privileged as normative—that is, as societal ideals. These ideals of masculinity, for instance, are referred to as **hegemonic masculinity**. Industrialized societies, for example, often view traits such as athleticism, courage, rationality, and heterosexuality as markers of an ideal "manliness."

Hegemonic masculinities are often used to construct gendered hierarchies in societies. For instance, those individuals who fall outside hegemonic gendered ideals are often labelled as "less masculine" than others, which leads to the proliferation of homophobia and/or the objectification of women. Canadian anthropologist David Murray, for instance, has studied how performances of a hegemonic masculinity on the Caribbean island of Martinique are dependent on "proving" one's heterosexuality through the aggressive pursuit of women, cat calling, and flirting with the opposite sex. Men who fail to pursue women aggressively are often labelled *macumé*, a derogatory word in Martinique that is equivalent to "sissy." In a society marked by intense homophobia, all men, whatever their sexual orientation, go to great lengths to uphold the norms of hegemonic masculinity in public settings. To be labelled *macumé* is a social liability, and a man risks physical and verbal abuse if he does not conform to societal ideals of gender.

Hegemonic masculinities are also constructed, performed, and maintained within societies through sports, competitions, and rituals. Fraternities, for instance, are a means of constructing hegemonic masculinities; they are also a way to promote often dangerous gendered hierarchies within university settings. This leads to the objectification, abuse, and marginalization of women.

Peggy Reeves Sanday, in her study of college fraternity gang rape, provides a vivid portrait of how male identity is defined and reinforced in American society. Gang rape, or "pulling train," as it is called in fraternities, begins with the coercion of a vulnerable young woman who is seeking acceptance. The ritual incorporates the man into a group whose activities reinforce a male identity, which is defined largely by the degradation of female identity through sexual conquest and physical abuse of women. Pulling train is both an expression of male sexuality and a display of the brotherhood's power to control and dominate women. In other words, gang rape is but one instance of the abuse and domination that begin during the initiation and that are continued later in relations with women and new pledges.

When she is too weak or intoxicated to protest, a "train" of men have sex with her. Gang rape is not limited to college campuses; it is also associated with sports teams, street gangs, and other groups of men for whom the act often serves, according to Sanday, as a male bonding ritual.

Sanday and her associates interviewed fraternity members, women who were associated with them, and victims of rape, seeking to explain what it was about male identity that encouraged these actions. Three things seemed to stand out in her account. First, there is a heavy emphasis in fraternities on male bonding and male-bonding behaviour, to the extent that a college man's self-esteem and social identity depend on gaining entry to a fraternity and being accepted by the brothers. Fraternities confer status; on most college campuses they are recognized as places "where the action is." They also provide reassurance, security, and a ready-made identity. Membership in a fraternity transforms outsiders into insiders.

Second, sex constitutes a major status and identity marker. Masculinity is defined and demonstrated by sexual conquest. In the fraternity in which the gang rape occurred, a major activity was persuading a woman to have sex. Men who had more success gained status, while those who often failed were in danger of being labelled "nerds" or, worse, "fags." Sex in this case is a public thing. Men in the fraternities that Sanday interviewed bragged publicly about their sexual conquests and arranged for brothers to witness them. Some fraternities posted weekly newsletters listing brothers' sexual conquests.

> **hegemonic masculinity**
> Refers to ideals and norms of masculinity in a society, which are often privileged over others.

A third element in the identity of fraternity men concerns their attitudes toward women. Many of the fraternity members in Sanday's study implied that women were sex objects to be abused or debased. A woman's identity among fraternity men was determined largely by her sexual interactions with them. Women who were sexually unresponsive were "frigid," women who allowed advances only up to a point were "cockteasers," and women who had sex with many men were "sluts" or "cunts." Such labels indicate that the role of girlfriend is virtually the only role with no negative connotations that a woman can play. In one fraternity, brothers marked women who attended their parties with "power dots," black, red, yellow, white, or blue stickers they attached to a girl's clothing at parties to indicate how easy the girl was to pick up.

For fraternity men, the debasement of women is interwoven with the themes of male bonding and sexual conquest. Part of the reason men bond in college, says Sanday, is to achieve the domination and power they think is owed to males. One fraternity man explained how verbally harassing a girl increases male bonding. "I mean, people come back the day after a party and say, 'You should have seen me abuse this girl.' They're real proud of it in front of everyone."

Sanday uses the term phallocentrism, "the deployment of the penis as a concrete symbol of masculine social power and dominance," to describe the use of sex and the debasement of women to demonstrate masculinity. Phallocentrism as well as the themes of male bonding, sexual prowess, and the debasement of women are all manifested in the act of pulling train. It is a form of bonding, it publicly legitimizes a male's heterosexuality, and it makes women an object of scorn and abuse.

Sanday is quick to emphasize that not all college men subscribe to the ideology of phallocentrism and that not all fraternity men measure their masculinity by sexual conquest. In the case that initiated her study, all the women who knew them described the six men charged with gang rape as "among the nicest guys in the fraternity."

Individually, probably none of them would have committed the act they were charged with. In the context of the fraternity, however, gang rape was the credible outcome of a process of identity formation manifested in fraternity life in general and in the fraternity initiation ritual in particular.

Gender Stratification and the Feminization of Poverty

Throughout the world, gender and age are significantly related to whether a person lives in poverty. In *Women and Children Last* (1986), Ruth Sidel draws an analogy between the doomed ship *Titanic* and society in the United States at the end of the 1980s. Both, she says, were gleaming symbols of wealth that placed women and children at a disadvantage. When the *Titanic* went down, women and children were indeed saved first, but only those who were travelling in first- or second-class accommodations. Women and children in third class and steerage were not saved. Although only 8 percent of the women and 3 percent of the children in first and second class drowned on the night the *Titanic* sank, 45 percent of the women and 70 percent of the children in steerage died. As with the *Titanic*, Sidel says, certain women and children in the United States are not the first to be saved; instead, they are the first to fall into poverty.

Most of the world's poor are women and children. As Michael Todaro, an economist, explains: "[Women] are more likely to be poor and malnourished and less likely to receive medical services, clean water, sanitation, and other benefits" (2000, 172). Female-headed households make up the poorest segments of Third World populations. For instance, as of 2000, 40 percent of all households in Kenya and 20 percent in India had no male wage earners. The percentages have increased since then. Women's potential earnings are far below those of males. Women have less access to education and government employment programs and are more likely to be employed in the informal sector, where neither wages nor working conditions are regulated. Even in households where there is a male wage earner, women may not have access to the household income. In countries where there is a strong male bias—such as India and China—household resources may be distributed very unevenly. In India, it is estimated that "girls are four times more likely to suffer from acute malnutrition and boys are 40 times more likely to be taken to a hospital when ill" (2000, 173–74). This not only results in more female infant deaths, but also contributes to an extremely high female child mortality.

When gender is combined with other factors that contribute to poverty, such as indigenous status, women face a combination of risks. Linda Gerber argues that in Canada, Métis, Inuit, and "Indian" women face "multiple jeopardy"—first as women, then as members of a "visible minority," and finally "as residents of uniquely dependent communities" (1990, 72). In the area of education, 7.7 percent of all Canadian females have not completed grade nine, but the percentages are much higher for Métis women (34.8 percent), Inuit women (62 percent), and "Indian" women (35.9 percent) (1990, 75). Moreover, Métis women have an average income 70 percent that of Metis men, Inuit women earn 76 percent of what Inuit men earn, and "Indian" women have an average income 73 percent of the average income of "Indian" men (1990, 79).

Body Image and Gender Hierarchies

One of the most important identity features for many North Americans is body shape. Although desired body shapes vary cross-culturally and across historical periods, in the West today a thin person is judged to be superior to a heavier person. When researchers asked children aged six to nine to examine three body silhouettes and to describe the kind of person represented by each body type, the children described the "thinner" figure as friendly, kind, happy, and polite, while they described the heavier figure as lazy, lying, and cheating. When

ten- and eleven-year-olds were shown drawings of other children, they consistently ranked heavier figures lowest, even below drawings of children with missing limbs or a child in a wheelchair.

Weight is a handicap also in the educational system, where teachers perceive heavy children as having more behavioural problems than others and as being less well liked by their classmates. Later in life, people who are overweight face hostile work environments and job discrimination. Workers judged unattractive by their peers—especially women—are consistently described in more negative terms.

The relationship between self-image and body shape is particularly relevant for female adolescents, as anthropologist Mimi Nichter discovered during a three-year study among high school girls in Arizona. Adolescent girls are particularly vulnerable to body image issues because during adolescence girls will gain up to 11.5 kilograms of body fat and thus are likely to be more critical of their own bodies. Young girls, says Nichter, are embedded in a morality play in which thinness is good, fatness is bad, and dieting is the way to get in shape. Nichter found that most of the girls in her study were thinking about their bodies either "all of the time" (24 percent) or "a lot of the time" (31 percent) and that 90 percent of white girls in the study were dissatisfied with their weight.

The adolescent girls in Nichter's study formed their idea of the "perfect" body largely from television, films, and magazines, and, of course, Barbie. The ideal woman was tall (170 centimetres) and had long hair (preferably blond), long legs, a flat stomach, a clear complexion, and "good" clothes. However, weight was the key factor: being "thin" was believed to be the ticket to happiness and popularity. As with many adult women that Nichter knew, the girls seemed to see the world in terms of fat and thin.

The girls rarely talked about weight with classmates whom they judged to be "fat"; nevertheless, they made moral judgments about them, believing that if someone who was overweight

THE CULTURAL CONSTRUCTION OF SOCIAL HIERARCHY

EXERCISE 6.3

Men and Body Image

Men rarely talk about dieting, or at least not as much as women do. However, concerns about body image are certainly not restricted to women. How, then, do men address the gap between their body image and the cultural ideal represented in advertisements and the media? Do men talk about this issue, and, if so, how is it articulated?

really wanted to lose weight, they could. Not losing weight implied that the girl was unconcerned about her personal appearance or was lazy. The lack of respect for overweight girls, says Nichter, was a theme that repeatedly emerged in discussions with the students. One girl explained:

> *I have a friend that's overweight and I feel that she should—I mean, I don't have anything against her 'cause she's overweight—but I guess it makes me mad that she doesn't do anything about it. She could do something about it and she doesn't. It's like her responsibility … like last night I went over there and right when I walked in she had a bag of Doritos—she was just, I mean, it's just like she's constantly eating. She's addicted to food. She just can't stop.*
>
> *(Nichter 2000, 42)*

Language, Gender, and Racial Hierarchies

Societies provide a social landscape along with the symbols or codes through which a person's place on the landscape is conveyed to others. For individuals these symbols or codes serve as toolboxes from which to fashion an identity. Societies may vary in the extent to which people are allowed to negotiate their place on the landscape, but all allow people some leeway.

Language, as we mentioned, is one of the tools that people have to signal how they want to be placed in society. Voice pitch, for example, does tend to differ because men's vocal tracts are longer, thus giving men a deeper voice. But children, whose voice tracts do not yet differ in size, will unconsciously lower or raise their pitch to conform to gender expectations; that is why you can usually tell from their voice the gender of a child. As Penelope Eckert and Sally McConnell-Ginet point out in *Language and Gender* (2003), people use language to present themselves as a certain kind of person, to project an attitude or a style, along with gender. All parts of language can be used in this way. The phonology, that is, the sounds, of a language can convey gender. For example, the /s/ sound can be made by pressing the tip of the tongue against the teeth. When pressed against the teeth it is still recognized as /s/, but this creates a slight lisp associated among English speakers in the United States and Canada with femininity in women and gayness in men.

Grammar can signal gender. Thus in French, there are male and female forms of nouns; in English, the third-person singular he and she force us to differentiate gender. In Japanese there are sentence-final particles that add to or soften the force of an utterance, with so-called women's language characterized as more mild. Thus "I am going" can be said as a mild assertion (*iku wa*), as a neutral assertion (*iku*), or as an emphatic assertion (*iku ze/iku zo*), with the latter being characterized as more masculine.

Whether or not to speak can convey gender. Children, for example, are encouraged to speak or to remain silent. Among the Araucanians of Chile, men are encouraged to talk since it is a sign of masculine intelligence and leadership, while the ideal woman is submissive and silent in her husband's presence.

Conversational styles may also convey gender. Linguist Robin Lakoff was one of the first to draw attention to the way a woman's identity in society influences how she speaks. Women, said Lakoff, are constrained to minimize their expression of opinion with various linguistic devices such as tag questions ("This election mess is terrible, **isn't it**?"), rising intonations on declaratives ("When will dinner be ready? **Six o'clock**?"), the use of hedges ("That's **kinda** sad" or "It's **probably** dinnertime"), boosters or amplifications ("I'm **so** glad you're here"), indirection (e.g., saying "I've got a dentist's appointment then," to convey an inability or reluctance to meet at that time and asking the other to propose another time).

The general thrust of Lakoff's argument has to do with the relative powerlessness of women stemming from their relatively weak social position. Speaking "as a woman," suggests Lakoff, requires avoiding firm commitment or expressing strong opinions and, in general, being restricted to using a "powerless" language.

Language can also be used to construct others, groups from which people want to separate themselves. In a classic work, *Racism in the English Language* (1976), Robert B. Moore discusses how judgments about race are coded into the way we speak. Reference to the colour black is scattered throughout the English language, generally with negative meanings: having a "black" outlook, to "blackball" or "blacklist" or "denigrate" someone, or being a "black sheep." The word "tribal" is often applied to discussions of African politics but not to European affairs. Thus rivalries between Ibo and Hausa and Yoruba in Nigeria or between Hutu and Tutsi in Rwanda are referred to in the press as "tribal conflicts," but not conflicts between Serbs and Croats in the Balkans, between Protestants and Catholics in Northern Ireland, or between Basques and Southern Spaniards in Spain.

Ward Churchill discusses the consequences of naming sports teams the "Braves," "Chiefs," "Redskins," "Seminoles," and "Savages," names that he suggests are deeply demeaning to Native Americans. Since apologists claim that this is just "fun," with no harm intended, Churchill suggests that we spread the fun around and use nicknames from other groups to name sports teams, such as the Kansas City "Kikes," the Hanover "Honkies,"

the Dayton "Dagos," Wisconsin "Wetbacks," and so on. Churchill draws attention to the way we use language, often unknowingly, that stigmatizes the identities of others.

QUESTION 6.4: HOW DO PEOPLE LIVING IN POVERTY ADAPT TO THEIR CONDITION?

The position in a social hierarchy occupied by each person is like a window through which she or he sees the world: different windows, different worlds. Furthermore, in order to survive in the impoverished conditions that exist in the lower tiers of society, people adopt specific adaptive strategies. Anthropologist Oscar Lewis coined the term **culture of poverty** to describe the lifestyle and world view of people who inhabit urban and rural slums. Some anthropologists object to that term, since it implies that poverty is somehow rooted in the subcultural values passed on from one generation to another, rather than in the social and cultural values of the larger society of which the poor are only a part. The implication is that if it weren't for the culture of poverty, the poor would have no culture at all.

Modifying that view, some anthropologists maintain that the behaviour of people in poverty represents their adaptations to their socioeconomic condition—no money and no jobs. These conditions are the result of inequality, usually reinforced by racism, and further buttressed by an economic system that requires a source of cheap labour. Moreover, descriptions of poor families as broken, fatherless, or female-centred are misleading.

> **culture of poverty**
> A term coined by anthropologist Oscar Lewis to describe the lifestyle and world view of people who inhabit urban and rural slums.

Many of the behaviours of the poor that are viewed negatively by the dominant society are actually resilient responses to the socioeconomic conditions of those living in poverty.

Kinship as an Adaptation to Poverty

One of the classic studies of how families cope with poverty was conducted by anthropologist Carol B. Stack in the late 1960s. She worked closely with a predominantly black community she called The Flats, a section of a small, midwestern city in the United States of 55,000 people. Unemployment in The Flats was over 20 percent, and 63 percent of the jobs held were in low-paying service occupations such as maid, cook, and janitor. While only 10 percent of the whites in the city lived in housing classed as deteriorating, 26 percent of blacks did. Moreover, blacks had inadequate access to health care, and their infant mortality rate was twice that of whites.

Stack's interest was in how the residents responded to their impoverished conditions. She discovered that they fostered kinship ties and created fictive kinship links to form close, interlocking, cooperative groups that would ensure economic and social support in times of need. Few people earned a sufficient amount to provide them or their families with enough to eat or a place to stay on a regular basis; even welfare payments could not always guarantee food and shelter for a family. Accordingly, people in The Flats regularly "swapped" food, shelter, child care, and personal possessions. In this respect, the community resembled societies such as the Ju/'hoansi, in which a person shares with others but expects them to reciprocate at some later time. Anthropologists call this type of sharing **generalized reciprocity**, as distinguished from **balanced reciprocity**, in which items are exchanged on the spot; a direct trade of items would be an example. **Negative reciprocity** is an attempt to get something for nothing or make a profit. The advantage of generalized reciprocity is that widespread sharing ensures that nobody lacks

the basic needs for survival. People in The Flats cultivated diffuse kinship and friendship relations by giving when they could, so that others would give to them when they were in need. These networks were often framed in a kinship idiom, even when no biological kin ties existed.

Another adaptation to poverty in The Flats involved child care. Given the unpredictability of employment, the sometimes young age at which women had children, and the need to respond to unpredictable living conditions and substandard housing, a child might reside with three or four different adults. Often different people performed the roles of provider, discipliner, trainer, curer, and groomer. Stack points out that those who provided child care did so because they considered it a privilege as well as a responsibility. Children were valued, but they were considered the responsibility of a wide network of kin and friends.

Male and female relations were most affected by the difficulty that men had in finding steady employment. Generally a couple in The Flats would not marry unless the man had a steady job. Men in The Flats had accepted the mainstream model in the United States of the male provider, and being unable to find regular employment prevented their assumption of that role. Moreover, marriage removed people from the widespread sharing network, since after marriage their major obligations belonged to their husbands or wives. In addition, because a woman was cut off the welfare rolls if she married, kinship networks and welfare benefits offered a woman more security than a

generalized reciprocity
A form of exchange in which people share what they have with others but expect them to reciprocate later.

balanced reciprocity
A form of exchange in which items of equal or near-equal value are exchanged on the spot.

negative reciprocity
A form of exchange in which the object is to get something for nothing or to make a profit.

husband could. Nevertheless, men and women in The Flats did form intimate relationships out of which children were born. Moreover, the fathers took considerable pride in their children, as did the paternal grandparents, to whom the children often went for help. However, the mothers often regarded the fathers as friends who had failed to fulfill their paternal obligations. Thus, the conditions of poverty drew people into kinship and friendship networks, rather than nuclear family patterns valued by the larger society.

Challenge Issue

As self-aware and self-reflecting beings, humans face emotional and intellectual challenges born of the need to make sense of our place in the universe. We puzzle over truly big questions about time and space and wrestle with existential questions about our own fate, life, and death. For countless generations, our species has creatively engaged in such reflections on the unknown, the mysterious, the supernatural. We do this in sacred narratives and rituals—prayers, chants, dances, prostrations, burnings, and sacrificial offerings—the cornerstones of many religions. Here we see Christian pilgrims walking toward the shrine of the Virgin of Guadalupe, the patron saint of Mexico. For centuries, Nahuatl-speaking Mexican Indians have referred to this brown-skinned Saint Mary, the virgin mother of Jesus Christ, as Tonantzin ("Our Revered Mother"), their traditional name for an ancient Aztec earth and fertility goddess. Believers claim she manifested herself in a blaze of light to an Aztec youth in 1531, a decade after the Spanish destruction of the Aztec empire. Representing purity, hope, and motherly love, she embodies a longing for a world of social justice and interethnic tolerance. Annually, her shrine in Mexico City attracts more than 6 million devotees, making it one of the largest pilgrimage sites on earth.

Spirituality, Religion, and Shamanism

Religions play an important role in determining cultural identity in many societies across the globe, sometimes overruling other major identity markers such as kinship, social class, and ethnicity or nationality. From an anthropological point of view, spirituality and religion are part of a cultural system's *superstructure*, earlier defined as the collective body of ideas, beliefs, and values by which members of a culture make sense of the world and their place in it. In contrast to theology or other disciplines, anthropology examines the entirety of shared concepts concerning the ultimate shape and substance of reality in terms of a people's **worldview**.

Notably, just 16 percent of the world's population is categorized as nonreligious (**Figure 13.1**). A small minority in that category is atheist, a broad label covering a range of worldviews, including individually held spiritual beliefs that do not fit any formally institutionalized religion.

As touched on in earlier chapters, and here discussed in greater detail, the superstructure of cultural systems is intricately connected with the infrastructure and social structure. Guided by our barrel model, we therefore expect adaptations in the superstructure when there are technological, economic, social, and/or political changes. Based on that principle, worldwide transformations in the ideological landscape are to be anticipated as an integral component of globalization. Reviewing world history for the past few thousand years, scholars recognize radical transformations in religious and spiritual beliefs and rituals everywhere. Taking the long view, we discover that, like political states discussed in the previous chapter, most religions we know today are, in fact, not that old. And even those that appear to be old are quite different from when they began.

In this chapter we offer a cross-cultural review and comparative historical perspective on a wide range of spiritual traditions and religions. We explain how societies have developed worldviews concerning the non-ordinary, mysterious, transcendental, supernatural, or metaphysical—cultural superstructures with particular repertoires of spiritual beliefs, ritual practices, and religious institutions, often considered sacred or holy.

worldview The collective body of ideas that members of a culture generally share concerning the ultimate shape and substance of their reality.

IN THIS CHAPTER YOU WILL LEARN TO

- Articulate how religion is related to other parts of a cultural system.

- Distinguish a cross-cultural variety of supernatural beings and spiritual forces.

- Compare different types of rituals and their functions in society.

- Describe how religions legitimize spiritual leadership.

- Recognize why places become sacred sites and turn into pilgrimage destinations.

- Explain beliefs in evil magic, or witchcraft, linking this to fear and social control.

- Interpret why shamanic healing is thought to be effective.

- Analyze the connection between cultural upheaval and new religious movements.

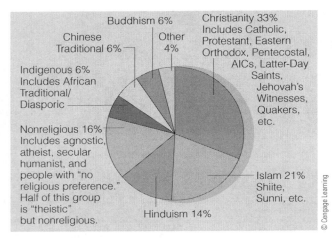

Figure 13.1 Major Religions of the World This chart shows the world's major religions with percentages of their adherents. The total adds up to more than 100 percent due to rounding. Two have enormous followings: Christianity, with almost 2.2 billion adherents (half of whom are Roman Catholic), and Islam, with about 1.7 billion (an overwhelming majority of whom are Sunnis). Within both religions are numerous major and minor divisions, splits, and sects.

Sources: adherents.com; Pew Research Center, 2011.

Roles of Spirituality and Religion

Among people in all societies, particular spiritual or religious beliefs and practices fulfill individual and collective psychological and emotional needs. They reduce anxiety by providing an orderly view of the universe and answers to existential questions, including those concerning suffering and death. They provide a path by which people transcend the burdens of mortal existence and attain, if only momentarily, hope and relief.

Spiritual or religious beliefs and practices also serve numerous cultural purposes. For instance, a religion held in common by a group of people reinforces community values and provides moral guidelines for personal conduct. It also offers narratives and rituals used to confirm a social hierarchy and sanction political power; conversely, it may allow for narratives *countering* the legitimacy of powerholders, even providing justifications and rituals to resist and challenge them. Last but not least, people often turn to religion or spirituality in the hope of reaching a specific goal, such as restoring health, securing a harvest, ending violence, or being rescued from danger (**Figure 13.2**).

Figure 13.2 Bugi Sailors Praying, Indonesia The Bugi of Sulawesi (Celebes) are famous for their oceangoing schooners. For generations, these Indonesian seafarers have plied the waters between Malaysia and Australia, transporting spices and other freight. Life at sea is risky—sudden storms, piracy, and other mishaps—and sailors pray for safety. This prayerful Bugi gathering in Jakarta on Java Island took place on a holiday ending Ramadan, the Islamic month of fasting. During that time Muslims refrain from eating, drinking liquids, smoking, and sexual activities, from sunrise to sunset. This taboo serves to purify thought and build restraint for Allah's sake.

Anthropologists recognize that not everyone believes in a supernatural force or entity, but they also agree that there is no known culture that does not provide some set of ideas about existence beyond ordinary and empirically verifiable reality, or—for lack of a better word—ideas concerning the supernatural or metaphysical. Because such ideas serve cultural purposes and fulfill emotional and psychological needs, it makes sense that spirituality and religion developed tens of thousands of years ago and spread across the globe.

In the wake of major technological inventions and new discoveries since the 1600s, European intellectuals predicted that magic, myth, and religion would be replaced by empirical research, proven facts, and scientific theories. They expected that as science progressed, beliefs and rituals based on what they argued to be ignorance and superstition would gradually disappear. Some even forecasted the end of religion altogether. But to date, and despite tremendous scientific achievements, that has not occurred. In many places, the opposite trend seems to prevail, in particular where radical technological, social, and economic transformations destabilize the long-established cultural order, challenge deeply embedded worldviews, and leave people feeling insecure and threatened. Confronted by sweeping changes over which people have little or no control, many turn to religion and spirituality.

Anthropological Approach to Spirituality and Religion

Worldwide, people are inspired and guided by strongly held ideas about the supernatural, putting into practice what they deeply believe to be true or right. It is not the responsibility of anthropologists to pass judgment on the metaphysical truth of any particular faith system, but it is their challenge to show how each embodies a number of revealing facts about humanity and the particular cultural superstructure, or worldview, within which these religious or spiritual beliefs are ideologically embedded.

Based on a cross-cultural and comparative historical perspective on worldviews, we define **religion** as an organized system of ideas about the spiritual sphere or the supernatural, along with associated ceremonial practices by which people try to interpret and/or influence aspects of the universe otherwise beyond their access or control. Similar to religion, **spirituality** is concerned with the sacred, as distinguished from ordinary reality, but it is often individual rather than collective and

does not require a formal institution. Both indicate that many aspects of the human experience are thought to be beyond natural or scientific explanation.

Because no culture, including those of modern industrial and postindustrial societies, has achieved complete certainty in controlling existing or future conditions and circumstances of human life, spirituality and/or religion continue to play a role in all known cultures. However, considerable variability exists globally (**Figure 13.3**).

At one end of the anthropological spectrum are food-foraging peoples, whose technological ability to control their natural environment is limited. Broadly speaking, they hold that nature is pregnant with the spiritual. Embedded and manifested in all aspects of their culture, spirituality permeates their daily activities—from food hunting or gathering to making fires, building homes, and conversations about life before or after death. It also mirrors and confirms the egalitarian nature of social relations in their societies, in that individuals do not plead with high-ranking deities for aid the way members of stratified societies more typically do. Their holistic worldview is often referred to as *naturalistic*, an imprecise but workable term.

At the other end of our spectrum are state societies with commercial or industrial economies, sophisticated technologies, and social stratification based on a complex division of labor. There, high-ranking social groups typically seek to control and manage the construction of a society's worldview as an ideological means of legitimizing and reinforcing their vested interests in its hierarchical structure. Usually featuring a ranked order of supernatural beings—for instance, God and (in some religions) the angels, saints, or other holy figures—it simultaneously reflects and reinforces the stratified system in which it is embedded. In such societies, religion tends to be less integrated into everyday activities, and its practice is usually confined to specific times, occasions, and locations.

Religions provide a powerful ideology justifying inequality in a state society, but may also inspire subordinated peoples to envision an alternative social order freeing them from exploitation, repression, and humiliation. Thus, religiously motivated social movements have challenged political establishments.

religion An organized system of ideas about the spiritual sphere or the supernatural, along with associated ceremonial practices by which people try to interpret and/or influence aspects of the universe otherwise beyond their control.

spirituality Concern with the sacred, as distinguished from material matters. In contrast to religion, spirituality is often individual rather than collective and does not require a distinctive format or traditional organization.

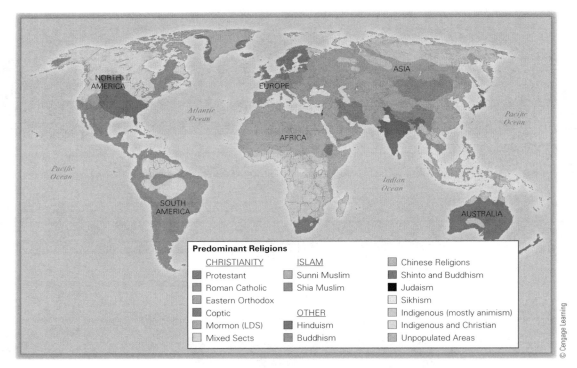

Figure 13.3 Global Distribution of Predominant Religions This map depicts only the global distribution of major religions, indicating where they predominate. In some areas, the mixture of different religions is such that no single faith is shared by most of that region's inhabitants. Not detailed enough to show pockets with significant numbers of a particular faith, it also omits many religions that are dispersed or eclipsed by others—including several worldwide ones such as Ahmadiyya (a Muslim sect, with 10 million adherents); Jehovah's Witnesses (a Christian sect with 7 million adherents); and Bahá'í (with 6 million adherents, emphasizing the spiritual unity of all mankind and recognizing divine messengers from various religions).

Myth and the Mapping of a Sacred Worldview

Because much remains beyond human capacity to actually observe and explain based on obvious or empirical evidence alone, people have creatively worked out narratives explaining the fundamentals of human existence—where we and everything in our world came from, why we are here, and where we are going. Describing a worldview, these narratives are referred to as **myths** (*mythos*, Greek for "word," "speech") and play a fundamental role in religious and spiritual beliefs. Mapping a people's *cosmology*—their understanding of the universe, its form and working—myths are believed to be true, even sacred, by those subscribing to the particular worldview engendering such narratives.

Typically, a myth features supernatural forces or beings engaged in extraordinary or miraculous performances. It may offer a morality play, providing an ethical code for its audience and guidelines for human behavior. For example, the Puranas (a body of religious texts, including cosmological myths, considered sacred by Buddhists and Hindus) are rich in such material. So are the Bible, Koran, and Torah, each held sacred in distinct but historically related religions originating in Southwest Asia. We will discuss myths further within the context of art in the next chapter, but here it is important to underscore that these stories, whether orally transmitted or in writing, have been passed on from generation to generation and inform believers with a sacred map of the cosmos or universe and their place in it.

Supernatural Beings and Spiritual Forces

A hallmark of religion is belief in spiritual forces and supernatural beings. Attempting to control by religious means what cannot be controlled in other ways, humans turn to prayer, sacrifice, and other religious or spiritual rituals. Their actions presuppose the existence of spiritual forces that can

---

myth A sacred narrative that explains the fundamentals of human existence—where we and everything in our world came from, why we are here, and where we are going.

Figure 13.4 Judeo-Christian God Giving Life to Adam The patriarchal nature of traditional Euramerican society is depicted on the ceiling of the Sistine Chapel in Rome, Italy. The image of a supreme male diety creating the first man, named Adam ("human being"), is culturally articulated and ideologically justified by its Judeo-Christian theology. Afterward, according to this biblical story, the first woman, named Eve, is formed from Adam's rib.

be tapped into, or supernatural beings interested in human affairs and available for aid. In many cultures, these supernatural forces or spiritual beings are associated with unique geographic locations valued as sacred sites—extraordinary rocks, lakes, wells, waterfalls, mountains, and so forth.

Supernatural beings can be divided into three categories: deities (gods and goddesses), ancestral spirits, and other sorts of spirit beings. Although the variety of deities and spirits recognized by the world's cultures is tremendous, it is possible to make certain generalizations about them.

Gods and Goddesses

Not all religions *anthropomorphize* the divine, but many do. Symbolically constructing a divine order that mirrors a society's gender structure, many religions recognize male and female deities. Gods and goddesses, or divinities, are the great and more remote supernatural beings. Generally speaking, cultures that subordinate women to men attribute masculine gender to the more powerful gods or supreme deity. For instance, in traditional Christian religions believers speak of God as a father who had a divine son born from a human mother but do not entertain thoughts of God as a mother or as a divine daughter (**Figure 13.4**). Such male-privileging religions developed in many societies traditionally based on the herding of animals or intensive agriculture, frequent warfare, and politics controlled by men.

Goddesses, by contrast, are likely to be prominent in societies where women play a significant role in the economy and enjoy relative equality with men. Such societies are most often those that depend on crop cultivation traditionally carried out solely or mostly by women. Typically, these may feature fertility and earth goddesses.

Some religions recognize deities represented as male–female combinations. For example, one of the Greek gods, also recognized in the Roman empire, was Hermaphroditus, the beautiful two-sexed son of Hermes (alias Mercury) and Venus (alias Aphrodite). A similar third-gender divinity is recognized by Hindus worshiping Ardhanarishvara ("the Lord who is half woman").

If a religion recognizes only one supremely powerful divinity as creator and master of the universe, we speak of **monotheism**. If it acknowledges more than one divinity, each governing a particular domain, we label it **polytheism**. Gods and goddesses of ancient Greece illustrate the latter: Zeus ruled the sky, Poseidon the sea, and Hades the underworld and the dead. In addition to these three brothers, Greek mythology features a host of other deities, both male and female, each similarly concerned with specific aspects of life and the universe. Athena and Nike, for instance, were goddesses of war and victory, respectively. A **pantheon**, or the collection of gods and goddesses such as those of the Greeks, is common in many religions, today most famously in Hinduism.

Because states typically have grown through conquest, often their pantheons have expanded, with local deities of conquered peoples being incorporated into the official state pantheon. A frequent feature of pantheons is the presence of a supreme deity, who may be all but totally ignored by humans. Aztecs of the Mexican highlands, for instance, recognized a supreme duo to whom they paid little attention. Assuming this divine pair was unlikely to be interested in ordinary humans, they devoted themselves to lesser deities thought to be more directly concerned with human affairs.

Ancestral Spirits

Beliefs in ancestral spirits support the concept that human beings consist of intertwined components: body/matter (physical) and mind/soul (spiritual). This dualistic concept carries with it the possibility of a spirit being freed from the body—through dream, trance, or death—and even having a separate existence. Frequently, where a belief in

monotheism The belief in only one supremely powerful divinity as creator and master of the universe.

polytheism The belief in multiple gods and/or goddesses, as contrasted with monotheism—the belief in one god or goddess.

pantheon All the gods and goddesses of a people.

ancestral spirits exists, these nonphysical beings are seen as retaining an active interest and membership in society.

Beliefs in ancestral spirits are found in many parts of the world, especially among people having unilineal descent systems with their associated ancestor orientation. In several African cultures, the concept is highly elaborate, and people believe ancestral spirits behave much like humans. They are able to feel hot, cold, and pain and may even die a second death by drowning or burning. Because spirits sometimes participate in family and lineage events, seats will be provided for them, even though they are invisible. If spirits are annoyed, they may send sickness or death. Eventually, they are reborn as new members of their lineage, so adults need to observe infants closely to determine just who has been reborn.

Ancestor spirits also play an important role in the patrilineal society of traditional China. Giving birth to sons is historically regarded as an obligation to the ancestors because boys inherit their father's ancestral duties. For the gift of life, a boy is forever indebted to his parents, owing them obedience, deference, and a comfortable old age. Even after their death, he has to provide for them in the spirit world, placing food, money, and incense on ancestral altars on the anniversaries of their births and deaths.

Other Types of Supernatural Beings and Spiritual Forces

Animism

One widespread concept concerning supernatural beings is **animism**, a belief that nature is enlivened or energized by distinct personalized spirit beings separable from physical bodies or the material substance they inhabit. Spirits such as souls and ghosts are thought to dwell in humans, animals, and plants, as well as human-made artifacts and natural features such as stones, mountains, and wells; for animists, the world is filled with particular spirits.

These spirit beings are a highly diverse lot. Less remote than gods and goddesses, they may be benevolent, malevolent, or just plain neutral. Involved in people's daily affairs, they also may be awesome, terrifying, lovable, or mischievous. Because they may be pleased or irritated by human actions, people are obliged to be concerned about them.

Animism is typical of those who see themselves as being a part of nature rather than superior to it (**Figure 13.5**). This includes most food foragers and food gardeners, among others. Deities, if they are believed to exist at all in such societies, may be seen as having created the world and perhaps making it fit to live in; but in animism, spirits are the ones to beseech when ill, the ones to help or hinder the shaman, and the ones whom the ordinary hunter may meet when off in the wilderness.

Animatism

Although supernatural power is often thought of as being vested in spirit beings, it does not have to be. Such is the case with **animatism**—the belief that nature is enlivened or energized by an impersonal force or supernatural energy, which may make itself manifest in any special place, thing, or living creature. This basic concept, which probably developed well before the first transition from food foraging to food production 10,000 years ago, is still present in many societies around the

Figure 13.5 Inuit Food Ritual Inuit of Arctic Canada refer to spirit beings as *anirniit* (singular *anirniq*, meaning "breath") and still obey certain taboos and perform rituals when killing game animals and dividing the meat. This is to avoid offending the animal's spirit (which remains alive and may take revenge on the hunter). Today, most Inuit are Christians, and their concept of *anirniq* is akin to "soul." But traditional food rituals continue. In this photo, Inuit at Baffin Island pray before a shared Easter feast of fish and seal meat.

© B & C Alexander/Photo Researchers, Inc.

world today. For example, in China it appears in the form of a concept known as *qi* (or *ch'i*), which may be translated as "vital energy." Inuit people in Arctic Canada think of this force in terms of a "cosmic breath-soul" they call *sila*. In northeastern America, Algonquian-speaking indigenous peoples refer to impersonal spirit power as *manitou*.

One of the best-studied examples of animatism can be found in the Pacific where Oceanic peoples inhabiting hundreds of islands share a concept they refer to as *mana*. Not unlike the idea of a cosmic energy passing into and through everything, affecting living and nonliving matter alike, *mana* is probably best defined as "supernaturally conferred potency" (Keesing, 1992, p. 236)—similar to "the force" in the *Star Wars* films. Traditional Maori, Tahitians, Tongans, and other Oceanic peoples typically attribute success (identified by actual achievements such as triumph in combat, bountiful harvest, abundant fish or game, and so on) to *mana*—and see it as proof of *mana*. In short, this metaphysical concept rests on pragmatic evidence.

Animism (a belief in distinct spirit beings) and animatism (which lacks particular substance or individual form) are not mutually exclusive and are often found in the same culture. This is the case among the Inuit pictured in Figure 13.5, who believe in spirit beings known as *anirniit* as well as in the impersonal spirit power they call *sila* (Merkur, 1983).

In many religious traditions, certain geographic places are thought to be spiritually significant or are held sacred for various reasons, including ideas here discussed in terms of animism and animatism. Typically, such sites are rivers, lakes, waterfalls, islands, forests, caves, and—especially—mountains. We revisit the topic of sacred sites later in the chapter.

Religious Specialists

Most cultures include individuals who guide others in their spiritual search and ritual practices. Thought to be inspired, enlightened, or even holy, they command respect for their skills in contacting and influencing spiritual beings and manipulating or connecting to supernatural forces. Often, they display unique personality traits that make them particularly well suited to perform these tasks for which they have undergone special training.

Priests and Priestesses

In societies with resources to support a full-time religious specialist, a **priest or priestess** will be authorized to perform sacred rituals and mediate between fellow humans and supernatural powers, divine spirits, or deities. In

many societies, they are familiar figures known by official titles such as *lama, kahuna, imam, priest, minister, rabbi, swami,* or *copa pitào*. How they dress, what they eat, where they live, and numerous other indicators may distinguish them from others in society and symbolically indicate their special status.

Reserving exclusive rights to exercise spiritual power, groups of priests and/or priestesses bond together in an effort to monopolize the means of sacred practice. This includes controlling holy sites of worship, supervising prescribed rituals, and maintaining possession of regalia, relics, statues, images, texts, and other representations of holiness. In so doing, they also create, promote, and maintain the ideological sources needed to symbolically construct the religious authority from which they derive their legitimacy.

When deities are identified in masculine terms, it is not surprising that the most important religious leadership positions are reserved for men. Such is the case in Judaism, Islam, as well as the Roman Catholic Church, the latter of which has always been headed by a male pope and his all-male council, the College of Cardinals.

Female religious specialists are likely to be found only in societies in which women are acknowledged to significantly contribute to the economy, and gods and goddesses are both recognized (Lehman, 2002). Also, all around the world women fully devoted to a religious life have formed their own gender-segregated institutions such as all-female convents headed by an abbess. Such nunneries not only exist in countries with longstanding Christian traditions, but were also founded in the Himalayas and many other Buddhist regions in southern and eastern Asia, including Taiwan, as described by American anthropologist Hillary Crane in the Biocultural Connection on the next page.

Spiritual Lineages: Legitimizing Religious Leadership

As with political institutions discussed in the previous chapter, religious organizations are maintained by rules that define ideological boundaries, establish membership criteria, and regulate continuity of legitimate leadership in the faith community. And, like other institutions, religions have always been challenged by changes. Even in a highly stable cultural system, every generation must deal with natural transitions in the life cycle, including death

---

animism The belief that nature is enlivened or energized by distinct personalized spirit beings separable from bodies.

animatism The belief that nature is enlivened or energized by an impersonal spiritual force or supernatural energy, which may make itself manifest in any special place, thing, or living creature.

priest or priestess A full-time religious specialist formally recognized for his or her role in guiding the religious practices of others and for contacting and influencing supernatural powers.

BIOCULTURAL CONNECTION

Change Your Karma and Change Your Sex?

By Hillary Crane

As Mahayana Buddhists, Taiwanese Chan (Zen) monastics believe that all humans are able to reach enlightenment and be released from reincarnation. But they believe it is easier for some because of the situation into which they are born—for example, if one is born in a country where Buddhism is practiced, in a family that teaches proper behavior, or with exceptional mental or physical gifts.

Chan monastics view contrasting human circumstances as the result of the karma accrued in previous lives. They believe certain behavior—such as diligently practicing Buddhism—improves karma and the chances of attaining spiritual goals in this lifetime or coming back

in a better birth. Other behavior—such as killing a living being, eating meat, desiring or becoming attached to things or people—accrues bad karma.

One way karma manifests itself is in one's sex. Taiwanese Buddhists believe that being born female makes it harder to attain spiritual goals. This idea comes, in part, from the inferior status of women in Taiwan and the belief that their "complicated bodies" and monthly menstruation cycles can distract them. Moreover, they believe, women are more enmeshed in their families than men, and their emotional ties keep them focused on worldly rather than spiritual tasks.

Taiwanese Buddhists who decide to become monks and nuns must break from their families to enter a monastery. Because women are thought to be more attached to their families than are men, leaving home is seen as a particularly big step for nuns and a sign that they are more like men than most women. In fact, a nun's character is considered masculine, unlike the frightened, indecisive, and emotional traits usually associated with women in Taiwan. When they leave home nuns even stop referring to themselves as women and call one another *shixiong* ("dharma brother"). They use this linguistic change to signal that they identify themselves as men and to remind one another to behave like men, particularly like the monks at the temple.

Monastics also reduce their attachments to worldly things like music and food. Nuns usually emphasize forsaking food and eat as little as possible. Their appearance, already quite masculine because they shave their heads and wear loose, gray clothing, becomes even more so when they lose weight—particularly in their hips, breasts, and thighs. Also, after becoming monastics, they often experience a slowing or stopping of their menses. Although these physical changes can be attributed to change in diet and lifestyle, the nuns point to them as signs they are becoming men, making progress toward their spiritual goals, and improving their karma.

BIOCULTURAL QUESTION

The Zen Buddhist ideal of enlightenment, realized when the soul is released from reincarnation, prescribes an extreme ascetic lifestyle for nuns that makes them physically incapable of biological reproduction. Do you think that their infertility allows these female monastics to emotionally adapt to a way of life that denies them motherhood?

Written expressly for this text, 2008. For a more detailed treatment of this topic, see Crane, H. (2001). Men in spirit: The masculinization of Taiwanese Buddhist nuns. *Ph.D dissertation, Brown University.*

---

of religious leaders. In many religions, spiritual leadership is thought to be vested in divine authority, representing or even embodying the divine itself. How do religions secure legitimate successors and avoid disruption and confusion?

Several major religions follow a principle of leadership in which divine authority is passed down from a spiritual founding figure, such as a prophet or saint, to a chain of successors who derive legitimacy as religious leaders from their status in such a lineage. Here identified as **spiritual lineage**, this principle has been worked out in numerous cross-cultural variations over the course of thousands of years. It not only applies to leadership of entire religions but to segmental divisions of religions, such as sects and orders.

spiritual lineage A principle of leadership in which divine authority is passed down from a spiritual founding figure, such as a prophet or saint, to a chain of successors.

Whereas kings in traditional political dynasties derive legitimacy from their ancestral blood lineage, religious leaders obtain it from their spiritual line of descent as specified in each particular religious tradition. The longer these lineages have existed, the greater their opportunities for building up a fund of symbolic capital—ideas and rituals, including sacred gestures, dances, songs, and texts. This fund also includes regalia, paintings, statues, and sacred architecture such as shrines, tombs, and temples, along with the land on which they stand. Thus, some religious leaders and their followers have accumulated a considerable amount of material wealth utilized in the exercise of religious authority, in addition to the immaterial holdings of traditional knowledge and sacred rituals.

Here, to illustrate the cross-cultural range of spiritual lineages, we distinguish four major forms. First, in some religions, spiritual leaders or high-ranking priests claim divine authority based on recognized biological descent from a common ancestor believed to have been a prophet, saint, or otherwise sacred, holy, or even divine being. Such is the case with *kohanim*, high-ranking Israelite priests, claiming patrilineal descent from the legendary high priest Aaron believed to have lived about 3,500 years ago.

In other religions, leaders personally groom, train, and appoint a spiritual heir, a successor tasked with guarding and continuing the spiritual legacy of the order or sect as established by its founder. For example, a sect of Muslim mystics known as Sufi is widely dispersed across Asia and North Africa and historically divided into many dozens of orders, or brotherhoods. Each brotherhood is headed by a master teacher, known by an honorific title such as *sheikh*. The sheikh derives his spiritual authority from his position in a *silsila* (Arabic, meaning "chain"), named after a founding saint who originally laid down a particular method of prayer and ritual practiced by followers seeking oneness with God (Abun-Nasr, 2007; Anjum, 2006).

A third form of legitimizing the authority of a religious leader is by election. In such cases, a group of leading elders comes together in a ritual gathering at a traditionally designated location and chooses one of their own to succeed the deceased leader. One of the best-known examples in world history is the election of a pope by a group of cardinals—"princes" of the Roman Catholic Church who proclaim the new pope to be the divinely ordained spiritual heir of St. Peter, Vicar of Christ. Believed by 1.2 billion Christians to hold the sacred key to heaven, the pope is traditionally addressed as "Holy Father." The current Pope Benedict XVI is the 265th holder of this nearly 2,000-year-old religious office.

A fourth and final example of spiritual lineage is found in Tibetan Buddhism, divided into four major orders or schools. Each has its own monasteries, monks of various ranks from novice to lama, and a wealth of ancient texts, ritual practices, meditations, and other sacred knowledge passed on largely by oral tradition. Highest in rank among the monks are reincarnated saints. These are individuals who, fully emanating the divine Buddha spirit, achieved enlightenment during their lifetime; led by compassion, they chose to give up *nirvana* ("eternal bliss") after death to return to life on earth. To fulfill this role, such a saintly person must be recognized. Toward this end, a select group of high-ranking lamas guided by omens seeks out a newborn boy believed to be a *tulku* ("emanated incarnation") of a recently deceased saintly lama in their spiritual lineage. Once they find the little boy, they ritually induct and enthrone him and begin grooming him for his designated spiritual leadership position in the Buddhist order (**Figure 13.6**).

Of about 500 *tulku* lineages in Tibetan Buddhism, the most famous is the Dalai Lama ("teacher who is spiritually as deep as the ocean"). This illustrious lineage traces its origins to a high-ranking monk named Gendun Drup (1391–1474), thought to have embodied the Buddha spirit of compassion. A few years after the death of the thirteenth Dalai Lama in 1933, high-ranking monks from his order identified a 2-year-old boy in a small farming village as his reincarnated "wisdom mind." Renaming him Tenzin Gyatso, they later enthroned the little *tulku* as His Holiness, the fourteenth Dalai Lama—the highest-ranking political and spiritual position among Tibetan Buddhists for centuries.

Shamans

Societies without religious professionals have existed far longer than those that have them. Although lacking full-time specialists, they have always included individuals considered capable of connecting with supernatural beings and forces—individuals such as shamans. That capacity, partially based on learned techniques, is also based on personality and particular emotional experiences that could be described as "mystical." Supplied with spiritual knowledge in the form of a vision or some other extraordinary revelation, they are believed to be supernaturally empowered to heal the sick, change the weather, control the movements of animals, and foretell the future. As they perfect these and related skills, they may combine the role of a diviner and a healer, becoming a shaman.

Originally, the word *shaman* referred to medical-religious specialists, or spiritual guides, among the Tungus and other Siberian pastoral nomads with animist beliefs. By means of various techniques such as fasting, drumming, chanting, or dancing, as well as hallucinogenic mushrooms (*fly agaric*), these shamans enter into a trance. In this waking dream state, they experience visions of an alternate reality inhabited by spirit beings such as guardian animal spirits who may assist with healing. Similar spiritual practices exist in many indigenous cultures outside Siberia, especially in the Americas. For that reason, the term *shaman* is frequently applied to a variety of part-time spiritual leaders, diviners, and traditional healers active in many other parts of the world (Kehoe, 2000).

107

VISUAL COUNTERPOINT

Figure 13.6 Buddhist Lama Dilgo Khyentsé Rinpoche and His Reincarnation Dilgo Khyentsé Yangsi Rinpoche There are many spiritual lineages in Tibetan Buddhism not as well known as that of the Dalai Lama. The monk on the left is a reincarnation of a Buddhist master identified as the first Khyentsé ("Compassionate Wisdom"). In 1832 at age 12, the first Khyentsé was recognized as the combined incarnation of an 8th-century Tibetan religious king and a profoundly learned Buddhist master. Renamed Jamyang Khyentsé Wangpo and receiving intensive training, he was ordained throne-holder of a major Tibetan monastery and became a living saint. Dying in 1892, he reincarnated in 1910 as a little boy—a *tulku* renamed Dilgo Khyentsé Rinpoche (*Rinpoche*, a title given to *tulkus*, means "Precious One"). Before Dilgo Khyentsé passed away at the Shechen Monastery in Nepal at age 81, he gave subtle indications concerning how and where his "wisdom mind" would be reincarnated. After his death, another high-ranking lama in his order, who had been his close friend and disciple, had visions and dreams. Guided by these instructions, a search party identified a boy born in Nepal in the summer of 1993 as his reincarnation. The boy (*right*) was renamed Dilgo Khyentsé Yangsi in 1996. With his legitimate status in this *tulku* lineage confirmed by the Dalai Lama, the young monk was enthroned at his predecessor's monastery the following year.

Anthropologist Michael Harner (see Anthropologist of Note feature), a modern-day shamanic practitioner famous for his participant observation among Shuar (or Jivaro) Indian shamans in the Amazon rainforest, defined a **shaman** as someone who at will enters an altered state of consciousness "to contact and utilize an ordinarily hidden reality in order to acquire knowledge, power, and to help other persons. The shaman has at least one, and usually more, 'spirits' in his or her personal service" (Harner, 1980, p. 20).

shaman A person who at will enters an altered state of consciousness to contact and utilize an ordinarily hidden reality in order to acquire knowledge, power, and to help others.

Shamanic Experience

Someone may become a shaman by passing through stages of learning and practical experience, often involving psychological and emotional ordeals brought about by isolation, fasting, physical torture, sensory deprivation, and/or *hallucination* (Latin, for "mental wandering"). Hallucinations may occur when one is in a trance state; they can come about spontaneously, but they can also be induced by drumming or consuming mind-altering drugs such as psychoactive vines or mushrooms.

Because shamanism is rooted in altered states of consciousness and the human nervous system universally produces these trance states, individuals experience

ANTHROPOLOGIST OF NOTE

Michael J. Harner (b. 1929)

A world-renowned expert on shamanism, American anthropologist **Michael Harner** studied at the University of California, Berkeley. Starting out in archaeology and collaborating with Alfred Kroeber on Mohave pottery research, he later switched to ethnography. Intrigued by the Jívaro, legendary for shrinking human heads, he ventured into eastern Ecuador's tropical forest in 1956, at age 27. For nearly a year, he lived among these Amazonian Indians, now better known as Shuar. They still subsisted on food gardens and by hunting and gathering; they fiercely guarded their freedom and launched raids on enemy tribes.

Holding an animistic worldview, the Shuar distinguish between what Harner has identified as ordinary and non-ordinary realities. They believe that supernatural forces govern daily life and that spirit beings can be perceived and engaged only by shamans capable of entering non-ordinary reality. They access this reality by drinking *natema*, a bitter brew made from a jungle vine known as *ayahuasca* ("vine of the soul"). As they told Harner, drinking this hallucinogenic potion, shamans enter an altered state of consciousness in which they perceive and engage what they believe are the "true" forces governing sickness and health, life and death.

Harner returned to the Upper Amazon in 1960 for more ethnographic fieldwork, this time among the Conibo in eastern Peru. Seeking greater insight on *ayahuasca's* psychological impact on the native cosmology, he drank the magic brew. Passing through the door of perception into the shamanic view of reality, he found himself in a world beyond his "wildest dreams": a supernatural landscape inhabited by spirit beings. Singing incredibly beautiful music, they began to carry his soul away and he felt he was dying. Coming out of this experience, and later ones with Conibo shamans, Harner realized that anthropologists had seriously underestimated the powerful influence hallucinogenic drugs had on Amazonian Indian ideologies and practices.

In 1963, Harner earned his doctorate at UC Berkeley, and the next year went back to Shuar country for additional shamanic experience. In 1966, having taught at UC Berkeley and served as associate director of the Lowie Museum of Anthropology, he became a visiting professor at Yale and Columbia Universities. In 1969, he did fieldwork among a neighboring Jivaroan-speaking tribe, the Achuara, and the following year joined the graduate faculty of the New School for Social Research in New York City. Over the next few years he published his monograph, *The Jívaro: People of the Sacred Waterfalls*, an edited volume titled *Hallucinogens and Shamanism*, and numerous academic articles.

Continuing cross-cultural research on shamanism, Harner became interested in drumming as an alternative means of achieving what he now identifies as SSC (shamanic state of consciousness). Learning and using this method of monotonous percussive sound ("sonic driving"), he began offering training workshops and in 1979 founded the Center for Shamanic Studies. A year later, he published *The Way of the Shaman*, a groundbreaking book now translated into a dozen languages.

Collaborating with his wife, clinical psychologist Sandra Harner, he established the Foundation for Shamanic Studies, a nonprofit charitable and educational organization dedicated to the preservation, study, and transmission of shamanic knowledge. Its Urgent Assistance program supports the survival of shamanic healing knowledge among such indigenous peoples as the Canadian Inuit, Scandinavian Sámi, and Tuvans of central Asia and Siberia.

Since resigning from his university professorship in 1987, this anthropologist has been fully devoted to shamanic studies and healing practice, training others, including physicians, psychotherapists, and other health care professionals. The Foundation's faculty assists him in this work.

In his most recent book, *Cave and Cosmos: Shamanic Encounters with Spirits and Heavens* (2013), Harner recounts and compares experiences of shamanic "ascension" and offers instructions on his core-shamanism techniques.

Michael Harner—anthropologist, shaman, and founder of the Foundation for Shamanic Studies in Mill Valley, California.

Figure 13.7 **Traditional Shaman in Mongolia** This female shaman in Mongolia, bordering Siberia, uses a drum crafted from the wood of a tree struck by lightning and covered with leather made from a female red deer. It is believed that when the shaman goes into a trance, her drum transforms into a magical steed that carries her into the dark sky of her ancestors.

similarly structured visual, auditory, somatic (touch), olfactory (smell), and gustatory (taste) hallucinations. The widespread occurrence of shamanism and the remarkable similarities among shamanic traditions everywhere are consequences of this universal neurological inheritance. But the meanings ascribed to sensations experienced in altered states and made of their content are culturally determined; hence, despite their overall similarities, indigenous traditions typically vary in particular details (Figure 13.7).

Shamans can be contrasted with priests and priestesses in that the latter serve dieties of the society. As agents of divine beings, priests and priestesses order believers what to think and do, whereas shamans may challenge or negotiate with the spirits. In return for services rendered, shamans may collect a fee—money, fresh meat, or some other valuable. In some cases, shamans are rewarded by the prestige that comes as a result of a healing or some other extraordinary feat.

Shamanic Healing

Shamans are essentially spiritual go-betweens who acts on behalf of some human client, often to bring about healing or to foretell a future event. Typically, they enter a trance state, experience the sensation of traveling to the alternate world, and see and interact with spirit beings. Shamans try to impose their will upon these spirits, an inherently dangerous contest, considering the superhuman powers that spirits are thought to possess.

An example of this can be seen in the trance dances of the Ju/'hoansi Bushmen of Africa's Kalahari Desert. Traditional Ju/'hoansi belief holds that illness and misfortune are caused by invisible arrows shot by spirits.

The arrows can be removed by healers, those who possess the powerful healing force called *n/um* (the Ju/'hoansi equivalent of *mana*). Some healers can activate *n/um* by solo singing or instrument playing, but more often this is accomplished through the medicinal curing ceremony or trance dance (Figure 13.8).

Acting on behalf of a client or patient, a shaman may put on a dramatic performance; such an artful

Figure 13.8 **Ju/'hoansi Shaman Healer and Helper in Trance Dance** Ju/'hoansi shamans may find their way into a trance by dancing around a fire to the pulsating sound of melodies sung by women. Eventually, sometimes after several hours, "the music, the strenuous dancing, the smoke, the heat of the fire, and the healers' intense concentration cause their *n/um* to heat up. When it comes to a boil, trance is achieved. At that moment, the *n/um* becomes available as a powerful healing force to serve the entire community. In trance, a healer lays hands on and ritually cures everyone sitting around the fire" (Shostak, 2000, pp. 259–260).

demonstration of spiritual power assures members of the community that prevailing upon supernatural powers and spirits otherwise beyond human control can bring about invulnerability from attack, success at love, or the return of health.

The precise effects of the shamanic treatment are not known, but its psychological and emotional impact is thought to contribute to the patient's recovery. For healing to occur, the shaman needs to be convinced of the effectiveness of his or her spiritual powers and techniques. Likewise, the patient must see the shaman as a genuine healing master using appropriate techniques. Finally, to close the triangle's "magic field," the community within which the shaman operates on the patient must view the healing ceremony and its practitioner as potentially effective and beneficial. From an anthropological perspective, shamanic healings can be understood by means of a three-cornered model: the *shamanic complex* (**Figure 13.9**). This triangle is created by the interrelationship of the shaman, the patient, and the community to which both belong.

Shamanic healing ceremonies involve social-psychological dynamics also present in Western medical treatments. Consider, for example, the *placebo effect*—the beneficial result a patient experiences after a particular treatment, due to the person's expectations concerning the treatment rather than from the treatment itself. Notably, some people involved in modern medicine work collaboratively with practitioners of traditional belief systems toward the healing of various illnesses (Harner & Harner, 2000; Offiong, 1999).

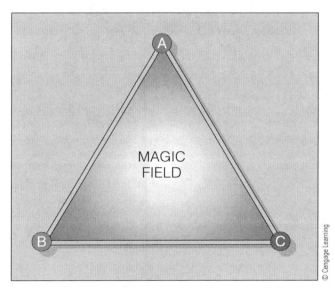

Figure 13.9 The Shamanic Complex Shamanic healing takes place within a "magic field" created when the shaman (A) and patient (B), as well as their community (C), are all convinced that the shaman is a genuine healing master using appropriate techniques that are effective and beneficial. Similar psychological processes are involved in Western medical treatments.

Ritual Performances

Rituals are culturally prescribed symbolic acts or procedures designed to guide members of a community in an orderly way through personal and collective transitions. Relieving anxiety and tensions in crises, rituals provide symbolic means of reinforcing a group's social bonds. Not all of them concern the sacred (consider, for example, college graduation ceremonies in North America). But those that do are ideologically linked to beliefs in the supernatural, playing a crucial role as spirituality or religion in action.

Anthropologists have classified several different types of ritual. These include rituals of purification, rites of passage, rites of intensification, and magical rituals, including witchcraft.

Rites of Purification: Taboo and Cleansing Ceremonies

In many religious and spiritual traditions, rituals have been developed to symbolically restore one's place in the cosmic order, removing "dirt," washing "impurity," and making "clean" in body, mind, and soul. Anthropologists specializing in comparative religion have been intrigued by the cross-cultural variation in cultural categories classifying certain animals, plants, objects, or acts as unclean or dirty and others as dangerous.

In every society, people follow certain culturally prescribed rules about what is dirty or filthy, or whichever term symbolically represents pollution—rules that say what they cannot eat, drink, touch, talk, or even think about. For instance, many millions of Hindus eat pork but avoid beef because they regard the cow as a sacred animal. On the other hand, many millions of Muslims consume beef but avoid pork because in Islam swine is considered unclean. In the words of British anthropologist Mary Douglas, "Dirt offends against order. Eliminating it is not a negative movement, but a positive effort to organise the environment" (1966, pp. 2–3).

Culturally prescribed avoidances involving ritual prohibitions are known as **taboo**, a term derived from the Polynesian word *tabu* (or *tapu*). Among Pacific Islanders it refers to something that has supernatural power and is to be avoided. It can apply to an object (such as food), a person (such as a high-ranking noble), or a place (a shrine or temple). Especially applied to blood and anything associated with sickness and death, taboos are

ritual A culturally prescribed symbolic act or procedure designed to guide members of a community in an orderly way through personal and collective transitions.

taboo Culturally prescribed avoidances involving ritual prohibitions, which, if not observed, lead to supernatural punishment.

taken very seriously. When a taboo is violated, believers expect supernatural punishment will follow. This penalty may come in magical form as misfortune—an unlucky accident, resulting in loss, sickness, or death. It is also possible that the taboo breaker will be punished by designated members in the community and may be ordered to undergo a purification ritual and make a sacrifice. Sometimes, the ultimate sacrifice is demanded, and the offender is executed.

For complex historical reasons of their own, some societies stress taboos much more than others. For instance, as discussed in the previous chapter, the traditional hierarchy in the Hindu caste society is religiously reinforced by strict rules against ritual pollution that govern the lives of members of the different *varnas*.

Whether someone has violated a taboo, or is otherwise no longer clean, many cultures have developed **rites of purification** to establish or restore purity. These may involve one person, but many are group or community ceremonial affairs. As symbolic acts, purification rituals are filled with spiritual or religious meaning. They impact participants emotionally and psychologically (restoring a sense of inner peace and cosmic harmony), as well as socially, such as by establishing or restoring harmony within their family, community, or some other group.

A cross-cultural comparison of these spiritual or religious ceremonies shows that the four elements of water, air, fire, and/or earth have been used in a wide range of rituals for thousands of years all across the globe. For instance, cleansing by water is very common in many forms of baptism, hot steam is used in sweat lodges, burning fragrant organic matter (such as plant leaves or resins) is used in smoking and smudging ceremonies. The human body and mind may also be subjected to rituals of internal purification by means of prayer, meditation, chanting, fasting, or dancing (**Figure 13.10**).

Figure 13.10 A Sufi *Sema* (Prayer Dance) in Aleppo, Syria Sufism, a mystical Muslim movement that emerged a thousand years ago, emphasizes the surrender of individual ego and attachment to worldly things in order to be receptive to God's grace. Known as "whirling dervishes," these Sufi dancers are part of the Mevlevi brotherhood, a spiritual lineage founded by the Persian Sufi master (*mawlana*) Jalal ad-Din ar-Rumi in the 13th century. According to Mevlevi tradition, during the *sema* the soul is freed from earthly ties and is able to jubilantly commune with the divine. (*Dervish* literally means "doorway" and is thought to be an entrance from the material world to the spiritual.) The felt hat represents personal ego's tombstone, and the wide skirt symbolizes its shroud.

Rites of Passage

Rites of passage are rituals marking important ceremonial moments when members of a society move from one distinctive social stage in life to another, such as birth, marriage, and death. When crossing the boundary (*limen*) between such stages, people briefly cease to be part of the stage left behind and have not yet become integrated into the next. Like travelers passing through a border area between two countries not controlled by either of them, they are neither here nor there. Guiding people through such uncertain transit zones, rituals associated with changing social status unfold in three phases: *separation* (pre-liminary), *transition* (liminary), and *incorporation* (post-liminary).

Phase one is the ceremonial removal of the individual from everyday society, phase two a period of ritual isolation, and phase three the formal return and readmission back into society in his or her new status (Van Gennep, 1960). Because certain transitions in the human life cycle are crucially important to the individual as well as to the social order of the community, these rituals may involve a religious specialist, such as a priest or priestess.

This sequence of phases occurs in a great array of rites of passage all around the world—from wedding ceremonies marking the transition from single to married status to ceremonies identifying the transference of religious leadership in a spiritual lineage to a designated heir to ceremonies initiating new members into a distinctive group. An example of the latter, described in an earlier chapter, is when young Maasai men in East Africa's grasslands move into the Warrior age grade; they are removed from their families and ritually initiated by circumcision, returning weeks later as *moranes*, armed warriors with a distinctive hairstyle and dress.

Likewise, when Mende girls in West Africa's savannahs begin menstruating, they are ritually prepared for womanhood. Separated from family, they spend weeks in seclusion. Discarding their childhood clothes, they learn the moral and practical responsibilities of motherhood from senior women. Believing circumcision enhances a girl's reproductive potential, these elders are tasked with removing each girl's clitoris (considered a female version of a penis). A good deal of singing, dancing, storytelling, and food accompany the ordeal and the training, which produces a strong sense of sisterhood. The girls emerge from their initiation as women in knowledgeable control of their sexuality, eligible for marriage and childbearing.

Rites of Intensification

Rites of intensification are rituals that take place during a crisis in the life of the group and serve to bind individuals together. Whatever the precise nature of the crisis—a drought that threatens crops, the sudden appearance of an enemy war party, the onset of an epidemic—mass ceremonies are performed to ease the sense of danger.

Figure 13.11 Hindu Cremation Ceremony in Bali, Indonesia Balinese people deal with death by turning what could be a painful emotional experience of grief and loss into a joyous celebration of life's progressive continuity through rebirth in a future existence. As a social reminder of Hindu caste differences, the family of a deceased relative uses this ceremony to display wealth and social rank. Funeral pyres built for members of a noble or royal family on the island are duly impressive.

This unites people in a common effort so that fear and confusion yield to collective action and a degree of optimism. The balance in the relations of all concerned is restored to normal, and the community's values are celebrated and affirmed.

An individual's death might be regarded as the ultimate crisis or point of separation in that person's life, but it is, as well, a point of separation for the entire group, particularly if the group is small. A member of the community has been removed, so its composition has been seriously altered. The survivors, therefore, must readjust and restore balance. They also need to reconcile themselves to the loss of someone to whom they were emotionally tied. As such, a funerary ceremony is an example of an intensification ritual that permits the surviving family and community to express in nondisruptive ways their emotional upset over the death while providing for social readjustment (**Figure 13.11**).

rite of purification A symbolic act carried out by an individual or a group to establish or restore purity when someone has violated a taboo or is otherwise unclean.

rite of passage A ritual that marks an important ceremonial moment when members of a society move from one distinctive social stage in life to another, such as birth, marriage, and death. It features three phases: separation, transition, and incorporation.

rite of intensification A ritual that takes place during a crisis in the life of the group and serves to bind individuals together.

Rites of intensification do not have to be limited to times of overt crisis. In regions where human activities change in accordance with seasonal climatic shifts, these rites take the form of annual ceremonies. They are particularly common among horticultural and agricultural peoples. Ritually articulating traditional ideas about the role of the supernatural in the cyclical return of rain, the light and warmth of the sun, and other factors of nature vital to healthy and bountiful crops, these ceremonies are staged to correspond with the crucially important planting and harvesting seasons. A similar cultural linkage between the annual subsistence cycle and the ceremonial calendar with its rites of intensification can be found in societies based on seasonal fishing and herding or hunting of migratory animals.

Magical Rituals

People in many cultures believe that supernatural powers can be compelled to act in certain ways for good or evil purposes by recourse to specified formulas. In short, they believe in **magic** and carry out magical rituals to ensure positive ends such as good crops, fertility of livestock, replenishment of hunted game, prevention of accidents, healing of illness, protection against injury, promise of victory, and the defeat of enemies, real or imagined. In traditional societies many of these rituals rely on *fetishes*—objects believed to possess magical powers (**Figure 13.12**).

Magical rituals are also popular in wealthy industrialized societies. Individuals commonly seek "good luck" when the outcome is in doubt or beyond one's influence—from lighting a votive candle for someone going through a hard time, to wearing lucky boxers on a hot date, to the curious gesturing baseball pitchers perform on the mound.

Anthropologists distinguish between two fundamental principles of magic. The first principle—that like produces like—is identified as **imitative magic** or *sympathetic magic*. In Myanmar (Burma) in Southeast Asia, for example, a rejected lover might engage a sorcerer to make an image of his would-be love. If this image were tossed into water, to the accompaniment of certain charms, it was expected that the girl would go mad and suffer a fate similar to that of her image.

The second principle is that of **contagious magic**—the idea that things or persons once in contact can influence each other after the contact is broken. The most

© SSPL/The Image Works

Figure 13.12 Congolese Fetish This 100-year-old carving from the Democratic Republic of Congo is a *nkondi*, with supernatural power coming in part from magic herbs hidden inside by a diviner. Such fetishes are traditionally used to identify wrongdoers, including thieves and witches responsible for mishaps, diseases, or death. A *nkondi* is activated by provocations (such as hammering nails into it) or invocations urging magic punishment of the suspects.

common example of contagious magic is the permanent relationship between an individual and any part of his or her body, such as hair, fingernails, or teeth. For instance, the Basutos of Lesotho in southern Africa were careful to conceal their extracted teeth to make sure they did not fall into the hands of certain mythical beings who could harm the owners of the teeth by working magic on them. Related to this is the custom in Western societies of treasuring things that have been touched by special people. Such items range from a saint's relics to possessions of other admired or idolized individuals, from rock stars to sports heroes to spiritual gurus.

magic Specific formulas and actions used to compel supernatural powers to act in certain ways for good or evil purposes.

imitative magic Magic based on the principle that like produces like; sometimes called *sympathetic magic*.

contagious magic Magic based on the principle that things or persons once in contact can influence each other after the contact is broken.

Figure 13.13 Assessing Ch'i Energy Feng shui master R. D. Chin determines the *ch'i* of a new office space in a Manhattan skyscraper, one side of which faces the city's central *ch'i* point—the Empire State Building. The consultant is planning the space, with the location of stairways and the CEO's office to be determined.

Divination: Omens and Oracles

Designed to access or influence supernatural powers, magical rituals have also been developed to prepare for the uncertain future—for the unseen and for the not yet present. Fears of pending dangers—for example, storms, attacks, betrayals, diseases, and death—call for precautionary measures, such as what to avoid and where to go. How does one find and interpret the signs, or *omens*, foretelling the future? The answer, as developed in many cultures, is through **divination**, a magical ritual designed to discover what is unknowable by ordinary means, in particular signs predicting fate or destiny.

Various ancient methods of divination exist, including *geomancy* (from Greek, *geo* for "earth" and *manteia* for "divination"), a technique traditionally considered sacred and practiced by shamans, prophets, fortunetellers, or other oracles in communication with supernatural forces. Skilled to interpret omens, a diviner practicing geomancy may toss a handful of sand or pebbles, for example, and then analyze its random patterns, searching for information hidden to ordinary people. Other divination methods include decoding flame or smoke patterns in a fire (*pyromancy*), wind and cloud formation in the air (*aeromancy*), or colors, ripples, and whirls in water (*hydromancy*).

Whereas Mongolian and Chinese shamans traditionally use an animal shoulder blade (*scapulamancy*) for divination purposes, Aymara *yachajs* ("possessors of knowledge") in the Andean highlands may probe sacred coca leaves or the convoluted pile of intestines of a slaughtered guinea pig for omens. Much better known, of course, is the divination technique involving palm reading (*chiromancy*), perhaps most famously practiced by female Gypsy fortunetellers. So-called mediums are popular, too, also in the United States, where many people believe them to be capable of contacting spirits of deceased relatives ready to pass on messages from beyond by means of an ancient ritual method known as *necromancy*.

Believed to possess knowledge hidden from ordinary people, diviners are feared in many cultures. However, they are also in high demand among those who believe in diviners' capacity to predict the future, and those believers may seek consultation before undertaking something important or risky. An example of this is *feng shui*, an ancient Chinese divination technique. Literally translated as "wind-water," its traditional Chinese characters signify "tao of heaven and earth." In the past few decades, this method has grown in popularity in North America as well, in particular in California, where homebuilders and buyers frequently hire feng shui consultants to help them design or redesign homes and offices to conform to the principle of *qi* or *ch'i* ("vital energy") (**Figure 13.13**).

In some religious traditions, including Christianity, fortunetelling and other divination rituals have long been viewed with suspicion, and in many places these practices have been prohibited. Especially when performed by individuals functioning in other religious or spiritual traditions believed to be false or worse, divination is condemned as evil magic, sorcery, or witchcraft.

Witchcraft: Anxiety and Fears of Evil Magic

Magical rituals intended to cause misfortune or inflict harm are often referred to as sorcery, or **witchcraft**, believed to be practiced by individuals embodying evil

divination A magical procedure or spiritual ritual designed to discern what is not knowable by ordinary means, such as foretelling the future by interpreting omens.

witchcraft Magical rituals intended to cause misfortune or inflict harm.

spirit power or those collaborating with malevolent supernatural beings. In contrast to magic-working experts inclined to do good, these individuals inspire awe, or even fear. Historically, such dangerous magic-working individuals are known in English under a variety of names such as *wizard, sorcerer*, or simply *witch*—imprecise terms often used interchangeably. This is also true for other languages using a variety of terms like *brujo* (Spanish), *uwisin* (Shuar), *umthakathi* (Zulu), *mchawi* (Swahili), and *wu* (Chinese).

Fear of witches is especially prevalent during periods of uncertainty and transition. When mysterious illnesses, devastating droughts, accidental deaths, economic uncertainties, and other upheavals disturb the cultural order, confusion may result in a surge of suspicion and a focus on disliked, unsociable, isolated individuals. Especially in patrilineal or patrilocal communities, the accused is often an older woman, typically single or widowed and without children. For instance, about 80 percent of the estimated 50,000 "witches" tried, tortured, and killed in Europe in the 16th and 17th centuries were female. Among matrilineal and matrilocal groups, however, people tend to think of witches as male.

Not all people suspected of mysterious malevolence are prosecuted, let alone executed, but witchcraft accusations clearly function as a social control mechanism, horribly reinforcing the moral code. Fear of being accused of being a witch encourages individuals to suppress as best they can those personality traits that are looked upon with disapproval. A belief in witchcraft thus serves as a broad control on what is believed to be antisocial behavior (Behringer, 2004).

Navajo Skin-Walkers

Beliefs in evil magic are widespread and take many forms. One interesting example comes from the Navajo, Native Americans historically surviving as sheepherders and small-scale irrigation farmers in the vast deserts of Arizona and New Mexico. The Navajo have a substantial repertoire of sacred rituals for healing victims of sorcery, all related to accusations of evil magic.

Among Navajos, who live in a residence group organized around a head woman, traditional belief holds that a person suffering from severe anxiety disorder, repetitive nightmares, or delusions is a victim of sorcery. The idea is that a ghost or some other evil spirit, traveling under cover of darkness, is responsible. And

according to the Navajo, the suspect is a powerful sorcerer, almost always a man, probably someone who has killed a relative and committed incest.

These dangerous Navajo sorcerers, resembling the werewolf of European folklore and the *nagual* in rural Mexico, are believed to be able to change themselves into animal form. Referred to as a *'ánt'įįhnii* ("skin-walker"), such a sorcerer stealthily goes to a secluded spot, such as a cave at night. There, he transforms into a coyote or wolf. Disguised in animal form, he emerges and runs fast toward his victim, bringing on *'ánt'į* ("the curse"). Having completed his accursed mission, the skin-walker swiftly returns to his hideaway, transforms again into human form, and slips back into his home before dawn (Kluckhohn, 1944; Selinger, 2007).

Sacred Sites: Saints, Shrines, and Miracles

Sacred sites are typically positioned in a transitional, or *liminary*, zone between the natural and supernatural, the secular and spiritual, earth and heaven. Reaching high into the sky, mountaintops are often considered to be magical places, shrouded in mystery. For instance, the Japanese view the snowcapped perfect volcanic cone of Mount Fuji ("Ever-Lasting Life") as a sacred place. Ancient Greeks considered Mount Olympus to be the mythological abode of Zeus, the king of all their gods. Likewise, Kikuyu view Mount Kenya as the earthly dwelling place of their creator god Ngai.

Some sites become sacred because they are places where ordinary human beings experienced something extraordinary—heard a divine voice or saw a guardian spirit, patron saint, or archangel. Often a site is declared sacred because believers associate it with a miracle-working mystic, saint, prophet, or other holy person. The tombs of such individuals often turn into shrines (*scrinium*, Latin for "round box" or "container," holding relics). For example, stories of miraculous events and special powers emanating from Muslim tombs are common wherever Sufism, a far-reaching mystical branch of Islam, is popular (Gladney, 2004).

Based on the principle of contagious magic, any material substance physically linked to a miraculous event or individual may itself become revered as holy or sacred. This may include bones, fingernails, hair, or any other body part believed to have belonged to a saint, or something the person wore, possessed, or simply touched. All these things may be treasured as holy relics and safeguarded in a shrine, inspiring the faithful.

Burial sites of saints often gain such importance that people feel inspired to construct a very large shrine for the saint's entombment; termed a *mausoleum*, some of these are large enough for the interment of lesser saints and pious individuals desiring proximity to the sacred saint after death. However large or small, shrines are religious focal points for prayer, meditation, and sacrifice.

Figure 13.14 Pilgrims at Mount Kailash in Tibet
Rising 6,700 meters (over 22,000 feet), this mountain has been sacred for many generations to Buddhists and Hindus, as well as Jains and followers of Bön (Tibet's indigenous religion). Every year a few thousand pilgrims make the tortuous 52-kilometer (32-mile) trek around it, some of them by crawling the entire distance.

© Alexander van der Made

Pilgrimages: Devotion in Motion

Every year, many millions of devotees of many religions—including Buddhism, Christianity, Hinduism, Islam, and their many branches—walk, climb, or even crawl to a sacred or holy site. Whether it is a saint's tomb, a mountain, lake, river, waterfall, or some other particular place believed to be metaphysically significant, *pilgrims* (from Latin *peregrinus*, meaning "wanderer") travel there seeking enlightenment, proving their devotion, and/or hoping to experience a miracle.

On their sacred journey, pilgrims participate in a religious drama, performing ritually prescribed acts such as prayers, chants, or prostrations. A devotion in motion, the **pilgrimage** demands personal sacrifices from the travelers. Enjoying little comfort, they may suffer from thirst and hunger, heat and cold, pain and fear while on the road, sometimes for many days or even months. Pilgrims often travel through unfamiliar territories where they may run into problems, including robbery, kidnapping, starvation, and even death. To identify their status as spiritually inspired travelers, some wear special clothes, shave their heads, carry amulets, chant prayers, or perform other prescribed rituals along the way.

One of the most challenging pilgrimages is the climb up the slopes of a mountain range in the Himalayas where Mount Kailash rises 6,700 meters (over 22,000

feet). Located in western Tibet, this black, snowcapped mountain stands out boldly in a dramatic landscape sacred to Hindus and Buddhists, as well as Jains and Bönpos (**Figure 13.14**). The latter, who practice an ancient Tibetan shamanic religion, refer to this hallowed mountain as Tisé ("Water Peak") because it is the source of four sacred rivers. For Hindus, it is the holy abode of Lord Shiva, the destroyer of ignorance and illusion and the divine source of yoga. Jains view Kailash as the sacred place where their divine cultural hero Rishabha ("Bull")—an incarnation of Lord Vishnu—first achieved full enlightenment. Finally, Tibetan Buddhists revere it as Gangs Rinpoche ("Snow Lord") and believe it to be the abode of Khorlo Demchok ("Circle of Bliss")—a wrathful deity who uses his power to destroy the three major obstacles to enlightenment: anger, greed, and ignorance.

For all four of these religious traditions, climbing to the summit of this holy mountain is taboo. So, pilgrims demonstrate their devotion by means of a ritual encirclement, or circumambulation—clockwise by Buddhists and Hindus, and in reverse by Jains and Bönpos. The rugged, 52-kilometer (32-mile) trek is seen

---

pilgrimage A devotion in motion. Traveling, often on foot, to a sacred or holy site to reach for enlightenment, prove devotion, and/or experience a miracle.

as a sacred ritual that removes sins and brings good fortune. Each year thousands follow the ancient tradition of encircling the mountain on foot. The most devout pilgrims turn their circumambulation into a sacrificial ordeal: Prostrating their bodies full length, they extend their hands forward and make a mark on the ground with their fingers; then they rise, pray, crawl ahead on hands and knees to the mark, and then repeat the process again and again.

One of the world's largest pilgrimages is the *hajj*—a performance of piety now made by 1.8 million Muslims traveling to Mecca in Saudi Arabia each year from all across the globe. The largest contingent of hajjis—about 300,000 a year—comes from Indonesia. One of the five pillars of Islam, the hajj brings all of these pilgrims together for collective prayers and other sacred rituals at the Kaaba in Mecca, their religion's holiest site.

Christianity, originating in what was an eastern province of the Roman empire about 2,000 years ago, has created a sacred landscape dotted with dozens of major pilgrimage sites in Southwest Asia and Europe. As in other ancient religions, these sites are symbolically associated with miracles and legendary holy men and women. For example, for nearly a millennium Christian pilgrims from all over Europe have made the long and difficult journey to Santiago de Compostela. Tens of thousands travel to this Spanish seaport each year—most by foot, some by bicycle, and a few on horseback like their medieval counterparts. About 180,000 pilgrims walk the final 100 kilometers to the old cathedral with the shrine containing the sacred remains of the apostle Saint James venerated as Santiago (Santo-Iago) since the Middle Ages and recognized as the official patron saint of Spain. Many more Roman Catholics make pilgrimages to shrines devoted to Saint Mary, as described following.

Female Saints: Divine Protection for the Weak

Many religions consider the divine order primarily or exclusively as masculine, as noted earlier. Ideologically reproducing the hierarchical social order dominated by men, this arrangement reflects the worldview of traditional cultures that revere male deities, prophets, and saints in officially sponsored cults and devotions. But religions are not monolithic, and some provide flexible spiritual space for alternatives, such as Christian cults devoted to female saints such as Mary, the virgin mother of Jesus Christ, the son of God.

More powerful than the pope in Rome, Mary has been loved and adored as a holy mother residing in heaven. Worldwide, Roman Catholic multitudes look up to her for divine protection. Like other Christian saints, she is thought to perform miracles and to be capable of physically manifesting herself at places and times of her choosing. Through the centuries, many believers claim to have witnessed such holy moments, some officially reporting the miracle. Typically, these believers are young members of the underclass—herders, peasants, or fishermen, for example. Beyond stories about the female saint manifesting herself to such low-status rural folk, the discovery of sacred relics (such as a drowned or buried statue representing Mary) may also generate excitement and hope in difficult times.

Stories and relics religiously associated with miracles performed by saints such as the Virgin Mary quickly attract popular attention and turn into myths. Inspired or led by individuals claiming divine authority based on immediate revelation, devotees typically build a shrine to commemorate the encounter or to safeguard the sacred relic. Developing outside the power structure of established religious institutions, these local devotions may turn into popular cults. Difficult if not impossible to stop, these cults may spawn mass movements, leading church authorities to consider whether to formally approve of the cult and take control of the Marian (Saint Mary) devotion. Sanctioned by the church or not, these shrines attract pilgrims in search of divine forgiveness, protection, healing, and compassionate love.

Among the best known Marian pilgrimage sites are the ones in Lourdes (France) and Fatima (Portugal), along with the Mexican shrine dedicated to the brown-skinned Virgin of Guadalupe detailed in the next section.

Black Madonnas and Brown-Skinned Virgin Mothers

As folk-based popular religious movements, Saint Mary cults not only developed across Europe, but also in Latin America, the Philippines, and other parts of the world historically colonized and dominated by Roman Catholics originating from Europe. The religious ideas and rituals of Catholicism changed many indigenous cultures—and were also changed by them. Of particular interest in this shifting religious landscape are Black Madonnas: brown or dark-colored clay or wooden statues, or painted images, representing the virgin mother. One of the many Black Madonna statues is enshrined in Aparecida, Brazil, where a popular cult emerged in her honor in the mid-18th century and now attracts over 10 million pilgrims annually.

Another popular devotion involving brown-skinned Saint Mary concerns the Virgin of Guadalupe, highlighted in this chapter's opening photo. As mentioned there, this Mexican cult originated in 1531, a decade after the Aztec Indian empire had been conquered by a Spanish army. That year, a recently converted young

AP Images/Marco Ugarte

Figure 13.15 Virgin of Guadalupe Pilgrim, Mexico City On December 9, 1531, Saint Mary appeared to Mexican Indian Juan Diego, a recent Christian convert, as he passed by Tepeyac Hill in what is now Mexico City. At the site of this encounter, the Basilica of Our Lady of Guadalupe was built with a shrine containing sacred evidence of this miraculous apparition. Pictured here is a weary pilgrim, sleeping alongside images of the virgin outside the basilica.

Aztec Christian named Juan Diego proclaimed a remarkable encounter with a holy woman who appeared to him in a blaze of light. Speaking his native Nahuatl tongue, she identified herself as the virgin mother and asked that a shrine be built in her honor. After their miraculous meeting, he discovered her image mysteriously imprinted on the inside of his simple white-hemp *tilma* ("cloak"). Seen as divine proof of Mary's manifestation, this sacred relic was soon enshrined in the chapel built in her honor at the foot of the hill where she appeared—now part of Mexico City.

A few decades later, a powerful Spanish bishop imposing religious order in the Mexican colony became aware of the emerging brown-virgin cult and saw it as an ideological means of unifying and controlling a racially divided population. Eventually, in 1780 church authorities officially declared her patron saint of Mexico, even promoting her to the title of Empress of the Americas in 1945. In 2002, nearly 500 years after Juan Diego's mystical encounter started this Marian devotion, Pope John Paul II canonized him before a crowd of 12 million. Diego became the first Native American to be declared a Roman Catholic saint. Today, most of the 6 million pilgrims who visit the Virgin of Guadalupe's shrine each year to see the sacred *tilma* relic discovered by Diego are mestizo or indigenous Mexicans (**Figure 13.15**).

Desecration: Ruining Sacred Sites

Although popular shrines are destinations for believers from near and far, they are also potential targets of **desecration**. By means of such ideologically inspired violation of a sacred site, enemies aim to inflict harm, if only symbolically, on people judged to have impure, false, or evil beliefs and ritual practices. Desecrations have occurred across the globe for thousands of years, as evidenced in archaeological sites and recorded in oral traditions or historical documents.

For example, during the Protestant Reformation in the 16th and 17th centuries, Christian Protestant iconoclasts campaigning against idolatry in the Netherlands and England destroyed untold numbers of ancient Roman Catholic statues and other treasures kept in sacred shrines. More recently, in Afghanistan, Taliban religious authorities shattered two huge 1,500-year-old statues they considered to be idols. Carved into the side of a sandstone cliff in the high mountain valley of Bamiyan, one of them, representing a celestial wisdom Buddha ("the enlightened one") stood 55 meters (180 feet) high; the other, representing Siddhartha Gautama, the founder of Buddhism himself, rose to 37 meters (121 feet). In 2001, the Taliban obliterated both monuments with artillery and dynamite.

Destruction in the name of religion is not unique to Christian or Muslim puritans, as militant Hindus and others also engage in similar desecrations. All of this pales in comparison with China's Cultural Revolution in the 1960s, when masses of activists, swept up in state-sponsored antireligious fervor, went on a rampage destroying religious monuments, sculptures, carvings, and paintings, as well as a large number of age-old sacred shrines.

desecration Ideologically inspired violation of a sacred site intended to inflict harm, if only symbolically, on people judged to have impure, false, or even evil beliefs and ritual practices.

Cultural Dynamics in the Superstructure: Religious and Spiritual Change

New technologies, improved means of transportation, internationalization of production and labor markets, and worldwide movements of ideas and practices all contribute to challenging and even destabilizing long-established cultural systems and associated worldviews. Reacting to these challenges and radical upheavals, people often turn to the supernatural to allay the anxiety of a world going awry.

The need to find deeper meaning in life and to make sense of an increasingly complex, uncharted, confusing, and sometimes frightening existence drives humans to continue their explorations—religious and spiritual, as well as scientific. Some people bundle or devise their own spiritual beliefs and rituals. Others form or join new spiritual movements.

Reactionary religious movements are also on the rise in culturally destabilized societies. Typically, these call for a radical return to traditional foundations prescribed in sacred texts and narrowly interpreted by conservative spiritual leaders. Examples include Islamic fundamentalism in countries such as Afghanistan, Egypt, and Iran; Jewish fundamentalism in Israel and the United States; and Hindu fundamentalism in India. Christian fundamentalism is represented in the dramatic growth of evangelical denominations in the United States, Latin America, and sub-Saharan Africa.

Revitalization Movements

No anthropological consideration of religion is complete without some mention of **revitalization movements**—movements for radical cultural reform in response to widespread social disruption and collective feelings of great stress and despair.

As deliberate efforts to construct a more satisfying culture, revitalization movements aim to reform not just the religious sphere of activity but may also impact an entire cultural system. Many such movements developed in indigenous societies where European colonial exploitation caused enormous upheaval. They also occurred in 16th-century Europe—as evidenced in the emergence of Puritans, Mennonites, and other Protestant groups when traditional societies faced radical transformations triggered by early capitalism and other

forces. Likewise, revitalization movements emerged in response to the industrial revolution triggering similar radical transformations in agrarian societies in the 19th century, not only in Europe but also in the northeastern United States, where Mormonism, Jehovah's Witnesses, Seventh-Day Adventists, and others began as Christian revitalization movements.

Revitalization movements can be found in many religions. One of the best known among Muslims is Ahmadiyya, founded in South Asia during British colonial rule in the late 19th century when Christian missionaries were actively proselytizing in predominantly Hindu, Muslim, or Sikh communities. Known as Ahmadis, followers of this Muslim sect number about 10 million across the globe. They believe that Allah (God) sent Mirza Ghulam Ahmad (1835–1908) as a prophet, a divinely ordained reformer (*mujjaddid*) like Muhammad. As the long-awaited Messiah, he embodied the second coming of the Christ, sent to bring about, by peaceful means, the final triumph of Islam as the only true religion for humanity, end all religious strife, and restore divinely guided morality, justice, and peace.

Recent U.S. revitalization movements also include the revival or introduction of traditional American Indian ceremonies such as the sweat lodge now common on many tribal reservations in North America, as well as the spectacular Sun Dance ceremony held each summer at various reservations in the Great Plains. Similar cultural revivals of "spiritual neo-traditions" are on the rise in many parts of the world, including Europe (Prins, 1994). Tens of thousands of people in Great Britain, attracted to a naturalistic worldview, now practice forms of "ecospiritualism" (Prins, 1996, p. 206), which often involves a revival of the ancient pre-Christian Celtic tradition of Druidry (**Figure 13.16**).

A similar nature-centered revival of pre-Christian beliefs and rituals is under way in Germanic-speaking parts of northern Europe, such as among Asatru in Scandinavia. Seeking a sacred relationship with nature, they worship the earth, elements of the sky, and forces such as thunder, as well as spirits they believe arise from sacred places like mountains and rivers. Similar tradition-based ecospiritual movements are developing throughout the industrialized world, including the United States.

Syncretic Religions

In Africa, during and following the period of foreign colonization and missionization, indigenous groups resisted or creatively revised Christian teachings and formed culturally appropriate religious movements. During the past century, thousands of indigenous Christian churches have been founded in Africa. These churches are often born of alternative theological interpretations and new divinely inspired revelations. They also originate from disapproval

revitalization movements Social movements for radical cultural reform in response to widespread social disruption and collective feelings of great stress and despair.

Figure 13.16 Stonehenge, Wiltshire County, England In 2010, the neo-tradition of Druidry was officially recognized as a religion in Great Britain. Stonehenge, a 4,500-year-old Neolithic site, is one of its sacred centers. With 10,000 followers, modern Druidry is rooted in the pre-Christian tradition of the Celtic peoples indigenous to the British Isles.

by foreign missionaries concerning the preservation of traditional beliefs and rituals culturally associated with animism, ancestor worship, and spirit possession, as well as kinship and marriage.

Today, the African continent is as religiously and spiritually diverse as ever. Although at least 40 percent of the population is Christian, and more than another 40 percent is Muslim, myriad African indigenous religions persist and are often merged with Christianity or Islam.

Syncretic Religions Across the Atlantic: Vodou in Haiti

In almost four centuries of trans-Atlantic slave trading, African captives stolen from hundreds of towns and villages from Mauretania south to Angola and beyond were shipped without material belongings to labor on cotton, sugar, coffee, and tobacco plantations from Virginia to Brazil. Ripped from family and community, individual slaves clung to some of their ancestral beliefs and knowledge of rituals.

Sharing a life of forced labor, slaves from different ethnic, linguistic, and religious backgrounds formed small communities, pooled remembered religious ideas and rituals, and creatively forged a spiritual repertoire of their own. Founded on a mix of Yoruba and other African beliefs and practices, their emerging religions also incorporated Christian features, including terminology from the languages of slave-owning colonists. In some cases,

elements from a region's indigenous American cultures were also included.

Such creative blending of indigenous and foreign beliefs and practices into new cultural forms illustrates what anthropologists define as **syncretism**. Especially after slavery was abolished in the course of the 1800s, these syncretic spiritual repertoires developed into Afro-Caribbean religions such as Vodou in Haiti and Santería in Cuba, which resemble Candomblé in Brazil. All of these religions are spreading as adherents freely migrate across borders (Fernández Olmos & Paravisini-Gebert, 2003).

Vodou emerged in Haiti in the early 1800s after this small tropical country in the Caribbean Sea won its independence from France in a decade-long slave revolt. The name means "divine spirit" in the language of the Fon, a large ethnic group in Benin and southwestern Nigeria. Providing an escape from the indignities of poverty and hopelessness, Vodou was developed by ex-slaves speaking French-based Creole. Now mostly poor black peasants, they are nominal Roman Catholics who, like their African ancestors across the Atlantic, believe in spirit possession.

Vodou rituals center on the worship of what Haitians refer to as *loas*—also known by Creole terms such as *anges* ("angels"), *saints* ("saints"), or simply as *mystères* ("mysteries"). This tradition is essentially based on a belief in

syncretism The creative blending of indigenous and foreign beliefs and practices into new cultural forms.

Figure 13.17 Haitian Women in a Vodou Bathing Ritual In mid-July every year, thousands of Haitian pilgrims journey to a sacred waterfall in the mountains north of Port-au-Prince, Haiti, in reverence to a Black Madonna known as Our Lady of Carmel. This Marian devotion is ritually associated with a major *loa*, or Vodou spirit, named Erzulie Dantor, who mysteriously appeared on a palm tree at this waterfall about 150 years ago. Since then, an important devotional activity is bathing in this sacred water, a deeply spiritual experience in which Vodou practitioners like these women enter a trance filled with divine grace.

a reciprocal relationship between the spirits of the living and those of the dead, representing multiple expressions of the divine. Spirits of deceased ancestors and other relatives can be summoned by means of drumming in a temple. Dancing to the beat, worshipers enter into trance. This is when a person's spirit temporarily vacates the human body, replaced by a *loa* from the spirit world who takes possession—the moment of divine grace (**Figure 13.17**).

Religious Pluralism and Secularization

Although Christianity in Europe is losing ground as a result of Islam's rise, a much more substantial decline is due to **secularization.** In this process of cultural change, a population tends toward a nonreligious worldview, ignoring or rejecting institutionalized spiritual beliefs and rituals. Over the last few decades, growing numbers of western Europeans have declared themselves to be without religion.

Secularization is especially noteworthy in a prosperous capitalist country like Germany, which has been for many

centuries predominantly Lutheran and Roman Catholic. Today, almost 40 percent of Germans identify themselves as nonreligious, compared to a mere 4 percent forty years ago. In contrast, religion is becoming *more* important in many parts of eastern Europe where atheism was communist state ideology for several generations in the 20th century.

Secularization also takes place in other wealthy industrialized countries. In the United States, for example, 20 percent of all adults are religiously unaffiliated—and the figure jumps to about 35 percent among adults under 30. Their ranks include more than 13 million self-described atheists and agnostics—nearly 6 percent of the U.S. public (Pew Research Center, 2012). As in other large countries, there are regional contrasts, with the secularization trend among New Englanders far outpacing several areas in the southeastern United States, where 80 to 85 percent claim that religion plays an important role in their lives.

With over 2,000 distinctive faiths, the U.S. religious landscape is highly diversified, and the country has given birth to many new religions, a few of which have gone global. Moreover, in the past few decades, Asian immigrant groups have greatly added to the religious diversification in North America as well as in Europe. In response, even global finance business is adapting to the changing ideological landscape, as illustrated in this Original Study on Shariah-compliant banking.

secularization A process of cultural change in which a population tends toward a nonreligious worldview, ignoring or rejecting institutionalized spiritual beliefs and rituals.

Sacred Law in Global Capitalism BY BILL MAURER

I will never forget my introduction to Islamic banking. It happened at a 1998 conference when I happened into a darkened room where the founder of an Islamic investment firm was showing a clip from the old Hollywood classic movie, *It's a Wonderful Life*. On the screen, George Bailey, played by Jimmy Stewart, faces an anxious crowd of Bedford Falls citizens, who have rushed into his Building and Loan, passbooks in hand, desperate to get their money. There is about to be a run on the bank.

One of the townspeople says he wants his money, *now*. George protests, "But you're thinking of this place all wrong—as if I had the money back in a safe. The money's not *here*. Why, your money's in Joe's house that's right next to yours, and in the Kennedy house, and Mrs. Macklin's house, and in a hundred others. You're lending them the money to build and then they're gonna pay it back to you as best they can. . . . Now, we can get through this thing all right. We've got to stick together, though. We've got to have faith in each other." The people cry, "I've got doctor's bills to pay!" "Can't feed my kids on faith!"

Then Mary, George's newlywed bride, shouts from behind the counter, "I've got two thousand dollars!" and holds up a wad of bills. It is the money for their honeymoon. George chimes in, "This'll tide us over until the bank reopens tomorrow." He proceeds to disburse money based on people's stated needs ("Could I have $17.50?" one woman asks meekly) and guaranteed only by his trust in them.

Seconds before six o'clock, the last client leaves. George has just two dollars left. He, Mary, his Uncle Billy, and two cousins count down the seconds and then lock the doors. They have managed to stay in business for one more day. They place the two remaining dollars in a tray, and George offers a toast: "To Mama Dollar and to Papa Dollar, and if you want this old Building and Loan to stay in business you better have a family real quick." "I wish they were rabbits," says Cousin Tilly.

At this point in the film, the conference host paused the video and said, "This is the first *lariba* movie." A murmur went through the crowd. No one quite knew what he meant. Most of the audience was Muslim; this was a Christmas movie. What was our host trying to say?

I now know that *lariba* is Arabic for "no increase." The Koran invokes the term *riba* (increase) twenty times, and the term is often translated as interest or usury (excessive interest). Islamic banking and finance aim to avoid *riba* through profit-and-loss sharing, leasing, or other forms of equity- or asset-based financing.

We are all aware of the recent global financial crisis, which led to the collapse of major corporations, the nationalization of big banks and car companies, massive unemployment, and unnerving insecurity for many people in the United States and around the world. One of the leading causes of the crisis was the marketing of debt to people who probably could not repay, and the packaging of those debts into complicated financial instruments that were supposed to curb risk but instead increased it.

What, you might ask, does anthropology have to contribute to the study of the financial markets, money, and the wider economy? Quite a lot, actually. Among other things, anthropologists have repeatedly demonstrated that economic decisions thought to be purely rational and self-interested are actually deeply embedded in social relationships, cultural values, and religious beliefs.

Take securitized debt instruments, for example—loans like mortgages, chopped up and rebundled together into salable commodities. When they started to go sour, many commentators blamed the instruments' complexity and called for a return to an economy based on real things instead of abstract tradable debt. However, we know from our research across the globe that peoples in different cultures do not always differentiate the real from the abstract in the same way. A person's reputation might be deemed more solid and real than a piece of gold. And a piece of gold has real value only because people agree to it as a convention.

After that 1998 conference, I began my study of global Islamic banking, including the efforts of American Muslims to create a new kind of "Islamic" mortgage that enables devout Muslims to buy a home in accordance with Islam's prohibition of interest. Instead of financing a home purchase with interest-bearing debt, Islamic alternatives rely on either leasing contracts (a sort of rent-to-own arrangement where the bank owns the house and the purchaser buys out the bank's share over time) or a partnership arrangement (like a joint business venture). Rather than having debt and interest at the center of the mortgage, as in a conventional loan, the house itself and its fair market rental value are at the center. The purchaser buys out the bank's share over time. At the center is the asset—the real thing—not the debt.

Of course, there is no reason why a joint partnership to own a piece of property is any more "real" or less "abstract" than bundling together debt. It depends on one's point of view, and one's precommitments to certain values—prohibiting interest and sharing risk, for example, or distributing risk onto others. In Islamic finance, the former is seen as "Shariah compliant," or in accord with Islamic law; and the latter, as unjust because it offloads one's own share of risk onto others.

Until the early 1990s, millions of Muslims throughout the world had few investment opportunities due to the ethics derived from Shariah law. Since then, hundreds of Islamic financial institutions have emerged in over fifty countries. Big American and European banks, including Citibank, have also entered the Islamic banking business in order to tap into the rising oil wealth. Today, Shariah-compliant banks manage well over $750 billion globally. Here we see three Muslim women in Kuala Lumpur, Malaysia.

At the same time, Islamic mortgages often require relatively large down payments; this excludes poorer people from achieving the American dream of homeownership. So, we need to ask ourselves whether the virtues of adherence to the precepts of one's religion outweigh broader social goals of financial inclusion.

Global Islamic banking today owes much to the immigration of Middle Eastern and South Asian students and professionals to the United States and western Europe since the 1970s, and the consolidation of large U.S.–Muslim organizations. The oil boom in the Middle East during the 1970s, which sparked renewed interest in Islamic banking in many Muslim-majority countries, also encouraged the development of a loosely knit interconnected network of Muslim international businessmen, who, working for oil and chemical companies as well as financial firms, gained experience in Western regulatory and business environments.

Islamic home financing expanded greatly after the 2001 terrorist attack on New York's World Trade Center and the Pentagon; these attacks sent shockwaves through the capitalist world system dominated by Wall Street. First of all, Americans in general, Muslims included, took their money out of the stock market after the attack and started investing in real estate, buoyed by low interest rates and feeding the speculative real estate bubble. Second, Islamic mutual funds had been able to maintain their "Islamicity" in part by contributing a portion of their profits to charity in order to religiously "cleanse" the funds; however, as charities came under governmental suspicion for terrorist money laundering, many Muslims withdrew their investments from these funds. Third, home financing, American Muslims told me, is the cornerstone of the "American dream," and they were eager to demonstrate their commitment to that dream.

People involved in Islamic banking and finance are continually engaged in an effort to define precisely what their field is. Is *riba* simply Arabic for "interest," or does *riba* refer only to "excessive interest" or usury? Does the prohibition say something about justice, or does it moralize about proper market relationships? Like any aspect of culture—economy included—Islamic banking is always a field of debate. And more debate, not less, may help us all to find just, peaceful, and profitable ways out of the various catastrophes we continually make for ourselves, as we create the abstractions and realities that mutually determine our lives together.

Written expressly for this text, 2010.

In this cross-cultural survey of religion and spirituality, we explored and contrasted numerous worldviews with their symbolic constructs of the universe and our place in it. Made and remade in the course of history, all of these ideological systems reflect human wonderings and ponderings—about life and death, health and illness, past and future, real time and dream time, the known and unknown. Dynamic and inherently complex as the superstructure of a cultural system, a worldview provides imaginative answers, even as it creates mysteries of its own. Whatever its symbolic substance or form, it plays a powerful role in social bonding and control, forging ideological ties that bind and divide.

Religions, as explained and illustrated in this chapter, are not just about spiritual beliefs and rituals, however important these may be. They are also fundamental in the symbolic construction of social identities—the ways in which billions of people see themselves—and motivate people to act or not act in prescribed ways. Performing religion or spirituality, individually or collectively, people not only express what they feel and think but also *who* they are. By tradition or choice, this provides them with another identity marker, beyond features such as gender, speech, kinship, place, or status. Given the cultural variations and historical changes, different markers are stressed or recognized as socially significant.

The cultural upheavals triggered by globalization have made the anthropological study of religion not only fascinating but crucial in our efforts to better understand our species in all its creative and destructive cultural capacity.

CHAPTER CHECKLIST

What are religion and spirituality, and what role do they play in a cultural system?

⬤ Religion is an organized system of ideas about the spiritual sphere or the supernatural, and it is a key part of every culture's worldview. Religion consists of beliefs and practices by which people try to interpret and/or influence aspects of the universe otherwise beyond their control.

⬤ Like religion, spirituality is concerned with sacred matters, but it is often individual rather than collective and does not require a distinctive format or traditional organization.

⬤ Among food-foraging peoples, religion is intertwined in everyday life. As societies become more complex, religion may be restricted to particular occasions.

⬤ Spiritual and religious beliefs and practices fulfill numerous psychological and emotional needs, such as reducing anxiety by providing an orderly view of the universe and answering existential questions, including those concerning suffering and death.

⬤ Myths are narratives that explain the fundamentals of human existence—where we and everything in our world came from, why we are here, and where we are going.

⬤ A traditional religion reinforces group norms and provides moral sanctions for individual conduct. Its narratives and rituals confirm the existing social order, but it may also provide vehicles for challenging that order. People often turn to religion or spirituality in the hope of reaching a specific goal such as restoring health.

What types of supernatural beings and forces are included in the worldview of humans?

⬤ Religion is characterized by a belief in supernatural beings and forces, which can be appealed to for aid through prayer, sacrifice, and other rituals. Supernatural beings may be grouped into three categories: major deities (gods and goddesses), ancestral spirits, and other sorts of spirit beings.

⬤ Gods and goddesses are great but remote beings that control the universe. Whether people recognize gods, goddesses, or both has to do with how men and women relate to each other in everyday life.

⬤ Monotheism holds that there is one supreme divinity; polytheism acknowledges more than one deity.

⬤ Belief in ancestral spirits is based on the dualistic idea that human beings consist of a body and a soul, or vital spirit. Freed from the body at death, the spirit continues to participate in human affairs. This belief is characteristic of descent-based groups with their associated ancestor orientation.

⬤ Animism, the belief that nature is animated (enlivened) by distinct personalized spirit beings separable from bodies, is common among peoples who see themselves as part of nature rather than superior to it.

⬤ Animatism, sometimes found alongside animism, is a belief that nature is energized by an impersonal spiritual force—as in the Chinese concept of *ch'i*.

What are the different types of religious specialists?

⬤ Priests and priestesses are full-time religious specialists authorized to perform sacred rituals and mediate with supernatural powers on behalf of others.

● Priests and priestesses typically hold their position by way of spiritual lineage in which divine authority is passed down from a spiritual founder to a chain of successors.

● There are four major forms of spiritual lineage: biological descent, training and appointment by religious leaders, election, and recognition of a reincarnated saint.

● Shamans are individuals skilled at entering an altered state of consciousness to contact and utilize an ordinarily hidden reality in order to acquire knowledge and supernatural power to help other people. Their special powers have come to them through some personal experience.

What are religious rituals and rites, and what purposes do they serve?

● A religious ritual is a culturally symbolic act or procedure designed to guide members of a community in an orderly way through personal and collective transitions. It is religion in action—the means through which people relate to the supernatural.

● Rites of purification are rituals performed to establish or restore purity when someone has violated a taboo or is otherwise unclean.

● Rites of passage are rituals marking an important stage in an individual's life cycle, such as birth, marriage, and death. They feature three phases: separation, transition, and incorporation.

● Rites of intensification are rituals that ease anxiety and bind people together when they face a collective crisis or change.

What are magic, divination, and witchcraft?

● People in many cultures believe in magic: the idea that supernatural powers can be compelled to act in certain ways for good or evil purposes through specified formulas.

● Many societies have magical rituals to ensure good fortune. Magic is considered to be both imitative (like produces like) and contagious.

● Divination is a magical procedure or spiritual ritual designed to find out what is not knowable by ordinary means, particularly through signs foretelling fate or destiny. Examples include geomancy and chiromancy (palmistry).

● Witchcraft—magical rituals intended to cause misfortune or inflict harm and often referred to as sorcery—is believed to be practiced by people who embody evil spirit power or collaborate with malevolent supernatural beings.

● Belief in witchcraft is widespread, takes many forms, and is especially common during periods of uncertainty.

What are sacred sites and pilgrimages?

● Sacred sites come in many forms. Some are places where ordinary people experienced something extraordinary. Others are associated with a holy person, including shrines or burial sites. Exceptional natural places, especially mountaintops, are often considered magical or sacred.

● A pilgrimage is a devotion in motion—a journey, often on foot, to a sacred site by individuals reaching for enlightenment, proving devotion, and/or hoping to experience a miracle. Among the largest pilgrimages is the hajj made by 1.8 million Muslims traveling to Mecca in Saudi Arabia each year from all around the world.

● Many pilgrimages center on cults of the Virgin Mary. These include Black Madonnas—dark-colored clay or wooden statues or painted images representing the virgin mother. One of them, the Virgin of Guadalupe in Mexico City, draws 6 million pilgrims annually.

● Sacred sites are potential targets of desecration—ideological violation of a sacred site aimed at harming, if only symbolically, people judged to have impure, false, or evil beliefs and ritual practices.

What are revitalization movements, and how are they connected to social upheaval?

● Revitalization movements, which can happen in any culture, arise when people seek radical cultural reform in response to widespread social disruption and collective feelings of anxiety and despair.

● Revitalization movements are not restricted to indigenous peoples historically dominated by colonial powers. They include the 19th-century rise of Mormonism in the United States and ecospiritualism in many Western nations, such as the rise of Druidry in England.

● The revival of traditional American Indian ceremonies such as the sweat lodge and Sun Dance ceremony are other revitalization examples.

● Syncretism, the creative blending of indigenous and foreign beliefs and practices into new cultural forms, can be found worldwide. This includes the practice of Vodou among former slaves in Haiti, which features elements of Roman Catholicism and traditional African beliefs such as spirit possession.

What is secularization?

● Secularization is a process of cultural change in which a population tends toward a nonreligious worldview, ignoring or rejecting institutionalized spiritual beliefs and rituals.

● Fairly common in wealthy countries, secularization has become especially prevalent in western Europe.

QUESTIONS FOR REFLECTION

1. There is more to culture than making survival possible, as humans also search for meaning in the universe and their place in it. Many put their faith in spirit forces, supernatural beings, or deities, seeking existential answers and praying for protection and support. Christian pilgrims in Mexico put their faith in a holy mother figure in heaven. Does your worldview provide you with the same or a similar spiritual support in times of hardship or suffering?

2. People in every culture experience anxiety, fear, and social tension, and many attribute accidents, illnesses, or other misfortunes to evil magic practiced by malevolent individuals such as witches or sorcerers. Do you believe people really possess such supernatural powers to inflict harm?

3. Do the basic dynamics of the shamanic complex also apply to preachers or priests in modern churches and medical doctors working in modern hospitals? Can you think of some similarities among the shaman, preacher, and medical doctor in terms of their respective fields of operation?

4. Graduation is a rite of passage, also known as commencement or convocation, when a high-ranking university official presents students who have completed their studies an academic degree. Can you identify the three phases in this ceremony?

5. Revitalization movements occur in reaction to the upheavals caused by rapid colonization and modernization. Do you think that the rise of religious fundamentalism among Christians, Muslims, Jews, and Hindus is a response to such upheavals as well?

ONLINE STUDY RESOURCES

CourseMate

Access chapter-specific learning tools, including learning objectives, practice quizzes, videos, flash cards, glossaries, and more in your Anthropology CourseMate.

Log into **www.cengagebrain.com** to access the resources your instructor has assigned and to purchase materials.

Body Ritual among the Nacirema

HORACE MINER
University of Michigan

THE anthropologist has become so familiar with the diversity of ways in which different peoples behave in similar situations that he is not apt to be surprised by even the most exotic customs. In fact, if all of the logically possible combinations of behavior have not been found somewhere in the world, he is apt to suspect that they must be present in some yet undescribed tribe. This point has, in fact, been expressed with respect to clan organization by Murdock (1949: 71). In this light, the magical beliefs and practices of the Nacirema present such unusual aspects that it seems desirable to describe them as an example of the extremes to which human behavior can go.

Professor Linton first brought the ritual of the Nacirema to the attention of anthropologists twenty years ago (1936:326), but the culture of this people is still very poorly understood. They are a North American group living in the territory between the Canadian Cree, the Yaqui and Tarahumare of Mexico, and the Carib and Arawak of the Antilles. Little is known of their origin, although tradition states that they came from the east. According to Nacirema mythology, their nation was originated by a culture hero, Notgnihsaw, who is otherwise known for two great feats of strength-the throwing of a piece of wampum across the river Pa-To-Mac and the chopping down of a cherry tree in which the Spirit of Truth resided.

Nacirema culture is characterized by a highly developed market economy which has evolved in a rich natural habitat. While much of the people's time is devoted to economic pursuits, a large part of the fruits of these labors and a considerable portion of the day are spent in ritual activity. The focus of this activity is the human body, the appearance and health of which loom as a dominant concern in the ethos of the people. While such a concern is certainly not unusual, its ceremonial aspects and associated philosophy are unique.

Body Ritual Among the Nacirema by Horace Miner from *American Anthropologist*, June 1956, pages 503-507, American Anthropological Association.

The fundamental belief underlying the whole system appears to be that the human body is ugly and that its natural tendency is to debility and disease. Incarcerated in such a body, man's only hope is to avert these characteristics through the use of the powerful influences of ritual and ceremony. Every household has one or more shrines devoted to this purpose. The more powerful individuals in the society have several shrines in their houses and, in fact, the opulence of a house is often referred to in terms of the number of such ritual centers it possesses. Most houses are of wattle and daub construction, but the shrine rooms of the more wealthy are walled with stone. Poorer families imitate the rich by applying pottery plaques to their shrine walls.

While each family has at least one such shrine, the rituals associated with it are not family ceremonies but are private and secret. The rites are normally only discussed with children, and then only during the period when they are being initiated into these mysteries. I was able, however, to establish sufficient rapport with the natives to examine these shrines and to have the rituals described to me.

The focal point of the shrine is a box or chest which is built into the wall. In this chest are kept the many charms and magical potions without which no native believes he could live. These preparations are secured from a variety of specialized practitioners. The most powerful of these are the medicine men, whose assistance must be rewarded with substantial gifts. However, the medicine men do not provide the curative potions for their clients, but decide what the ingredients should be and then write them down in an ancient and secret language. This writing is understood only by the medicine men and by the herbalists who, for another gift, provide the required charm.

The charm is not disposed of after it has served its purpose, but is placed in the charm-box of the household shrine. As these magical materials are specific for certain ills, and the real or imagined maladies of the people are many, the charm-box is usually full to overflowing. The magical packets are so numerous that people forget what their purposes were and fear to use them again. While the natives are very vague on this point, we can only assume that the idea in retaining all the old magical materials is that their presence in the charm-box, before which the body rituals are conducted, will in some way protect the worshipper.

Beneath the charm-box is a small font. Each day every member of the family, in succession, enters the shrine room, bows his head before the charm-box, mingles different sorts of holy water in the font, and proceeds with a brief rite of ablution. The holy waters are secured from the Water Temple of the community, where the priests conduct elaborate ceremonies to make the liquid ritually pure.

In the hierarchy of magical practitioners, and below the medicine men in prestige, are specialists whose designation is best translated "holy-mouth-men." The Nacirema have an almost pathological horror of and fascination with the mouth, the condition of which is believed to have a supernatural influence on all social relationships. Were it not for the rituals of the mouth, they believe that their teeth would fall out, their gums bleed, their jaws shrink, their friends desert them, and their lovers reject them. They also believe that a strong relationship exists between oral and moral characteristics. For example, there is a ritual ablution of the mouth for children which is supposed to improve their moral fiber.

The daily body ritual performed by everyone includes a mouth-rite. Despite the fact that these people are so punctilious about care of the mouth, this rite involves a practice which strikes the uninitiated stranger as revolting. It was reported to me that the ritual consists of inserting a small bundle of hog hairs into the mouth, along with certain magical powders, and then moving the bundle in a highly formalized series of gestures.

In addition to the private mouth-rite, the people seek out a holy-mouth-man once or twice a year. These practitioners have an impressive set of paraphernalia, consisting of a variety of augers, awls, probes, and prods. The use of these objects in the exorcism of the evils of the mouth involves almost unbelievable ritual torture of the client. The holy-mouth-man opens the client's mouth and, using the above mentioned tools, enlarges any holes which decay may have created in the teeth. Magical materials are put into these holes. If there are no naturally occurring holes in the teeth, large sections of one or more teeth are gouged out so that the supernatural substance can be applied. In the client's view, the purpose of these ministrations is to arrest decay and to draw friends. The extremely sacred and traditional character of the rite is evident in the fact that the natives return to the holy-mouth-men year after year, despite the fact that their teeth continue to decay.

It is to be hoped that, when a thorough study of the Nacirema is made, there will be careful inquiry into the personality structure of these people. One has but to watch the gleam in the eye of a holy-mouth-man, as he jabs an awl into an exposed nerve, to suspect that a certain amount of sadism is involved. If this can be established, a very interesting pattern emerges, for most of the population shows definite masochistic tendencies. It was to these that Professor Linton referred in discussing a distinctive part of the daily body ritual which is performed only by men. This part of the rite involves scraping and lacerating the surface of the face with a sharp instrument. Special women's rites are performed only four times during each lunar month, but what they lack in frequency is made up in barbarity. As part of this ceremony, women bake their heads in small ovens for about an hour. The theoretically interesting point is that what seems to be a preponderantly masochistic people have developed sadistic specialists.

The medicine men have an imposing temple, or *lati pso,* in every community of any size. The more elaborate ceremonies required to treat very sick patients can only be performed at this temple. These ceremonies involve not only the thaumaturge but a permanent group of vestal maidens who move sedately about the temple chambers in distinctive costume and headdress.

The *lati pso* ceremonies are so harsh that it is phenomenal that a fair proportion of the really sick natives who enter the temple ever recover. Small children whose indoctrination is still incomplete have been known to resist attempts to take them to the temple because "that is where you *go* to die." Despite this fact, sick adults are not only willing but eager to undergo the protracted ritual purification, if they can afford to do so. No matter how ill the supplicant or how grave the emergency, the guardians of many temples will not admit a client if he cannot give a rich gift to the custodian. Even after one has gained admission and survived the ceremonies, the guardians will not permit the neophyte to leave until he makes still another gift.

The supplicant entering the temple is first stripped of all his or her clothes. In everyday life the Nacirema avoids exposure of his body and its natural functions. Bathing and excretory acts are performed only in the secrecy of the household shrine, where they are ritualized as part of the body-rites. Psychological shock results from the fact that body secrecy is suddenly lost upon entry into the *lati pso*. A man, whose own wife has never seen him in an excretory act, suddenly finds himself naked and assisted by a vestal maiden while he performs his natural functions into a sacred vessel. This sort of ceremonial treatment is necessitated by the fact that the excreta are used by a diviner to ascertain the course and nature of the client's sickness. Female clients, on the other hand, find their naked bodies are subjected to the scrutiny, manipulation and prodding of the medicine men.

Few supplicants in the temple are well enough to do anything but lie on their hard beds. The daily ceremonies, like the rites of the holy-mouth-men, involve discomfort and torture. With ritual precision, the vestals awaken their miserable charges each dawn and roll them about on their beds of pain while performing ablutions, in the formal movements of which the maidens are highly trained. At other times they insert magic wands in the supplicant's mouth or force him to eat substances which are supposed to be healing. From time to time the medicine men come to their clients and jab magically treated needles into their flesh. The fact that these temple ceremonies may not cure, and may even kill the neophyte, in no way decreases the people's faith in the medicine men.

There remains one other kind of practitioner, known as a "listener." This witch-doctor has the power to exorcise the devils that lodge in the heads of people who have been bewitched. The Nacirema believe that parents bewitch their own children. Mothers are particularly suspected of putting a curse on children while teaching them the secret body rituals. The counter-magic of the witch-doctor is unusual in its lack of ritual. The patient simply tells the "listener" all his troubles and fears, beginning with the earliest difficulties he can remember. The memory displayed by the Nacirema in these exorcism sessions is truly remarkable. It is not uncommon for the patient to bemoan the rejection he felt upon being weaned as a babe, and a few individuals even see their troubles going back to the traumatic effects of their own birth.

In conclusion, mention must be made of certain practices which have their base in native esthetics but which depend upon the pervasive aversion to the natural body and its functions. There are ritual fasts to make fat people thin and ceremonial feasts to make thin people fat. Still other rites are used to make women's breasts larger if they are small, and smaller if they are large. General dissatisfaction with breast shape is symbolized in the fact that the ideal form is virtually outside the range of human variation. A few women afflicted with almost inhuman hypermammary development are so idolized that they make a handsome living by simply going from village to village and permitting the natives to stare at them for a fee.

Reference has already been made to the fact that excretory functions are ritualized, routinized, and relegated to secrecy. Natural reproductive functions are similarly distorted. Intercourse is taboo as a topic and scheduled as an act. Efforts are made to avoid pregnancy by the use of magical materials or by limiting intercourse to certain phases of the moon. Conception is actually very infrequent. When pregnant, women dress so as to hide their condition. Parturition takes place in secret, without friends or relatives to assist, and the majority of women do not nurse their infants.

Our review of the ritual life of the Nacirema has certainly shown them to be a magic-ridden people. It is hard to understand how they have managed to exist so long under the burdens which they have imposed upon themselves. But even such exotic customs as these take on real meaning when they are viewed with the insight provided by Malinowski when he wrote (1948:70):

> Looking from far and above, from our high places of safety in the developed civilization, it is easy to see all the crudity and irrelevance of magic. But without its power and guidance early man could not have mastered his practical difficulties as he has done, nor could man have advanced to the higher stages of civilization.

REFERENCES CITED

LINTON RALPH
    1936 The Study of Man. New York, D. Appleton-Century Co.

MALINOWSKI BRONISLAW
    1948 Magic, Science, and Religion. Glencoe, The Free Press.

MURDOCK GEORGE
    1949 Social Structure. New York, The Macmillan Co.

THE CULTURAL CONSTRUCTION OF CONFLICT AND VIOLENCE

© Bilderbuch/Design Pics/Thinkstock

Canadian memorials to fallen soldiers, such as the Canadian National War Memorial, often evoke the sentiment "Lest We Forget." In the second half of the 20th century, Canada saw itself as a peacekeeper nation, striving to prevent or diminish violent conflict. However, as Richler notes, Canada has more recently become a "warrior nation," especially since it has taken on a combat role in Afghanistan. How do Canadians make sense of our ambivalent relationship with war?

Often it is illuminating to see how history puts on different disguises even as the underlying habits of a place are fundamentally unaltered. This is to say either that Canada today is a "warrior nation"—that the peacekeeping version of Canada was a fifty-year aberration and a public that believes otherwise genuinely has ignored Canada's long military history—or that the Canada with an innate disposition toward "soft power," "making a difference" and the sort of peacekeeping work that is now so disparaged is the underlying constant and the "warrior nation" is the fiction.

Noah Richler, What We Talk About When We Talk About War *(2012)*

PROBLEM 8

How do societies give meaning to and justify collective violence?

INTRODUCTION

The Justification of Violent Conflict

When the Spaniards invaded the New World in the 16th century, they met fierce resistance from the Carib. A warlike people, the Carib inhabited the northeastern part of South America around what is now Venezuela and Guyana. The neighbours of the Carib recognized their ferocity by calling them "sons of the tiger's teeth." Moreover, the Carib were cannibals. To prepare for war, a Carib chief would hold a feast during which women urged the dancing warriors to be fierce and avenge their dead. The dancing was intended to encourage the tiger spirit, Kaikusi-yuma, to take possession of the warriors, and when they went to war, it was the spirit of Kaikusi-yuma that killed, not them. A warrior could rid himself of the possession only by tasting the blood and flesh of a dead enemy.

From our perspective, the acts of the invading Spanish, like the acts of the Carib, were horrific. The Spanish invaders murdered and enslaved thousands of indigenous people, and the Carib devoured human flesh. But both the Europeans and the Carib considered their acts to be moral and proper: the Spaniards justified their killing and enslavement as the work of God; the Carib defined their killing as the act of an animal possessing a human body. Both peoples constructed meanings for their acts that distanced them from the consequences of their violence. Although we may condemn these acts, we live in a world in which governments construct systems of meaning that allow them to plan and contemplate the use of weapons that are much more deadly than the clubs, spears, crossbows, and primitive firearms of the Carib and Spaniards—weapons capable of incinerating millions of people.

Violence, "a category in between peaceful disputing, and major planned warfare and fighting" (Stewart and Strathern 2002, 1), seems to be an intrinsic feature of human societies. In fact, it is difficult to find societies that do not sanction violence for one reason or another. But why is collective violence so universally sanctioned? Some suggest that human beings have an innate instinct toward aggression and that the roots of war and collective violence lie somewhere in the biological mechanisms that animals and humans have in common. Violent conflict is regarded as a part of human nature. Others reject this explanation as simplistic; collective violence, they say, is above all a cultural construction whose roots lie in the human mind, not in the genes. Although there may be some innate aggressive impulse, human beings can choose whether they will give meaningful form to that impulse.

The fact that human beings construct systems of meaning to justify violent conflict and to distance themselves from its consequences suggests that it has little to do with a natural aggressive impulse. Acts of collective violence are rationalized as purposeful, noble, or inevitable, not as evidence of wanton cruelty. The problem is to discover how societies construct meanings for violent conflict that mask its consequences and that convince people it is right and proper.

To evaluate this issue, the first question to be addressed is how societies create a bias in favour of collective violence. That is, what kinds of meanings are constructed to encourage people to commit violence against others? Then, if there are societies without collective violence, how do they create a bias against it? If violent conflict is not natural and inevitable but culturally constructed, it may

be possible to learn from societies in which there is little if any violence. The question is, are there significant social, economic, or political differences between violent and peaceful societies? And also, what is the relationship between violence and the nation-state? Since collective violence is sanctioned in North American societies, it is instructive to ask how we have created a bias toward violent conflict and constructed meanings that allow us to contemplate, plan for, and pursue the destruction of millions of people in other nations. Finally, we will explore the potential pitfalls and possible insights to be gained by conducting participant observation of, and during, violent conflicts.

QUESTIONS

8.1 How do societies create a bias in favour of collective violence?

8.2 How do societies create a bias *against* violent conflict?

8.3 What are the economic, political, and social differences between peaceful and violent societies?

8.4 What is the relationship between violence and the nation-state?

8.5 How is it possible to justify the construction of weapons of mass destruction?

8.6 How do anthropologists do fieldwork in the midst of violent conflict?

QUESTION 8.1: HOW DO SOCIETIES CREATE A BIAS IN FAVOUR OF COLLECTIVE VIOLENCE?

Horses, Rank, and Warfare Among the Kiowa

One way societies create a bias toward collective violence is by rewarding it. Among the Native

Americans of the western plains, for example, raiding other groups for horses was a means by which a man gained status. Horses symbolized wealth, and in many groups a man's importance was measured by the number of horses he owned and gave to others as gifts.

Horses are not indigenous to North America; they were brought to the continent by the Spaniards in the 1500s. Native American groups such as the Kiowa captured some horses and acquired others in trade with the Spaniards. The Kiowa also obtained horses by attacking other Native American groups with horse-raiding parties of as many as thirty men. The objective of these raids was to secure as many of the enemy's horses as possible and, as well, to demonstrate bravery. Among the Kiowa, rank was determined in two ways: by the number of horses a man possessed and by the honours accruing to him in warfare.

Kiowa society was divided into four ranks or grades. In the top rank were *ongop*, men who were generous, who held considerable wealth, and, most important, who had distinguished themselves in war.

In the second rank were *ondeigupa*, men who had property (especially horses), who were generous, but who had not yet distinguished themselves in war. The lower ranks of Kiowa society were occupied by *keen* or *dupom*, people who were poor, propertyless, or helpless. To rise in status, a young Kiowa male needed to acquire a horse. Often he began his climb through the ranks of Kiowa society by borrowing a horse from a kinsperson to go on a raid, hoping to repay the loan with another horse he had captured. With a horse of his own, he could participate in more raids, gradually obtaining enough horses to rise to the rank of *ondeigupa*, or, as the Kiowa put it, "rise out of the bush of *keen*." Several years of raiding might bring him twenty or thirty horses, at which point people would begin speaking of him with respect.

To rise to the top rank of *ongop*, however, also required the accumulation of honours won in war. The Kiowa had a very elaborate system of battle honours divided into three groups of brave deeds, with group I being the most honored (see Table 8.1). Counting first coup, for example,

TABLE 8.1 KIOWA RANKING AND HONOURS

Group I	Group II	Group III
Counting first coup	Killing an enemy	Dismounting, turning horse loose, and fighting on foot
Charging an enemy while the party is in retreat, thus covering the retreat	Counting second coup	Counting third and fourth coup
Rescuing a comrade while the party is retreating before the enemy	Receiving a wound in hand-to-hand combat	Serving as raid leader
Charging the leading man of the enemy alone before the parties have met		Success in stealing horses
		Efficiency in war camp life

Source: Information from Bernard Mishkin, *Rank and Warfare Among the Plains Indians* (Seattle: University of Washington Press, 1940).

involved charging the enemy alone and striking one of them with a stick. The number of feathers a man wore in his headdress was a measure of his heroic exploits.

Anthropologist Bernard Mishkin (1940) estimates that approximately 10 percent of the men would rise to the top rank of Kiowa society by obtaining a significant number of horses and accumulating sufficient battle honours. In this way, the Kiowa rewarded aggressive behaviour and bravery in battle.

Good Hosts Among Yanomamo

Another way societies create a bias in favour of collective violence is by making it a necessary means for protecting valuable resources. As we discussed in Chapter 1, a classic (but contentious) example is the Yanomamo of Venezuela. The Yanomamo live in villages of from 40 to 250 people and practise slash-and-burn (swidden) agriculture, living primarily on the crops they grow in their gardens.

Warfare between villages is endemic among the Yanomamo. Anthropologist Napoleon Chagnon, who has worked with them since 1964, reports that one village of 200 people was attacked twenty-five times, and that ten people were killed during a period of fifteen months, representing a loss of 5 percent of the village population. He estimates that 20 to 25 percent of all male deaths are the result of warfare.

For the Yanomamo, women and children are valuable resources. The men believe that to protect themselves and their resources, they must be fierce, and raiding another village is one way for them to demonstrate their ferocity. Raids may be conducted to avenge the death of a village member at the hands of an enemy village or as the result of an act of sorcery by an enemy. Raids may also be made to capture women or children. Violence can also take the form of inviting members of another village to a feast and—usually with the aid of allies from another village—killing the guests and abducting their women. Raiding by other villages forces them to move fairly frequently, and sometimes they take refuge from their enemies in the villages of their allies. This practice is risky, however, because host villages generally expect sexual access to the wives of their guests or expect unmarried female guests to marry men of their village. These expectations often lead to open hostilities between hosts and guests.

Expressions of ferocity may be directed among village members as well. For example, men often vent anger and demonstrate their ferocity by beating their wives. A man who accuses another of cowardice or of making excessive demands for goods or women may challenge his opponent to a chest-pounding duel in which they take turns hitting each other in the chest as hard as they can. The duel generally ends when one of the contestants is too injured to continue. Fights with clubs are another form of settling disputes between men, although these generally result in free-for-alls—which can be deadly.

In this environment, where each man strives to acquire women from others, it is necessary to adopt an antagonistic stance toward others. This in turn encourages the development of what the Yanomamo call *waiteri* (ferocity). The *waiteri* complex, as Chagnon calls it, is evidenced in ways other than direct conflict. The Yanomamo express it in their origin myth, which tells how the original people were created from the blood of the moon, which had been shot with an arrow by beings who believed their children's souls were being devoured by the moon. The first Yanomamo born of the blood of the moon were exceptionally fierce and waged constant war on one another.

The Yanomamo also socialize male children to be aggressive and hostile. Boys are teased to strike tormentors and to bully girls. At one gathering of two villages attended by Chagnon, men were to satisfy their grievances against each other with a chest-pounding duel. Prior to the duel the men gathered all the boys between the ages of eight and fifteen and forced them to fight each other. At first, says Chagnon, the boys were reluctant and tried to run away, but their parents dragged them back and insisted that they hit each other. At the first blows the boys cried, but as the fight progressed, fear became rage, and they ended up pounding each other while they screamed and rolled in the dirt, to the cheers and admiration of their fathers.

Constructing Religious Justifications for Violence

Another way to justify violence is by framing it as a cosmic struggle between good and evil. Most modern religions contain sacred texts describing violent confrontations between the forces of good and the forces of evil. The Book of Revelation with its description of the forces of Satan and the ultimate battle between good and evil provides one of the most powerful (and most violent) metaphors of war and redemption in Western literature. As Elaine Pagels notes, the characterization of one's enemies as "Satanic" and of oneself as God's people has long been a formula for justifying hatred and mass slaughter.

So it should not be surprising that people use religious rhetoric to justify violent acts. But when devout adherents to Christianity, Judaism, Sikhism, Buddhism, or Islam commit violent acts in the name of God or some spiritual mission, they are often responding also to social, political, or economic grievances as well. Osama bin Laden sought the establishment of an Islamic caliphate, but he was also protesting the Israeli occupation of Palestinian territories, the stationing of U.S. troops in Saudi Arabia, and the American support for oppressive governments in the Middle East.

All major religions have their violent militants. On 20 March 1995, five members of the Aum Shinrikyo movement, all of whom had scientific training, walked into the Tokyo subway and, with sharpened umbrellas, punctured plastic bags filled

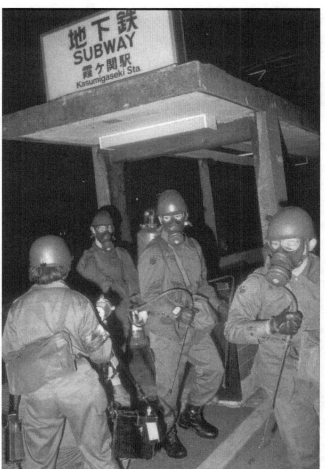

Aftermath of Tokyo subway Sarin attack in 1995.

with deadly sarin gas, killing 12 people and poisoning more than 5,500. The group's members explained to Mark Juegensmeyer that Aum Shinrikyo represented for them a critique of Japanese religion and the "hierarchical" Japanese social system. The movement was founded by Shoko Asahara based on the idea that a world catastrophe would occur, a Third World War or "Armageddon," in which the forces of good and evil would confront each other and members of Aum Shinrikyo would survive.

Asahara justified his acts by reference to Tibetan Buddhism and the concept of *phoa*. Instead of focusing on the effect that killing has on the killer's moral purity, this doctrine focuses on the one who is killed and on the merit that comes after death. According to Asahara, if a person is a scoundrel or is part of an evil social system, he or she is accumulating negative karmic debt. Killing such people represents a mercy killing that allows their souls to move to a higher plane than if they continued to exist in sin.

Juegensmeyer (2004) asks under what conditions people are likely to use religious justifications for violence. He suggests that by locating a struggle on a cosmic scale, aggressors elevate its importance beyond local concerns and, instead, invoke legendary battles between good and evil. Osama bin Laden justified violence by projecting the struggle as one between the forces of Islam and those trying to destroy it. The rhetoric of wars of good versus evil is even part of the U.S. political mainstream, with terms such as "axis of evil."

There is real power, suggests Juegensmeyer, in elevating a political conflict to a cosmic war. To live in a state of war, he writes,

> is to live in a world in which individuals know who they are, why they have suffered, by whose hand they have been humiliated, and at what expense they have persevered. The concept of war provides cosmology, history, and eschatology and offers the reins of political control. Perhaps most important, it holds out the hope of victory and the means to achieve it. In the images of cosmic war this victorious triumph is a grand moment of social and personal transformation, transcending all worldly limitations. One does not easily abandon such expectations. To be without such images of war is almost to be without hope itself. (2000, 154–55)

The Archangel Michael defeating Satan (oil on canvas), Reni, Guido (1575–1642)/Private Collection/ The Bridgeman Art Library

There is real power in elevating a political conflict to a cosmic war.

EXERCISE 8.1

Examples of group-sanctioned conflict are readily available in reports in newspapers and on the Internet. To examine the justifications for such conflict, follow a daily newspaper or news website for a couple of days and document the instances you find of group-sanctioned violence and the reasons attributed for it.

QUESTION 8.2: HOW DO SOCIETIES CREATE A BIAS *AGAINST* VIOLENT CONFLICT?

Anthropologist Thomas Gregor (1990) suggests that since war is so widespread in human societies, the task of the social scientist is not so much to explain war as to explain peace. Peaceful societies, he says, are difficult to find. By peaceful, he means a society that is not involved in internal collective violence and in which there is little interpersonal violence. A peaceful society has no special roles for warriors and places a positive value on nonaggressive behaviour and the peaceful resolution of conflict. Societies that have been characterized as relatively peaceful include the Ju/'hoansi, the Semai of Malaysia, and the Xinguano of the Amazon.

Characteristics of Peaceful Societies

Peaceful societies avoid conflicts over material resources through a strong emphasis on sharing and cooperation. It is understood that everyone in the group has a legitimate claim to what the group possesses. Among the Ju/'hoansi the person whose arrow kills an animal is considered to be the owner of the game, but he is obligated to distribute it. The Ju/'hoansi will share arrows with the understanding that if they kill an animal with an arrow given to them by someone else, they will give the owner the game to distribute. This also works to spread out the responsibility for meat sharing and the glory (and perhaps the hostility) that accompanies meat distribution.

The Semai of Malaysia are known for their nonaggressiveness and avoidance of physical conflict. The approximately 15,000 Semai live in hamlets of fewer than one hundred people each. Understanding Semai nonviolence, says anthropologist Clayton Robarchek (1990), requires understanding the Semai notion of *pehunan*, a state of being in which a person is unsatisfied in regard to some need or want, such as food or sex. The Semai believe that to refuse a request and deny a person a need intensifies the danger to both the individual and the group; for that reason, the group is obligated to help. The idea of *pehunan* encompasses a depiction of the community as nurturant caregivers. Instead of saying that it is each person's obligation to meet his or her own needs, the Semai believe that it is the obligation of all members of the community to help and give nurturance to others. Thus, Semai values stress affiliation, mutual aid, and the belief that violence is not a viable option for settling disputes.

Another way that people in peaceful societies create a bias against violence is by condemning those who boast or who make claims that can be interpreted as a challenge to others. Among the Ju/'hoansi, for example, no one is praised for gathering food or making a kill, and people go out of their way to minimize their accomplishments. Those who make boastful claims are ridiculed. Anthropologist Richard Lee painfully learned this lesson himself when, to show his appreciation to the Ju/'hoansi for the help they had given him, he brought a fine ox to be slaughtered and distributed at a Christmas feast. The Ju/'hoansi, much to Lee's chagrin, ridiculed the ox, claiming it was thin and unappetizing. Lee later realized that they were acting toward him as they would have to one of their own. They were letting him know that he wasn't as important as the gift and the killing of the ox made him think he was.

Thomas Gregor says that villagers in the Xingu basin of the Amazon maintain harmony by purposely sanctioning village monopolies in the production of certain goods such as shell belts, stone axes, salt, cotton, fish spears, and ceramic pots. In this way, each village has something that other villages need. The villages therefore maintain good relations, since to alienate another village might deprive one's own village members of a desired good. Moreover,

THE CULTURAL CONSTRUCTION OF CONFLICT AND VIOLENCE

trade is positively valued in itself. When villagers are asked why they don't make the goods they need themselves, they reply that this might anger those who do make them. Or they may claim that they do not have the knowledge to produce the items, although when they are temporarily cut off from a supply, they seem to learn how to make or acquire them very quickly. Gregor says it is unlikely that any village could not produce the goods desired, since marriage between groups is common so that each village contains people with the skills of other villages.

The Xinguanos place a strong negative value on aggression and on things that symbolize aggression. Killing is wrong because it produces blood; even animal blood is considered defiling. Most game animals are considered inedible, and even fish must be well cooked so that there is no blood. The Xinguanos also hold strong negative stereotypes of aggressive groups. They consider non-Xingu Indians to be "wild Indians" who are violent; they beat their children, rape their women, and shoot arrows at white men's planes. The wild Indian has almost the status of an animal and represents everything a Xinguano doesn't want to be. When Xingu villages have been the object of aggression by others, they have defended themselves, but successful warriors take no trophies and are given no special honour. In fact, they have to take special

This Xinguano will ensure that his catch is well cooked, to ensure there is no blood.

© Ueslei Marcelino/Reuters

medicine to cleanse themselves of the defilement of the blood of their victims.

Peaceful societies also minimize violence and conflict through ceremony. The Ju/'hoansi believe that everyone has "medicine" or power. In the same way that nearby Bantu tribes have witchcraft and sorcery, and Europeans have pills and syringes, the Ju/'hoansi have *n/um*, a substance they say lies in the pit of the stomach. *N/um* has the capacity to keep people healthy and to help cure people who are sick. Most important, *n/um* can be transferred from someone who is acting as a healer to others through the medium of the trance dance, their most common ceremony. The idea of the dance is for a person to "heat up" his or her *n/um* by dancing; as the person dances, the *n/um* in the stomach is vaporized and travels up the spinal cord into the brain, which causes the dancer to go into a trance. The dancer then goes from person to person laying on hands and transferring power to those who are touched, thereby enabling them to ward off sickness and death. Anyone can be a healer among the Ju/'hoansi; in a lifetime, each person is likely to serve as a healer at one time or another.

The trance dance has meanings that go beyond the power to heal, however. Some Ju/'hoansi are thought to have special powers that allow them to see the ghosts of dead ancestors who hover around the fires, to see distant scenes, to see through things, and, in special cases, to change themselves into lions and stalk the veldt in search of human prey. Trance dances are most frequent when large numbers of people come together (from about once a month in small groups, up to four times a week in large camps) and during certain occasions such as the arrival of visitors to a camp, the presence of meat, or sickness. The congregation of large numbers of people, the presence of meat, and the arrival of new people are all occasions that in one way or another create the potential for interpersonal conflict. The fact that trance dances are more frequent during such times seems to indicate that they may serve to heal social conflict as well as individual maladies. By bringing people together in the ceremony, by the sharing of *n/um* and the ritual recognition of common threats, the trance dance unites people and symbolizes the relationship between group harmony and individual well-being.

In sum, peaceful societies create a bias against violence by sharing, by valuing nonaggressive behaviour, by building relations of dependence between individuals and groups, and by engaging in collective behaviours that promote harmony. They are not, of course, always successful, and even among some so-called peaceful societies, there is violence. Lee collected accounts of twenty-two homicides among Ju/'hoansi groups during a thirty-five-year period from 1920 to 1955, for example, but found little if any sanctioned group violence.

QUESTION 8.3: WHAT ARE THE ECONOMIC, POLITICAL, AND SOCIAL DIFFERENCES BETWEEN PEACEFUL AND VIOLENT SOCIETIES?

Thomas Hobbes, a 17th-century philosopher, proposed that human beings in their natural state, without government or laws, are driven by greed and the quest for gain. Without some common power to keep them in awe, Hobbes said, they live in a state of war, with every person against every other person. Here is one of the more famous passages from *Leviathan*, in which Hobbes describes his vision of life before civilization:

> *Whatsoever therefore is consequent to a time of warre, where every man is enemy to every man; the same is consequent to a time, wherein men live without other security, than what their own strength and their own invention shall furnish them withall. In such a condition there is no place for Industry; because the fruit thereof is uncertain; and consequently no Culture of the Earth [agriculture]; no navigation, nor use of the commodities that may be imported by sea; no commodious Building; no Instruments of moving, and removing such things as require much force; no Knowledge of the face of the Earth; no account of Time; no Arts; no Letters; no Society; and which is worst of all, continual feare, and danger of violent death; And the life of man, solitary, poore, nasty, brutish, and short. (Hobbes 1881[1651], 94–96)*

Hobbes saw human beings as having a natural inclination to be violent, an inclination that can be controlled only by some form of centralized authority. However, as anthropologists have discovered, societies with little formal government, such as the Ju/'hoansi and the Semai, are among the most peaceful in the world (as discussed earlier). Also, these peaceful societies are small in scale and make their living primarily by hunting and gathering or by swidden agriculture. Most are relatively isolated and lack formal mechanisms for resolving conflict once it begins. There are no courts, no police, no jails, and no formally sanctioned threats of violence, even against wrongdoers. Since there is little that people in these societies can do once violence begins, they go to great lengths to avoid it.

Had Hobbes known the Yanomamo, however, he might have found that his vision of a stateless society, "where every man is enemy to every man," had been verified. Their social and economic life closely resembles that of the Semai, and they live in virtually the same environment and are neighbours of the peaceful Xinguano. But Yanomamo society creates attitudes favouring collective violence in order to protect its women and children, which suggests that Hobbes may have been correct, at least in part. In this case, the lack of any centralized control or formal mechanisms for putting an end to conflict results in unrestrained violence rather than the avoidance of conflict.

The Need to Protect Resources

In societies without any form of centralized control and a bias toward collective violence, such as that of the Yanomamo, individuals must protect their own resources through force. Because the Yanomamo, for example, do not effectively control intravillage conflict, men of their own as well as other villages are constantly seeking to seduce one another's wives. Consequently, the men, individually or in groups, must build a reputation for fierceness in order to protect themselves and their families. Failure to control conflict and the need for men to build a reputation for aggressiveness in order to protect their resources combine to produce a society that places a positive value on violent behaviour.

The conditions that give rise to violent conflict among the Yanomamo are not unlike those that promote violence in street gangs in the United States. When Lincoln Keiser worked in the 1960s with the Vice Lords, a Chicago street gang (or "club," as they preferred to call themselves), he concluded that boys joined gangs because alone they could not protect themselves from shakedowns or safeguard their interests in girls. Where the Yanomamo encouraged *waiteri*—fierceness—the Vice Lords valued heart—a willingness to follow any suggestion regardless of personal risk. Where a Yanomamo demonstrated fierceness through chest-pounding duels, axe fights, and raids against enemy villages, members of street gangs in Chicago confirmed their heart in gang fights, or "gangbangs." Street gangs even formed alliances against other gangs, as do Yanomamo villages with each other. The similarities in the dynamics and values of violent conflict among Yanomamo and among street gangs in Canada and the United States illustrate how under certain conditions individuals form groups to protect themselves against other

groups. To discourage attacks from others in the absence of protection from other agencies, these groups cultivate a reputation for violence.

The gang violence that Keiser observed in Chicago during the late 1960s has escalated since, and weapons more typical of armed soldiers in the military are now being used. Alex Kotlowitz, in *There Are No Children Here* (1991), reported how the Vice Lords, one of three gang factions in Chicago in the early 1990s, made use of an arsenal that included Uzis and grenades. The purpose was the same, although the stakes were higher. Drugs have become the major source of contention among Chicago gangs (the head of one Vice Lord faction grossed $50,000 to $100,000 a week). When drug wars erupt over territory, the violence reflects the increased stakes and more massive firepower. A couple of years ago, four members of the Vice Lords came upon a rival gang member in the lobby of a housing project and shot him five times with an Uzi, two sawed-off shotguns, and a .25-calibre automatic handgun to establish their dominance in the neighbourhood.

The social and political conditions that characterize the societies of the Vice Lords and

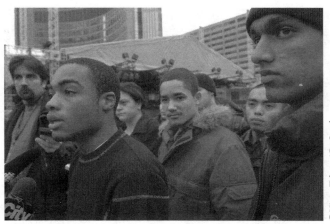

One reason for gang warfare may be a lack of other ways to protect valued resources or to settle disputes, but innocent bystanders may also be killed. Here, spokespeople for Toronto youth groups plead for help from municipal politicians to combat unchecked gang violence.

© Vince Talotta/GetStock.com

the Yanomamo are such that in each of them, individuals must mobilize and use force to protect or acquire desired resources. In neither case is there any effective centralized authority to guarantee the safety of resources or to stop violence once it begins. There is a centralized force in Chicago—the police—but they rarely intervene in gang violence, because they are unwilling or do not have the resources to do so, or because local residents are afraid or reluctant to report violence.

Creating the Conditions for Violence

Napoleon Chagnon characterized Yanomamo warfare as a "truly primitive cultural adaptation … before it was altered or destroyed by our culture." It was, he said, the normal state of affairs before it was suppressed by colonial governments. However, there is considerable evidence that Yanomamo warfare and aggression were less a product of their existence or nature than it was a consequence of Western contact.

Brian Ferguson (1995) maintains that the period of Chagnon's fieldwork (1964 to 1972), on which he based his best-selling ethnography, *The Fierce People* (1968), was one of the most turbulent in Yanomamo history. Violence and aggression, writes Ferguson, were a product of three major changes: (1) the presence of new outpost settlements of government agents, missionaries, and researchers; (2) competition for Western manufactured goods, particularly steel cutting tools, and (3) a breakdown of social relations brought about by epidemics and the depletion of game and other food resources.

The Yanomamo, Ferguson points out, had been in contact with outsiders for centuries. Europeans began raiding Yanomamo villages for slaves as early as the mid-17th century and continued to do so until around 1850. In the late 19th century, the rubber boom in the Amazon—a horrendous period for indigenous groups, who were forced to collect rubber under the threat of torture and death—brought the Yanomamo into increased contact and

conflict with other indigenous groups. After the Amazon rubber boom collapsed in the 1920s as a result of competition with Asian rubber plantations, the area in which the Yanomamo lived was relatively peaceful until the 1950s and 1960s, when influenza and measles epidemics swept the area, leaving only one-quarter of the children with both parents. But more disruptive yet was the presence of new, Western outposts.

The new outposts made available manufactured items desired by the Yanomamo (such as steel knives, machetes, aluminum pots, and shotguns). Steel cutting tools, for example, were ten times more efficient than the stone cutting tools they had long been using. Shotguns were effective both for hunting and for raiding. The Yanomamo could obtain these items in various ways. They could relocate their villages near the outposts, they could send trading parties on long voyages to get them, or they could raid other groups for them. But the greatest advantage went to what Ferguson called "anchor villages," those that relocated near outposts. The result was a hierarchy of settlements ranging from anchor villages whose members were able to monopolize the new desired goods to more isolated settlements whose members had fewer and lower quality goods.

Yanomamo in anchor settlements traded Western items to distant groups for local handicrafts such as cotton hammocks, spear points, or manioc flour. But trading parties were also targets of raids by groups desiring Western goods. To protect themselves and their monopoly on Western trade goods and to discourage raiding, Yanomamo groups found it advantageous to cultivate reputations for violence and aggression. A reputation for fierceness was also an advantage in negotiating for desired goods. Thus one man told of the number of people he had killed on raids just before demanding a machete.

Proximity to Western outposts incited violence in other ways. For example, once people relocated their village near an outpost settlement, they were reluctant to move. One way that small-scale, mobile societies such as the Yanomamo avoid conflict is by moving villages away from enemies when conflict is threatened. But since moving would mean giving up access to and a monopoly on Western goods, members of anchor villages were reluctant to move, and hence needed to protect themselves and the goods they obtained from Westerners. In addition, more permanent settlements quickly depleted game resources, resources that had been used in reciprocal exchanges with other people and groups. Thus sharing patterns, which as we noted ealier are crucial for maintaining peaceful relations, began to break down, leading to more conflict.

In these ways, deaths from disease and war disrupted traditional social relations, the depletion of game weakened traditional patterns of sharing and cooperation, and access to Western technology provided new sources of conflict. Furthermore, the new technology introduced a new way of ordering society and enhanced the ability of people in anchor villages to make war.

Access to Western goods also explains the aggressive attitudes of Yanomamo men to women. Traditionally, Yanomamo practised brideservice; grooms were obligated to work for their bride's family from one to four years. But families of grooms in anchor villages were able to substitute Western goods for brideservice, one result being a movement of wives to villages with greater access to Western goods. This, combined with the Yanomamo practice of female infanticide and polygamy, resulted in a shortage of and greater competition for females and the more frequent raiding of other villages for women. In addition, Yanomamo wives go to live in their husband's family villages, particularly where Western goods take the place of brideservice. The result is that women are removed from the protective influence of their families and are more likely to be victims of abuse.

In sum, many of the patterns of Yanomamo warfare, violence, and aggression cannot be understood without knowledge of their history of contact with Western society and the contact conditions that increased the likelihood of violence and war. Even the power of chiefs, whose feast giving played such an important role in Chagnon's descriptions of alliance formation and aggression, was largely a function of Western contact. Outsiders, following traditional customs, brought gifts to local leaders. But the gifts that outsiders brought were far more valuable. Thus Chagnon gave one chief a gift of twenty-five machetes, providing him with items that he could use to enhance his power. And thus, as Ferguson says, "if villages were not anchored to outposts but were able to move freely, if long-established marital alliances were not disturbed by massive mortality, if communal sharing of meat were still the norm, and, above all, if necessary technology were widely and equally available, my theoretical expectation is that there would be little collective violence among the Yanomami" (1992, 225).

Sexism and Violent Conflict

Another difference between peaceful and violent societies that has been suggested has to do with gender roles. Among the Ju/'hoansi, the Xinguano, and the Semai, men and women are relatively equal and there is little institutionalized violence against women. In contrast, the Yanomamo and the Vice Lords are characterized by male dominance, and both sanction violence against women. Several reasons have been advanced to support the link between sexist values and violent conflict. First, it is men that make war, though women may fill certain positions in the armed forces. While there have been societies in which women engage in armed combat, these instances are the exception rather than the rule. During the Sandinista rebellion in Nicaragua in the 1980s, women took an active role in combat, but they were banned from active combat once the Sandinistas gained power. Second, there is a strong cross-cultural link between patriarchy and violent conflict. After examining information on more than one thousand societies, William Tulio Divale and Marvin Harris (1976) concluded that the intensity of collective violence is significantly higher in societies characterized by a strong male bias—patrilocal residence, patrilineal descent, polygyny, postmarital sex restrictions on females, male secret societies, and men's houses. Finally, there is evidence that societies characterized by sexual violence against women tend to be more warlike and prone to collective violence. Peggy Sanday's 1981 study of 95 societies in which there was evidence of frequency of rape supports this conclusion. The question is, does a sexist ideology promote violent conflict, or does the incidence of violent conflict promote sexism?

Those who claim that sexism promotes violent conflict make that connection in various ways. Betty Reardon (1985) and Leslie Cagan (1983) suggest that societies that relegate women to an inferior position explicitly or implicitly sanction violence against women. Moreover, violence toward women serves as what they call a "primal" paradigm for violent warfare against other peoples. That is, once violence is allowed as a means of domination of one group such as women, it can serve as a model for dominance and violence against other groups.

For Peggy Sanday, and for many others, sexism and violent conflict both have their roots in competition over scarce resources. During periods in which resources are not scarce, males and females are valued equally. When there is an imbalance between food supply or distribution and needs, or when groups are competing for resources, males become of greater value, females become objects to be controlled, and sexual violence becomes one way that men demonstrate their dominance. Among cattle-herding people in East Africa, for example, raiding for cattle was common and sometimes led to violent conflict between groups. Violence was defined as a manly activity, leading East African societies to place great emphasis on masculinity and manliness. Manliness, however, was tested not only in battle but in male–female relations as well, for sex was a way of demonstrating strength.

In sum, factors such as a lack of centralized control, competition over scarce resources, private

EXERCISE 8.3

There is some suggestion of a link between militarism and competitive sports; that is, societies that are prone to collective violence are more likely to value games in which men aggressively compete against other men. How does this apply to North American societies? Which sports in North America most closely resemble or promote the values of militarism and war? Does the language of these sports reflect militaristic values? Do gender roles reflect these values? In what ways does Canada differ from the United States on these issues?

property, and sexism may lead societies to construct an ideological bias toward violence. Examining the effects of violent conflict to see if they produce changes in societies may provide insights into the factors that promote violent conflict.

QUESTION 8.4: WHAT IS THE RELATIONSHIP BETWEEN VIOLENCE AND THE NATION-STATE?

The Evolution of the Nation-State

Anthropologists suggest that violent conflict may encourage certain forms of political organization. Robert Carneiro argues, for example, that in the course of human history violent conflict has been the primary agent that has transformed human societies from small-scale, autonomous communities into vast, complex nation-states. He reasons that war has promoted the consolidation of isolated, politically autonomous villages into chiefdoms of united villages and into states. At first, war pits village against village, resulting in chiefdoms; then it pits chiefdom against chiefdom, resulting in states; then it pits state against state. War, he says, began as the effort to oust a rival from a territory but soon evolved into an effort to subjugate and control an enemy. As the process continued, warfare became the mechanism by which the number of political units in the world began to decline. Carneiro predicts that if the number of political states continues to decline as it has in the past, by the year 2300 there should be only a single world state.

The rise of the Zulu state in Africa illustrates Carneiro's theory. The Zulu state took form in southeastern Africa in the early 19th century. Prior to that time, the region was inhabited by small, sometimes warring groups. About 100,000 people lived in an area of about 80,000 square miles by practising agriculture and cattle herding. While there were separate entities that Westerners labelled tribes, the largest political unit was the clan. Warriors from these clans raided one another for cattle, but there was no conquest of land.

Warfare increased between 1775 and 1800 as the population of southeastern Africa increased. The strongest groups were those that could muster the most warriors and organize and discipline them effectively. The process of state formation whereby these separate groups combined into a larger political unit was begun by a leader of the Mtetwa tribe named Dingiswayo. He developed new ways to organize his troops and began to take control of the lands of those he defeated. After he conquered an area, he appointed a person from the head family of the group he had conquered to rule for him. Using new techniques of war and political control, he achieved dominance over a wide area. His reason for extending his control, according to one 19th-century writer, was to make peace among warring groups. Dingiswayo, it was said, "wished to do away with the incessant quarrels that occurred amongst the tribes, because no supreme head was over them to say who was right or who was wrong."

By the early 1800s, Dingiswayo had conquered and united some thirty different groups. He was aided by a young officer named Shaka Zulu, the son of the chief of the Zulu clan. When the Zulu chief died, Dingiswayo installed Shaka as the head of the clan, and when Dingiswayo was killed by a rival, Shaka took over the army and established his Zulus as the dominant clan. By 1822 Shaka had defeated every rival and was master of all of the present South African province of Kwa-Zulu Natal.

Violence and the Nation-State

As we discussed in Chapter 7, the symbolic barriers of excluded Others, infrastructure, and education are essential for nation building. The use of violence or the threat of armed force is another key instrument in creating and maintaining the nation-state. Killing is the ultimate tool of nation-states. In fact, some anthropologists, among them Pierre van den Berghe, Leo Kuper, and Carol Nagengast, view the nation-state as a genocidal or ethnocidal institution, one that conspires to kill or remove those citizens who fail to (or refuse to) conform to the dictates of the imposed national culture. "Ethnic cleansing" is not a phenomenon of the late 20th century. For example, the United States, through policies of either aggressive extermination or benign neglect, attempted to kill all indigenous peoples and assimilate those who remained. Between 1975 and 1979, the government of Cambodia, the Khmer Rouge, systematically murdered two million of its seven million citizens, and in 1994 the Rwandan state slaughtered 800,000 of its citizens. According to Carol Nagengast,

> the numbers of people worldwide subjected to the violence of their own states are staggering. More than a quarter of a million Kurds and Turks in Turkey have been beaten or tortured by the military, police, and prison guards since 1980; tens of thousands of indigenous people in Peru and Guatemala, street children in Brazil and Guatemala, Palestinians in Kuwait, Kurds in Iraq, and Muslim women and girls in Bosnia have been similarly treated. Mutilated bodies turn up somewhere everyday. Some 6000 people in dozens of countries were legally

shot, hung, electrocuted, gassed, or stoned to death by their respective states between 1985 and 1992 for political misdeeds: criticism of the state, membership in banned political parties or groups, or for adherence to the "wrong" religion; for moral deeds: adultery, prostitution, homosexuality, sodomy, or alcohol or drug use; for economic offenses: burglary, embezzling, and corruption; and for violent crimes: rape, assault, and murder. (1994, 119–20)

Pierre van den Berghe contends that what is euphemistically called nation building is nothing but a blueprint for **ethnocide** (an attempt to destroy the culture of a people) at best and **genocide** (an attempt to exterminate a people) at worst. Social scientists, he writes, tend to ignore the genocidal character of the nation-state because of the widespread assumption that nation-states are necessary for maintaining peace and economic stability. Instead, he says, nation-states are, in effect, mafias or gangs that, through the use or threat of violence, extract booty for themselves or their elites from rival "gangs" and extract "protection money" from their own citizens.

Other anthropologists share van den Berghe's view of the nation-state as an instrument of force and violence. Nagengast examined not only state killing but also the use of torture, rape, and homosexual assault to draw the boundaries of the nation-state. State-sponsored violence, she says, serves not only to inflict pain but also to create "punishable categories of people"—that is, people whose existence creates and maintains an Other. These punishable individuals represent an ambiguous underclass believed capable of undermining the accepted order of society. Arrest and torture, she says, stigmatize people and mark them as people no one would want to be. Arrest and torture provide a way to symbolically mark, discipline, and stigmatize categories of people whose existence or demands threaten the idea, power, and legitimacy of the nation-state. Because torture and violence are committed only against "terrorists," "communists," or "separatists," these methods become legitimate. "We only beat bad people," said a Turkish prison official in 1984. "They are no good, they are worthless bums, they are subversives who think that communism will relieve them of the necessity of working." He described with apparent pride the order that he had given that "all prisoners should be struck with a truncheon below the waist on the rude parts, and warned not to come to prison again." "My aim," he said, "is to ensure discipline. That's not torture, for it is only the lazy, the idle, the vagabonds, the communists, the murderers who come to prison" (Nagengast 1994: 121).

One of the most recent instances of state violence against its own citizens occurred on the island of Timor on the southern edge of Indonesia. East Timor had been colonized by the Dutch and the Portuguese and was granted its independence by the Portuguese in 1975. Five days after a state visit by then U.S. Vice-President Gerald Ford and

ethnocide
The attempt to destroy the culture of a people.

genocide
The attempt to exterminate a people.

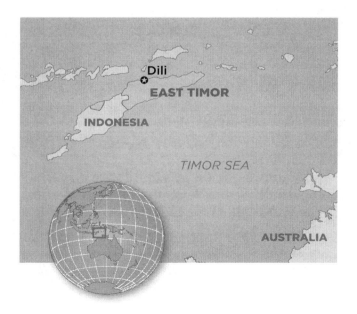

THE CULTURAL CONSTRUCTION OF CONFLICT AND VIOLENCE

Secretary of State Henry Kissinger, Indonesia invaded East Timor. Over the following two decades, Indonesians, especially members and friends of the ruling family, invested millions of dollars in various enterprises there. And, as many other countries have done, Indonesia embarked on a campaign of violence and terror in its attempt to integrate the East Timorese into the Indonesian nation-state.

Indonesian anthropologist George Aditjondro, who faced an indefinite jail term for criticizing Indonesian leaders, described the campaign of terror, violence, and torture embarked on by the Indonesian state against its most recent citizens. It included, among other things, a "pacification war" that lasted from 1975 to 1979 and repression that continued even after a 1999 UN-sponsored referendum in which 80 percent of the population voted for independence from Indonesia. Torture, says Aditjondro, was a standard method of subjugation. Techniques included physical beatings, the use of cigarette butts to burn holes in the skin, electric shock, crushing victims' hands and feet with chair or table legs, poking the victim's mouth with bamboo sticks, inflicting pain on the genitals (including raping females), and immersing victims in metal tanks filled with water charged with electricity. Torture was used for five reasons, according to Aditjondro. First, to obtain information from victims. Second, to crush the fighting spirit of freedom fighters. Third, to weaken the political power of the Catholic Church by obtaining "confessions" of church complicity in pro-independence politics or in sacrilegious or criminal acts. Fourth, to protect the business interests of Indonesians in East Timor. And finally, to minimize critical press reports from East Timorese newspapers.

But torture was not the only technique of state terror used by Indonesia. There was, for example, physical terror, including mass killings of guerrillas along with women and children that took place during the first decade of the Indonesian occupation. Some 200,000 people—around one-third of the population—were killed or died of deprivations brought about by the terror. Prisoners were thrown to their death from helicopters; people were killed by napalm bombings that also destroyed crops, and thousands died from resulting famines. Many people died in overcrowded prison barracks, some of which were covered with black canvas to turn them into human ovens.

Then there was a campaign to "depurify," as Aditjondro calls it, the bodies of Indonesian women through rape and forced fertility control. Rape was often committed against the wives or daughters of men suspected of being involved with the resistance. In other cases, rape was committed against women who failed to produce identity cards or who refused to accompany or submit to the sexual demands of soldiers. Other women were forced to spy on resistance forces while serving as sex slaves of Indonesian troops. In still other cases, East Indonesian women were forced into brothels for use by Indonesian troops. Rape, says Aditjandro, was also a way to destroy the East Timorese resistance by biologically depurifying their ethnic constituency.

Another way to biologically depurify the population was through forced contraception. Family planning programs were used as means to discipline the population; they symbolically represented state control over human bodies. Thus high school girls were injected with Depo-Provera, a birth control drug, without being told of its function.

Other forms of symbolic violence included erecting pro-Indonesian monuments and forcing citizens to participate in Indonesian political rituals (flag raisings, parades, and parties), subjecting them to arrest, interrogation, and physical torture if they resisted. Language itself was modified, with new linguistic expressions for torture and execution becoming common. *Jalan-jalan ke Jakarta* ("taking a trip to Jakarta") and *Berangkat studi lanjut ke Jawa* ("going for further study in Java") were euphemisms for executions. *Mani laut* ("taking a sea bath") referred to the practice of weighting the bodies of people with rocks and dumping them

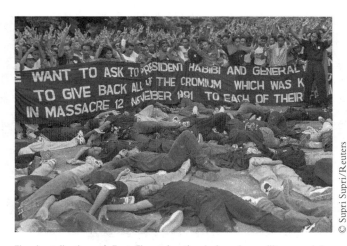

The brutalization of East Timor by the Indonesian military and by Indonesian-supported militia from 1975 to 1999 is but one example of how nation-states use force to control their citizens. Here, East Timorese youth are staging a drama portraying the killings of some 271 unarmed protesters by Indonesian troops at the Santa Cruz cemetery on November 12, 1991.

from a helicopter into the sea. *De-Santa Cruz-kan* ("Santa Cruz-ified") was an expression used by mothers to threaten their children with the sinister connotations of a notorious massacre of Indonesian high school students in 1991 who were protesting Indonesian occupation. Finally, 200,000 people were taken from East Timor and relocated to other parts of Indonesia.

Many East Timorese became **refugees**—forced to flee their home country to seek protection in another. Refugees living in **diaspora**—that is, dispersed and living outside their homeland—escape direct violence and harm; however, the effects of living through sustained, everyday violence are long lasting. Amanda Wise (2006) conducted fieldwork with the refugee diaspora in Sydney, Australia. She found that the experience of shared violence and trauma was a key element in the collective identity of the refugees, who came together to create what she called a "community of suffering." The embodied memories of pain and suffering drew the community together. The Indonesian military inflicted violence on the East Timorese, and "such practices symbolically and affectively bind the pain of the individual to the fate of the ethnic collectivity." The shared memory and common suffering became the foundation of solidarity among her informants (2006, 15).

East Timor finally regained its independence from Indonesia in 1999 after a UN–sponsored referendum in which 80 percent of the population voted for independence. But before they withdrew from East Timor in September 1999, the Indonesian military and military-trained and -supported militias laid waste to virtually the entire country, killing thousands of people and driving 200,000 people out of East Timor and into Indonesia, where many remain under the control of fleeing militia members. For Wise's informants, living in exile in Australia, independence opened up the possibility of a return to their homeland. But many of them, having spent so many years in Australia, had mixed feelings about where they belonged. They had developed a sense of identity based on collective suffering. An exiled journalist described these mixed feelings: "Perhaps the worst condemnation of all is to watch our country recede from our reach like a foreign, distant, indecipherable tide and to witness how indecisively our bodies begin to seek stability after many precarious years; our bodies, unconsenting and perhaps irremediably, grow accustomed to a country which they did not choose of their free will" (in Wise 2006, 163).

Canada's part in the tragedy of the East Timorese is documented in the video *Bitter Paradise: The Sellout of East Timor,* by Elaine Brière. Probably the last tourist to visit East Timor while it was still a peaceful, welcoming society in 1974,

refugees
Groups of people who have been forced from their homeland due to warfare, forced expulsion, acts of terrorism, or other factors.

diaspora
A population whose members are dispersed and living outside of their homeland.

THE CULTURAL CONSTRUCTION OF CONFLICT AND VIOLENCE

Brière dedicated her life to making the genocide public. The video followed Brière's journey into the business world, where she was told that Canadians who were commercially involved in Indonesia did not know about the genocide or believed that it was an exaggeration; to the world of the media, where she was told by the host of a talk show that Canadians didn't "connect" with the killing of East Timorese; and to Ottawa, where her questions were completely ignored by the External Affairs Minister. Canada continued to give enormous amounts of economic aid to the Suharto regime in spite of the killings and in spite of cutbacks in social programs at home, and Canadian businesses, such as Inco and Bre-X, continued to see Indonesia as a haven for international investment.

The tactics used by Indonesia to subdue people who resisted integration into the Indonesian nation-state are not unique. In fact, virtually all these tactics have been used by most, if not all, nation-states at one time or another. You can get some idea of how nation-states today sponsor violence against their citizens by going to the Internet, where information is readily available from organizations such as Amnesty International and Human Rights Watch.

EXERCISE 8.4

Protesting the Genocide in East Timor

Many Canadian students protested Canada's continued financial support of Indonesia with international aid. What do you think would have happened to Canada's ability to do business in Indonesia if Canada had stopped the aid? Do you think Canadian businesses should have continued to operate in Indonesia in spite of the genocide? Do you thank that if Canada had taken a stand against the genocide (stopped the aid, withdrawn all businesses), the rest of the world would have followed?

QUESTION 8.5: HOW IS IT POSSIBLE TO JUSTIFY THE CONSTRUCTION OF WEAPONS OF MASS DESTRUCTION?

Anthropologist Hugh Gusterson, who had been an antinuclear activist, wanted to know how nuclear weapons scientists could justify conducting research on and testing of weapons of mass destruction. What could create a world view that enabled people to justify performing that kind of work? To answer that question, he set out to study the culture of the Lawrence Livermore National Laboratory in Livermore, California.

Gusterson (1995) suggests that those who justify nuclear weapons and who question nuclear disarmament make four assumptions about the world. First, they claim that anarchy characterizes international relations. Second, they assume that states must rely on self-help since no one else is going to offer them protection. Third, they assume that nuclear weapons are the ultimate form of self-help, because they vastly increase the cost of aggression against them. And fourth, they assume that relatively little can be done in the short term to change the anarchistic nature of the international system.

Critics of nuclear weapons make very different assumptions. They argue that international relations are not as anarchistic as they are made out to be and that rules and norms that control aggression exist. Many critics see the nuclear arms race as "objective social madness." People who work in the area, they assume, must be in denial and must demonize the Other to justify their work.

Gusterson wanted to find out not so much who was "right," but rather how people came to hold such divergent opinions. When he began his research, he was surprised by the variety of political and religious viewpoints of people working at

Livermore. Political views ran the gamut from conservatives to active environmentalists, civil rights supporters, and women's rights advocates. How, he asked, could such a diverse population all agree on the value of nuclear weapons development, an agreement so profound that "they often asked me in puzzlement to explain why antinuclear activists were so afraid of nuclear weapons"?

Nuclear weapons scientists did not, says Gusterson, avoid the ethical concerns of their research. Most, however, accepted the central axiom that nuclear research is necessary to make the world safe. To some, working on nuclear weapons was more ethical than working on conventional weapons, since conventional weapons were more likely to be used. Nuclear weapons, the scientists assumed, were simply symbolic chips in a game, the goal of which was to avoid using them. When asked if he could ever foresee a circumstance in which nuclear weapons would be used, one scientist said, "No, even if we were under attack." In other words, deterrence was the only reason to develop nuclear weapons; if you were attacked, the whole enterprise had failed. Others rationalized their work more baldly, saying they were not responsible for how what they designed would be used. "Are automobile designers," they ask, "responsible for deaths caused by drunk drivers?"

When Gusterson asked people why they chose to work at Livermore, most cited the intellectual freedom they enjoyed working in a weapons laboratory. Almost all compared Livermore favourably to working in universities (which they characterized as "stodgy," "cutthroat," or "high-pressure") or in private organizations. Some also cited the challenges of weapons research and the opportunity to work with state-of-the-art equipment. Also, Livermore paid about twice as much as a university position.

Once a person was hired, secrecy played a major role in forging a person's identity. Livermore employees were investigated before being given security clearance to laboratory facilities. Personnel were divided into different security categories and given coloured badges indicating their level of clearance. "Q" clearance (a green badge) was necessary for classified research; "L" clearance (yellow badge) allowed access to classified areas but not to classified information. The labs themselves were divided into areas of lesser and greater security. As Gusterson put it, the laboratory was "an enormous grid of tabooed spaces and tabooed topics."

Without a green badge, a weapons scientist was not considered a full adult in the lab. The process of getting "Q" clearance was elaborate and could take six months to two years. Virtually every aspect of a person's life was subject to investigation in search of clues that he or she was unfit to handle classified material. But most people passed, and because secrecy was not that well guarded in practice, the security clearance process functioned mostly as a rite of passage that added to the mystique of weapons research and that disciplined the initiate.

Secrecy was one of the principal ways that the lab's diverse population was brought together. Knowing secrets, regardless of how mundane they might be, marked a person as a member of a special group and lent an air of drama and importance to one's work. Secrecy also served to limit discussion that could change a person's view of the work that they were doing. As Gusterson put it, "the laboratory's culture of secrecy does tend to produce certain effects in its scientists: it segregates laboratory scientists as a privileged but somewhat isolated elite; it inculcates a sense of group loyalty; and it thrusts on laboratory scientists an amorphous surveillance, which can become internalized" (1995, 68).

The process of testing nuclear weapons was in many ways the critical step in creating the nuclear scientist. Any Livermore scientist could propose a weapons test, but reviewers (senior scientists at the laboratory) selected only about one out of twenty ideas for testing. Approval of an idea for testing reaffirmed the scientist's membership in the group. Nuclear tests had elements of myth and ritual. Rarely in the narratives that Gusterson collected on testing did anyone note the importance of testing nuclear reliability. Instead, people spoke of the fulfillment of personal ambition, the struggle to master a new technology, the drama of creating something new, and the experience of community that each test created.

Testing produced not only weapons but also weapon designers. It was a way of producing the elite. The more tests one participated in, the greater the prestige and power that accrued. A successful test validated status and credentials and brought forth congratulatory support and reinforcement. Test provided a symbolic simulation of the reliability of the entire system of deterrence: "Each time a nuclear test is successfully carried off, the scientists' faith in human control over nuclear technology is further reinforced. Seen in this light, the 'reliability' the tests demonstrate has an expandable meaning, extending out from the reliability of the particular device being tested to the entire regime of nuclear deterrence" (1995, 161).

The Language of Nuclear Destruction

Carol Cohn (1987, 1991) spent one year studying the culture of a strategic studies institute, or "think tank," for government defence analysts who plan nuclear strategy. She began her study with this question: How are people whose job it is to plan nuclear destruction able to do it? One of her conclusions was that the planners used language to distance themselves from the consequences of the actions they were planning. The language they used obfuscated and reassembled reality in such a way that what was really being talked about—the destruction of human lives—was hidden behind metaphors and euphemisms.

During her first weeks at the centre, as she listened to the participants talking matter-of-factly about nuclear destruction, she heard language that she labelled *technostrategic*. This language included terms such as *clean bombs* (fusion bombs, which release more energy than fission bombs), *penetration aids* (technologies that help missiles get through enemy defences), *collateral damage* (human

deaths), and *surgical strikes* (bombing that takes out only military targets). Domestic metaphors were common in the technostrategic language: missiles were based in *silos*, piles of nuclear weapons in a submarine were *Christmas tree farms*, bombs and missiles were *re-entry vehicles* or *RVs*, and massive bombing was *carpet bombing*. According to Cohn, the domestic images were more than a way for people to distance themselves from the grisly reality they were discussing. Calling the pattern in which a bomb would fall a footprint removed the speakers from any position of accountability for the acts they were contemplating.

Cohn also discovered that the language and metaphors of those working at the institute seemed incapable of expressing certain realities. The aftermath of a nuclear attack was described in technostrategic language as "a situation bound to include EMP blackout, brute force damage to systems, a heavy jamming environment, and so on" (1987, 707). She contrasted this with eyewitness accounts of the bombing of Hiroshima (see the photo and description above). There was, Cohn wrote, no way of describing this experience in technostrategic language. It removed the speakers

This sketch of the effects of the U.S. bombing of Hiroshima was drawn by eyewitness Sawami Katagiri, who recalled, "I was walking among many dead people ... It was like hell ... This picture shows only a part of Hiroshima. The whole city was just like this at that time." Sawami Katagiri, from *The Unforgettable Fire*, NHK Publishing (Japan Broadcast Publishing Co., Ltd.).

from having to think about themselves as victims of nuclear war.

Cohn also discovered that she could not use ordinary language to speak to the defence analysts. When she tried, they acted as if she were ignorant or simpleminded. To communicate at all, she had to use terms like *subholocaust engagement* and *pre-emptive strike*. The word *peace* was not a legitimate part of the vocabulary; to use it was to brand oneself as a softheaded activist. The closest she could come to *peace* in the language of technostrategic was *strategic stability*.

Cohn encountered descriptions of nuclear situations that made little sense until she realized that different realities were being discussed. For example, the following passage describes a nuclear exchange in a situation in which missiles with more than one warhead are mutually banned: "The strategic stability of regime A (a scenario) is based on the fact that both sides are deprived of any incentive ever to strike first. Since it takes roughly two warheads to destroy the enemy silo, an attacker must expend two of his missiles to destroy one of the enemy's. A first strike disarms the attacker. The aggressor ends up worse off than the aggressed" (1987, 710).

By what type of reasoning, asked Cohn, could a country that had dropped a thousand nuclear bombs ten to one hundred times more powerful than the one dropped on Hiroshima end up "worse off" than the country it dropped the bombs on? This would be possible only if winning depended on who had the greatest number of weapons left.

To an anthropologist, the fact that people are limited by their culture, their language, and their point of view is, of course, no surprise. All cultures give a characteristic meaning to violent conflict, whether it is viewed as the act of an animal in possession of a human body, or as the will of God, or as a game. The more serious implication of Cohn's observations is that scientists, academics, and nuclear planners give weight to their claim that their perspective is "objective" and therefore has greater truth value than other perspectives.

Moreover, says Cohn, if one can speak to defence analysts only in the language of technostrategic, and if the language is constructed in such a way as to be incapable of expressing different realities, then there is no way for these analysts to appreciate or understand the other realities involved in the use of nuclear weapons.

QUESTION 8.6: HOW DO ANTHROPOLOGISTS DO FIELDWORK IN THE MIDST OF VIOLENT CONFLICT?

As often as possible, anthropologists try to learn about and understand various social and cultural phenomena through fieldwork and participant observation. However, attempting to understand violent conflict first-hand can be difficult at best and dangerous at worst. Often it is contentious as well. Should anthropologist place themselves in danger in the name of fieldwork? What if, through our very presence, we put others at risk or promote the conditions for further violence? Can we use ethnography to understand war from a soldier's perspective? Below, we discuss three different examples of the possibilities and pitfalls of studying violence and conflict, either directly or indirectly.

The Endangered Anthropologist

The risk of injury, disease, or hostile reactions has always been a feature of anthropological fieldwork. As anthropologists increasingly work in areas where human rights violations are common, these risks are intensified. At least four anthropologists have been murdered because of their fieldwork: In 1982, South African anthropologist and anti-apartheid activist Ruth First was killed by a mail bomb in her office at Maputo University in Mozambique. In 1984, Melanesian anthropologist Arnold Ap was tortured and killed by the Indonesian army, his body dumped by helicopter into the sea. In 1989, South African anthropologist David Webster was shot and killed by members of a pro-apartheid death squad. And in 1990, Guatemalan anthropologist Myrna Mack was stabbed to death by a soldier, ostensibly for her work with Mayan refugees and their experiences in the government's counterinsurgency war of the early 1980s, which killed hundreds of thousands of people. In addition, at least two anthropologists, Ricardo Falla and George Aditjondro, are in exile and under threat of assassination because of their work. These real dangers that anthropologists face may provide insights into how the people with whom they are working experience the threat of violence.

In 1989 and 1990, Linda Green was doing fieldwork in the Guatemalan community of Xe'caj. Like many similar communities, Xe'caj was only beginning to recover from some 35 years of violence. Beginning with a military coup orchestrated largely by the CIA against a democratically elected government in 1954, Guatemala experienced regular violence as the militarized state tried to suppress attempts to overthrow the military regime. Hundreds of thousands of Guatemalans were killed, mostly by the government, in an attempt to suppress the revolt. The late 1970s and early 1980s were particularly brutal as the government embarked on a campaign to destroy peasant villages and relocate people to government-controlled towns. In addition, paramilitary groups, largely supplied and supported by the regular military, embarked on campaigns of terror and torture in an attempt to control the peasant population.

The people of Xe'caj lived in a state of constant surveillance from the military encampment located above the town. Many of the residents had husbands, fathers, or sons taken away by the military. There were rumours of death lists. People had difficulty sleeping and reported nightmares of recurring death and violence. Soon, said Green, "I, too, started to experience nighttime hysteria, dreams of death, disappearances, and torture."

Green interviewed women who had been widowed by the conflict. Without prompting, the women recounted in vivid detail their stories of horror, the deaths and disappearances of husbands, fathers, sons, and brothers, as if they had happened last week or month rather than six to eight years ago.

Then one day when Green arrived to continue the interviews, the women were anxious and agitated. When she asked what had happened, they told her that the military commissioner was looking for her and that people were saying she was helping the widows and talking against other people in the community. When Green told the women she was going to go and see the commissioner, they pleaded with her not to do so, telling her that they knew of people who had gone to the military garrison and never returned. Green decided to visit the garrison alone, and that visit would provide a vivid experience of the fears confronted by the villagers. As she approached the garrison,

> I saw several soldiers sitting in a small guardhouse with a machine gun perched on a three-foot stanchion pointed downward and directly at me. The plight of Joseph K. in Kafka's *Trial* flashed through my mind, he accused of a crime for which he must defend himself but about which he could get no information. I didn't do anything wrong, I must not look guilty, I repeated to myself like a mantra. I must calm myself, as my stomach churned, my nerves frayed. I arrived breathless and terrified. Immediately I knew I was guilty because I was against the system of violence and terror that surrounded me. (1995, 116)

Fortunately the *commandante* said he knew nothing about why she was being harassed. He assured her that she could continue with her work, and everything went smoothly from there. But Green had gained a fuller understanding of the experiences of people who must live under the constant threat of violence.

Is There a Place for Anthropology/Military Collaborations?

In 2005, Montgomery McFate, a military adviser with a background in anthropology, published an article in *Military Review* arguing that there was a "culture gap" in our understanding of the conflict in Iraq caused by "the almost total absence of anthropology within the national-security establishment." She argued that successful counterinsurgency requires a total understanding of local culture. To achieve victory, the United States needed to understand Iraq's traditional authority structure and the competing interests of different groups such as the Shia, Sunni, and Kurds. In a second article, co-written with Andrea Jackson, McFate outlined a proposal to establish an "Office for Operational Cultural Knowledge," which would train teams to provide battlefield commanders with knowledge of local culture, or as it was being called, the "human terrain."

The need for cultural knowledge was echoed by retired Major General Robert H. Scales, Jr., who argued that these new conflicts required not technological superiority but "an exceptional ability to understand people, their culture, and their motivation."

One outcome of this interest in cultural knowledge was the development of Human Terrain Systems (HTSs). The centrepiece of the program was Human Terrain Teams (HTTs), each of which had a staff of five: an army officer serving as team leader, a cultural analyst, a regional studies analyst, a Human Terrain (HT) research manager, and an HT analyst. Each team studied the local culture, interviewed local people, and provided valuable information to the battalion commander. In 2008 the Canadian Forces began a similar program of "white situational awareness teams" (WSAT). In military terminology, white refers to the civilian population (as opposed to the "red" and "blue" of enemy and friendly forces, respectively). Each

WSAT team included two military intelligence officers and three civilian Department of Foreign Affairs employees, and aimed to provide a more nuanced understanding of the cultural terrain for military leaders and advisers (Fenton 2010).

Anthropologists who joined the HTS project explained their service as an attempt to do something meaningful. Marcus Griffin wrote: "I have an obligation to use my skills to learn about people and to share what I learn." Working as a member of an HTT in Iraq, Griffin saw his job as finding out what Iraqis needed and helping them meet those needs.

Not everyone, however, shared this positive assessment of HTS. The American Anthropological Association issued a formal statement in 2007 condemning the project, arguing that it would lead anthropologists to violate ethical standards and that it posed a danger to both anthropologists and the people they were studying. Another notable critic, Roberto Gonzales, pointed out a number of dangers of HTS. First, was it possible for informants to *consent* to their participation? Second, what type of information was being gathered by anthropologists, and how would it be used? Third, how well would informants be protected from retaliation from hostile groups or political

U.S. Army photo by SSG Michael Castell

A U.S. soldier takes notes as he talks and drinks tea with local Andar District Special Needs School administrators during a cordon and search of Nani, Afghanistan, in June, 2007. Can anthropological expertise be put to (good) use in a war zone?

rivals? Maximillian Forte, an anthropologist at Concordia University, also expressed concerns about HTS, WSAT, and the potential militarization of anthropology in general: "Their [WSATs'] job seems to be no different from that of HTS, except that for now the civilians they use are government employees, not academics. They have breached a barrier however: the idea that social and cultural knowledge can be useful for counterinsurgency, at least that door has now been opened in Canada" (in Fenton 2010).

What bothers many critics of HTS is that regardless of the efforts of the military and others to put a humanitarian face on the contributions of social scientists, the information gathered by HTTs is clearly going to be used for military purposes. HTS advocates want to make whatever information is gathered available to other agencies and to the governments of Iraq and Afghanistan, to "enable them to more fully exercise sovereignty over their country" (Gonzalez 2009, 74). This reminds many anthropologists of the disastrous CORDS program, implemented during the Vietnam War. Like HTS, CORDS was designed to gather cultural knowledge in order to win "hearts and minds." Using information from social scientists, military personnel exploited Vietnamese superstitions and religious beliefs to frighten and terrorize civilians. When CORDS data were given to the South Vietnamese government, they were used to target political opponents and dissidents. What precautions are being taken to ensure that the Iraqi and Afghan governments do not use HTT information to target political rivals or to create blacklists for personal vendettas?

The use of social scientists for HTTs in Iraq and Afghanistan raises a larger issue: the responsibility of anthropologists and other social scientists to be aware of how their data may be used. The Pentagon, for example, is using information collected by social scientists to help identify dangerous neighbourhoods in Baghdad and Kabul. This allows the military to predict which neighbourhoods are at risk for riots, gun violence, or bombings; it also helps them develop lists of possible participants and their relatives, friends, and associates.

Perhaps more ominous, the military is awarding grants to social scientists to forecast human behaviour. The U.S. Department of Defense is developing a project called Human Social and Culture Behavior Modeling (HSCB). Much of this work will be contracted out to private corporations eager to secure lucrative government contracts. One corporation, Aptima, in conjunction with Carnegie Mellon University, has developed "Social Network Analysis" (SNA) software. SNA has been used by the U.S. military "to predict a state's potential for instability or civil unrest in terms of nine key factors," which range from "lack of essential services" to "corruption level" to "tension."

One danger, of course, is that the philosophy of HTS, and the development of elaborate surveillance technologies using vast quantities of information now available on citizens, will move from military applications in places such as Iraq and Afghanistan to domestic uses that seriously undermine democratic freedoms. Gonzalez concludes his critique of HTS as follows:

What comes across from the accounts of many social scientists supporting counterinsurgency initiatives in Iraq and Afghanistan is a fundamental acceptance of modern warfare in general and the U.S.-led occupations in particular. Furthermore, they generally accept the false notion that counterinsurgency—the "graduate level of war" to quote one military enthusiast—is more antiseptic, more humane, less damaging than conventional warfare. As technicians of power, some adhere to Machiavellian principles: do not question the prince or his war, but instead use the most efficient means to help him achieve victory. War's inevitability is taken for granted. Basic assumptions are left unquestioned. Missing from these accounts is the question of whether war is appropriate at all today. (2009, 123–24)

Making Sense of Combat: Canadian Soldiers in Kandahar

Throughout this chapter, we have explored the ways in which people in various societies and cultures make sense of violent conflict. As we have seen, language and ritual are both employed, quite successfully, to make nuclear proliferation and the subsequent possibility of mass destruction seem both feasible and meaningful. As noted at the outset of the chapter, until recently, pride in peacekeeping was a key part of Canadian national identity. For the first time since the Korean War, however, Canada now has soldiers in active combat (in Afghanistan). In her work with Canadian Forces soldiers stationed in Kandahar, Anne Irwin analyzed the ways in which they use storytelling and ritual to make sense of their experiences in combat.

A former member of the Canadian Forces herself, Irwin spent many years studying Canadian soldiers, both while they trained for peacekeeping operations (Irwin 2002) and, more recently, with a unit that would undertake "full-spectrum operations," including combat (2012, 61). Irwin spent several months with the unit during its tour in 2006, living with them both at Kandahar's air force base and "outside the wire," on patrol and in combat. Irwin found that whereas time and routine on the base were quite structured, time outside the wire was completely disrupted—"there was no day-to-day routine for sleeping and eating, not even predictable shifts" (64). Even when there was no engagement—"troops in contact," in military parlance—the soldiers experienced all time outside the wire as being in combat, not least because of the omnipresent danger of IEDs (improvised explosive devices). Soldiers who spent time outside the wire together seemed to go through a rite of passage, and shared a liminal period together during combat (69). However, Irwin is reluctant to cast combat as a rite of passage that turns boys into men. Indeed, she argues that although combat has some of the elements of a rite of passage, soldiers who return to Canada seem to be both permanent adolescents (referring to themselves and their fellow soldiers as "the boys") and, at the same time, old men: prematurely aged, grief stricken, and often scarred or disabled (76).

Irwin has also collected and analyzed soldier's narratives about the war in Afghanistan. Often these address and link individual morality to social and political debates about Canada's combat role. One soldier, in telling the story of his experiences, said that "a lot of people in Canada think that we should not be here in Afghanistan, but those people don't see the remarkable changes happening here. One interpreter told me, 'Because Canada is here, our people are happy again.' So to all those Canadians who continue to harp about what they don't know—here's your straw, suck it up" (Cpl Sanders, in Pengelly and Irwin 2011, 52).

Here, the soldier has turned his combat experience into a morality tale, one that takes the qualities of a good solider—responsible, tough, and uncomplaining—and transposes them onto the Canadian public. Moreover, he is attempting to show the moral justness of the war by drawing on "the moral character of a helpful and caring Canada" (2011, 53). By examining these kinds of narratives, we can see how their circulation helps soldiers understand and justify their participation in this violent conflict. Moreover, when such combat narratives draw on a sense of national identity and pride, of Canada as "helpful and caring," we can begin to make sense of the rather rapid (though contested) shift, at the turn of the 21st century, of Canada's role from peacekeeper to warrior nation.

Systems of Political Organization

The term **political organization** refers to the way power is accumulated, arranged, executed, and structurally embedded in society, whether in organizing a whale hunt, managing irrigated farmlands, collecting taxes, or raising a military force. In short, it is the means through which a society creates and maintains social order. It assumes a variety of forms among the peoples of the world, but anthropologists have simplified this complex subject by identifying four basic kinds of political systems: bands, tribes, chiefdoms, and states (**Figure 12.1**). The first two are uncentralized systems; the latter two are centralized.

Uncentralized Political Systems

Until recently, many non-Western peoples have had neither chiefs with established rights and duties nor any fixed form of government, as those who live in modern states understand the term. Instead, marriage and kinship have formed their principal means of social organization. The economies of these societies are primarily of a subsistence type, and populations are typically small.

Leaders do not have real power to force compliance with the society's customs or rules, but if individuals do not conform, they may become targets of scorn and gossip or even be banished. Important decisions are usually made in a collective manner by agreement among adults. Dissenting members may decide to act with

TYPES OF POLITICAL ORGANIZATION

The symbol ➔ indicates that the attribute varies between less and more complex societies of that type.

	BAND	TRIBE	CHIEFDOM	STATE
MEMBERSHIP				
Number of people	Dozens and up	Hundreds and up	Thousands and up	Tens of thousands and up
Settlement pattern	Mobile	Mobile or fixed: 1 or more villages	Fixed: 2 or more villages	Fixed: Many villages and cities
Basis of relationships	Kin	Kin, descent groups	Kin, rank, and residence	Class and residence
Ethnicities and languages	1	1	1	1 or more
GOVERNMENT				
Decision making, leadership	Egalitarian	Egalitarian or Big Man	Centralized, hereditary	Centralized
Bureaucracy	None	None	None, or 1 or 2 levels	Many levels
Monopoly of force and information	No	No	No ➔ Yes	Yes
Conflict resolution	Informal	Informal	Centralized	Laws, judges
Hierarchy of settlement	No	No	No ➔ Paramount village or head town	Capital
ECONOMY				
Food production	No	No ➔ Yes	Yes ➔ Intensive	Intensive
Labor specialization	No	No	No ➔ Yes	Yes
Exchanges	Reciprocal	Reciprocal	Redistributive (tribute)	Redistributive (taxes)
Control of land	Band	Descent group	Chief	Various
SOCIETY				
Stratified	No	No	Yes, ranked by kin	Yes, by class or caste
Slavery	No	No	Some, small-scale	Some, large-scale
Luxury goods for elite	No	No	Yes	Yes
Public architecture	No	No	No ➔ Yes	Yes
Indigenous literacy	No	No	No ➔ Some	Often

© Cengage Learning

Figure 12.1 Four Types of Political Systems This figure outlines the four basic types of political systems: bands, tribes, chiefdoms, and states. Bands and tribes are uncentralized political organizations; chiefdoms and states are centralized.

the majority, or they may choose to adopt some other course of action, including leaving the group.

This egalitarian form of political organization provides great flexibility, which in many situations offers an adaptive advantage. Because power in these kin-ordered communities is shared, with nobody exercising exclusive control over collective resources or public affairs, individuals typically enjoy much more freedom than those who are part of larger and more complex political systems.

Bands

The **band** is a relatively small and loosely organized kin-ordered group that inhabits a common territory and that may split periodically into smaller family groups that are politically and economically independent. Typically, bands are found among food foragers and other small-scale migratory communities in which people organize into politically autonomous extended family groups that usually camp together as long as environmental and subsistence circumstances are favorable. Bands periodically break up into smaller groups to forage for food or visit other relatives. The band is the oldest form of political organization because all humans were once food foragers and remained so until the development of farming and pastoralism over the past 10,000 years.

Given their foraging mode of subsistence, band population densities are usually less than one person per square mile. Because bands are egalitarian and small, numbering at most a few hundred people, there is no real need for formal, centralized political systems. Everyone is related to—and knows on a personal basis—everyone else with whom dealings are required, so there is high value placed on getting along. Conflicts that do arise are usually settled informally through gossip, ridicule, direct negotiation, or mediation. When negotiation or mediation is used, the focus is on reaching a solution considered fair by all concerned parties, rather than on conforming to some abstract law or rule.

Decisions affecting a band are made with the participation of all its adult members, with an emphasis on achieving consensus—a collective agreement—rather than a simple majority. Individuals become leaders by virtue of their abilities and serve in that capacity only as long as they retain the confidence of the community. They cannot coerce others to abide by their decisions. A leader who exceeds what people are willing to accept quickly loses followers.

An example of the informal nature of band leadership is found among the Ju/'hoansi Bushmen of the Kalahari Desert, mentioned in earlier chapters. Each Ju/'hoansi band is composed of a group of families that live together, linked through kinship ties to one another and to the headman (or, less often, headwoman). The head, called the *kxau*, or "owner," is the focal point for the band's claims on the territory through which it traditionally

Figure 12.2 Band Leadership Toma Tsamkxao was the headman of a Ju/'hoansi band. Lightly armed, he led his migratory community of hunters and gatherers in the Kalahari Desert. They ranged the region freely much as their ancestors did for almost 40,000 years. About half a century ago, outsiders imposed radical changes on Bushmen bands. Some, guided by wise leaders like Tsamkxao, survived the upheaval and now subsist on a mix of livestock and crop farming, crafts and tourism, and some traditional foraging.

ranges as a migratory community (**Figure 12.2**). He or she does not personally own the land and natural resources but symbolically represents the ancestral rights of band members to them. If the head leaves the area to live elsewhere, people turn to someone else to lead them.

When local resources are no longer adequate to sustain a band, the leader coordinates and leads the move, selecting the new campsite. Except for the privilege of having first choice of a spot for his or her own fire, the leader of the band has few unique rewards or duties. For example, a Ju/'hoansi head is not a judge and does not punish other band members. Troublemakers and wrongdoers are judged and held accountable by public opinion, usually expressed by gossip, which can play an important role in curbing socially unacceptable behavior.

Through gossip—talking behind someone's back and spreading rumors about behavior considered disruptive, shameful, or ridiculous—people accomplish several

political organization The way power, as the capacity to do something, is accumulated, arranged, executed, and structurally embedded in society; the means through which a society creates and maintains social order and reduces social disorder.

band A relatively small and loosely organized kin-ordered group that inhabits a specific territory and that may split periodically into smaller extended family groups that are politically and economically independent.

objectives while avoiding the potential disruption of open confrontation. First, gossip underscores and reinforces the cultural standards of those who abide by the unwritten rules of proper conduct. At the same time, the gossip discredits those who violate standards of socially acceptable behavior. Furthermore, because gossip can damage a person's reputation and is often fueled by hidden jealousy or a secret desire to retaliate against someone considered too accomplished or successful, it may function as a leveling mechanism to reduce a real or perceived threat of an individual becoming too dominant.

Another prime technique in small-scale societies for resolving disputes, or even avoiding them in the first place, is mobility. Those unable to get along with others of their group may feel pressured to move to a different group in which existing kinship ties give them rights of entry.

Tribes

The second type of uncentralized authority system is the tribe. In anthropology, the term **tribe** refers to a wide range of kin-ordered groups that are politically integrated by some unifying factor and whose members share a common ancestry, identity, culture, language, and territory.

Typically, a tribe has an economy based on some form of crop cultivation or livestock raising. Tribes develop when a number of culturally related bands come together, peacefully settle disputes, participate in periodic visiting and communal feasting, and intermarry for purposes of economic exchange and/or collective self-defense against common enemies. For this reason, tribal membership is usually larger than band membership. Moreover, tribal population densities generally far exceed that of migratory bands and may be as high as 250 people per square mile. Greater population density introduces a new set of problems, as opportunities for bickering, begging, adultery, and theft increase markedly, especially among people living in permanent villages.

Each tribe consists of one or more self-supporting and self-governing local community (including smaller kin-groups earlier discussed as bands) that may then form alliances with others for various purposes. As in the band, political organization in the tribe is informal and temporary. Whenever a situation requiring political integration of all or several groups within the tribe arises—perhaps for defense, to carry out a raid, to pool resources in times of scarcity, or to capitalize on a windfall that must be distributed quickly before it spoils—groups come together to deal with the situation in a cooperative manner. When the problem is satisfactorily solved, each group then resumes autonomy.

In many tribal societies, the organizing unit and seat of political authority is the clan, composed of people who consider themselves descended from a common ancestor. Within the clan, elders or headmen and/or headwomen regulate members' affairs and represent their clan in interactions with other clans. As a group, the elders of all the clans may form a council that acts within the community or for the community in dealings with outsiders. Because clan members usually do not all live together in a single community, clan organization facilitates joint action with members of related communities when necessary.

Leadership in tribal societies is also relatively informal, as is evident in a wide array of past and present examples. Among these is the Big Man common in Melanesia, including New Guinea and other islands in the South Pacific. Heading up localized descent groups or a territorial group, the Big Man combines a measure of interest in his community's welfare with a great deal of cunning and calculation for his own personal gain. His power is personal, for he holds no political office in any formal sense, nor is he elected. His prestige as a political leader is the result of strategic acts that raise him above most other tribe members and that attract loyal followers who benefit from or depend on his success.

The Kapauku in the west central highlands of New Guinea typify this form of political organization. Among these Papua, the Big Man is called the *tonowi* ("rich one"). To achieve this status, one must be male, wealthy, generous, and eloquent. Physical bravery and an ability to deal with the supernatural are also common *tonowi* characteristics, but they are not essential (**Figure 12.3**).

A Kapauku Big Man functions as the headman of the village unit in a wide variety of situations within and beyond the community. He represents his group in dealing with outsiders and other villages and acts as negotiator and/or judge when disputes break out among his followers. As a *tonowi*, he acquires political power through giving loans. Villagers comply with his requests because they are in his debt (often interest-free), and they do not want to have to repay their loans. Those who have not yet borrowed from him may wish to do so in the future, so they, too, want to keep his goodwill. A *tonowi* who refuses to lend money to fellow villagers may be shunned, ridiculed, and, in extreme cases, even killed by a group of warriors. Such unfavorable reactions ensure that individual economic wealth is dispersed throughout the community.

A Big Man gains further support from his relatives and from taking into his household young male apprentices

---

tribe In anthropology, the term for a range of kin-ordered groups that are politically integrated by some unifying factor and whose members share a common ancestry, identity, culture, language, and territory.

of East Africa (discussed in the previous chapter), the Warrior age grade guards the village and grazing lands, whereas Judicial Elders resolve disputes. The oldest age grade, the Ritual Elders, advise on matters involving the well-being of all the Tiriki people. With the tribe's political affairs in the hands of the various age grades and their officers, this type of organization enables the largely independent kin-groups to solve conflicts and sometimes avoid feuding between the lineages.

The Pashtun, a large ethnic group with tribes on both sides of the border between Afghanistan and Pakistan, provide another example of decentralized political organization. Periodically, groups of male elders, each representing their kinfolk, gather to deal with collective challenges. In such a political assembly, known as a *jirga*, these Pashtun tribal leaders make joint decisions by consensus—from settling disputes, working out treaties, and resolving trade issues to establishing law and order in their war-torn homelands (**Figure 12.4**).

Centralized Political Systems

Political authority is not centralized in bands and tribes, but this changes when populations grow, individuals specialize, division of labor increases, and surplus is exchanged in expanding trade networks. This process creates opportunities for some enterprising individuals or groups to gain control at the expense of others. In such increasingly complex societies, political authority and power are concentrated in a single individual (the chief) or in a body of individuals (the state). In centralized systems, political organization relies more heavily on institutionalized power, authority, and even coercion.

Chiefdoms

A **chiefdom** is a politically organized territory centrally ruled by a chief heading a kin-based society with prestige ranking and a redistributive economy. Rank in such a hierarchical political system is determined by the closeness of one's relationship to the chief. Those closest are officially superior and receive deferential treatment from those of lower status. The office of the chief is usually for life and often hereditary. Typically, it passes from a man to his younger brother, a son, or his sister's son, depending on whether descent is traced patrilineally or matrilineally.

Unlike the headman or headwoman in bands and tribes, the leader of a chiefdom is generally a true authority figure with the power to command, settle disputes, punish, and reward. This chief serves to maintain peace and order within and between allied communities.

Chiefdoms have a recognized hierarchy consisting of major and minor authorities that control major and

Figure 12.3 Big Man from West Papua, New Guinea Wearing his official regalia, the *tonowi* is recognizable among fellow Kapauku and neighboring Papua highlanders as a man of wealth and power.

who receive business training along with food and shelter. He also gives them a loan that enables them to marry when the apprenticeship ends. In return, they act as messengers and bodyguards. After leaving, they remain tied to the *tonowi* by bonds of affection and gratitude.

Because a Big Man's wealth comes from his success at breeding pigs (the focus of the entire Kapauku economy, as described in the chapter on patterns of subsistence), it is not uncommon for a *tonowi* to lose his fortune rapidly due to poor management or simple bad luck with his pigs. Thus, the Kapauku political structure shifts frequently: As one man loses wealth and consequently power, another gains it and becomes a *tonowi*. These changes prevent any single Big Man from holding political power for too long.

Political Integration Beyond the Kin-Group

Age sets, age grades, and common-interest groups discussed in the previous chapter are among the political integration mechanisms used by tribal societies. Cutting across territorial and kin-groupings, these organizations link members from different lineages and clans. For example, among the Tiriki

---

chiefdom A politically organized society in which several neighboring communities inhabiting a territory are united under a single ruler.

Figure 12.4 Gathering of Tribal Leaders In traditional kin-ordered societies such as tribes, political power is neither centralized nor monopolized. Instead, social networks of extended families, lineages, or clans share political power. As shown in this photo of tribal elders attending a *Loya Jirga* ("Grand Assembly") in Afghanistan's capital city of Kabul, Pashtun leaders gather periodically to discuss and resolve conflicts and other collective challenges.

minor subdivisions. Such an arrangement is a chain of command, linking leaders at every level, with each owing personal loyalty to the chief. It serves to bind groups in the heartland to the chief's headquarters, whether it is a large tent, wood house, or stone hall. Although leaders of chiefdoms are almost always male, in some cultures a politically astute wife, sister, or single daughter of a deceased chief could inherit this powerful position as well.

Chiefs usually control the economic activities of those who fall under their political rule. Typically, chiefdoms involve redistributive systems, and the chief has control over surplus goods and perhaps even over the community's labor force. Thus, he (and sometimes she) may demand a share of the harvested crop from farmers, which may then be redistributed throughout the domain. Similarly, manpower may be periodically drafted to form battle groups, build fortifications, dig irrigation works, or construct ceremonial sites.

The chief may also amass a great amount of personal wealth and pass it on to offspring. Land, cattle, and luxury goods produced by specialists can be collected by the chief and become part of the power base. Moreover, high-ranking families of the chiefdom may engage in the same practice and use their possessions as evidence of superior social status.

Traditionally, chiefdoms have been unstable, with lesser chiefs trying to take power from higher-ranking chiefs, or rival chiefs vying for supreme power as paramount chiefs. In precolonial Hawaii, for example, where war was the way to gain territory and maintain power, great chiefs set out to conquer each other in an effort to become paramount chief of all the islands. When one chief defeated another, the loser and all his nobles were dispossessed of their property and lucky to escape alive. The new paramount chief then appointed his own supporters to positions of political power.

Among the many symbols indicating their supreme political rank, paramount chiefs carry a title of renown

not only recognized in their own domain but beyond. In English, the title *paramount chief* is often translated as "king." This covers a range of political authority figures—from the high-ranking ruler elected by an alliance of chiefs to the leader of a politically centralized society historically divided in chiefdoms. As such, indigenous royal titles—*malku* in Aymara for rulers in the Andean highlands of Bolivia; *raja* in Hindi for those in India; *gyalpo* in Tibetan for Himalayan rulers in Sikkim and Bhutan; *emir* or *sultan*, both Arabic, for rulers throughout Islamic Asia and North Africa; and *vorst* or *fürst* in Germanic Europe—are all translated as "king." Historically, the Indian subcontinent alone numbered 565 princely states, both large and small.

The political distinction between a paramount chiefdom, princely state, or kingdom by whatever name cannot be sharply drawn. As an intermediary form of political organization between tribes and states, most chiefdoms, paramount chiefdoms, and kingdoms have disappeared in the course of time. However, many hundreds still exist in parts of Asia and Africa, for example—albeit no longer as politically independent or sovereign domains. Subordinated to the state as a more powerful political system, those that endure do so as an enclosed territorial division such as a district or province, with its traditional rulers and their successors remaining in office, although with reduced authority.

Due to their wealth and prestige, and holding onto traditional titles and other high-status symbols, high-ranking chiefs and kings (or queens) are often well positioned to successfully adapt to the new order. Especially in pluralistic states with an ineffective or otherwise challenged centralized government, regional political rulers such as traditional paramount chiefs, emirs, and kings may (re)gain power and claim greater independence.

Such is the case with chiefs among the Kpelle, the largest ethnic group in Liberia, a pluralistic West African country

Figure 12.5 Paramount Chiefs and International Diplomacy
In a special diplomatic ceremony commemorating the bilateral relationship between Liberia and China and expressing appreciation for China's economic investment and financial aid in his domain, Paramount Chief Moses Galakrumah of the Kpelle chiefdom of Panta, Bong County, appointed the Chinese ambassador Zhou Yuxiao as honorary paramount chief. Together with Chief Elder Togba Gbonpelee, he briefed his high-ranking Chinese guest on the history of the Panta chiefdom and dressed China's senior envoy in a traditional Kpelle robe, along with a wooden sword and staff— symbols of power and bravery.

inhabited by about 30 ethnic groups. Traditionally, the Kpelle are politically divided in several independent paramount chiefdoms, each comprising an alliance of smaller chiefdoms. Whereas the Kpelle inhabit territories in Liberia's eastern interior, African Americans from the United States, including former slaves, colonized its coastal region. Aided by the American Colonization Society, these black settlers founded the Republic of Liberia in 1847, naming its capital Monrovia in honor of U.S. president James Monroe. Since then, these Americo-Liberians have dominated the country's political economy. However, they never fully succeeded in centralizing political power. This left traditional paramount chiefs among the Kpelle and their neighbors largely in control of regional affairs as salaried state officials, mediating between the inhabitants in their districts (traditional chiefdoms) and the central government.

Today, many Kpelle are rice farmers, but they also engage in wage labor. Their paramount chief, like those of other ethnic groups, receives government commissions on taxes and court fees collected within his district, plus a commission for providing laborers for Liberia's numerous foreign-owned mines and rubber plantations. He also gets a stipulated amount of rice from each farming household and gifts from people who approach him for favors. Moreover, he has the authority to settle disputes, and people compensate him for that as well.

In keeping with his high social status, a Kpelle chief has at his disposal uniformed messengers, a literate clerk, and the symbols of wealth: several wives, embroidered gowns, and freedom from manual labor. After a devastating civil war (1989–2003), Liberia's government has tried to rebuild the pluralistic country's economy by decentralizing some of its governing power, granting the traditional chiefs more political, legal, and administrative control. Some now even participate in international diplomacy for their country (**Figure 12.5**).

States

The **state** is a politically organized territory occupied by a class-stratified society with a centralized government and definite boundaries. The most formal of political systems, it is organized and directed by a government that has the capacity and authority to manage and tax its subjects, make laws and maintain order, and use military force to defend or expand its territories. Two of the smallest states today measure less than 2.5 square kilometers (1 square mile), whereas the largest covers about 17 million square kilometers (6.6 million square miles).

---

state A political institution established to manage and defend a complex, socially stratified society occupying a defined territory.

Often states are ruled by coalitions of well-connected and wealthy individuals or groups that have accumulated and fought over power. Possessing the resources (including money, weapons, and manpower), these ruling elites exercise power through institutions, such as a government and its bureaucracy, which allow them to arrange and rearrange a society's social and economic order.

A large population in a state-organized society requires increased food production and wider distribution networks. Together, these lead to a transformation of the landscape by way of irrigation and terracing, carefully managed crop rotation cycles, intensive competition for clearly demarcated lands and roads, and enough farmers and other rural workers to support market systems and a specialized urban sector.

Under such conditions, corporate groups that stress exclusive membership multiply rapidly, ethnic differentiation and ethnocentrism become more pronounced, and the potential for social conflict increases dramatically. Given these circumstances, state institutions—which minimally involve a bureaucracy, a military, and (often) an official religion—provide the means for numerous and diverse groups to function together as an integrated whole.

An important aspect of the state is its delegation of authority to maintain order within and outside its borders. Police, foreign ministries, war ministries, and other bureaucracies function to control and punish disruptive acts of crime, dissension, and rebellion. By such agencies the state asserts authority impersonally and in a consistent, predictable manner. Throughout history, neighboring states have often had conflicts over territorial boundaries (**Figure 12.6**).

States first began to emerge over 5,000 years ago. Often unstable, many have disappeared in the course of history, some temporarily and others forever. Some were annexed by other states, and others collapsed or fragmented into smaller political units. Although some present-day states are very old—such as Japan, which has endured as a state for almost 1,500 years—few are older than the United States, an independent country since 1783.

A key distinction to make at this point is between state and nation. A **nation** is a people who share a collective identity based on a common culture, language, territorial base, and history (Clay, 1996). Today, there are roughly 5,000 nations (including tribes and ethnic groups) throughout the world, many of which have existed since before recorded history. By contrast, there are about 200 independent states in the world today, most of which did not exist before the end of World War II (1945).

As these numbers imply, nation and state do not always coincide, as they do, for example, in Iceland, Japan, and Swaziland. In fact, about 75 percent of the world's states are *pluralistic societies*, defined in an earlier chapter as societies in which two or more ethnic groups or nationalities are politically organized into one territorial state but maintain their cultural differences (Van den Berghe, 1992). Typically, smaller nations (including tribes) and other groups find themselves at the mercy of one or more powerful nations or ethnic groups gaining political control over the state.

Frequently facing discrimination or repression, some minority nations seek to improve their political position by seceding and founding an independent state. In splitting the state's territory, they usually encounter stiff opposition with sometimes violent confrontations. So it is

Figure 12.6 Territorial Boundaries
After the British empire pulled out of South Asia over 60 years ago, that subcontinent erupted in warfare between Muslims and Hindus. The region was then carved up along religious lines into Pakistan and India. Since then, these countries have fought three wars against each other. The tense political relations between these nuclear-armed rivals are symbolically displayed in the military border-closing ritual at Wagah. Every evening, Pakistani Pathan guards, wearing black uniforms and fantailed headgear of the same color, face India's border guards, dressed in khaki uniforms and hats adorned with scarlet fantails. Brandishing rifles and parading in goosestep, they greet each other, lock gates, and lower their national flags.

© Reuters/Corbis

with the Tuareg, a nomadic Berber nation of Muslim herders and traders whose ancestral homeland stretches across a vast expanse of the Sahara Desert carved up by North African states such as Mali, Niger, Libya, and Algeria.

The Kurds are another nation whose ancestral homeland of about 200,000 square kilometers (77,000 square miles) has been subdivided. Like the Tuareg, many Kurds are willing to fight for political autonomy or even national independence, but they are forced to accept their minority status in the neighboring modern states of Turkey, Iraq, and Iran. With a population of about 27 million, they are much more numerous than Australians, for example. In fact, the total population of the four Scandinavian countries—Denmark, Finland, Norway, and Sweden—is less than that of the Kurds (**Figure 12.7**).

Forming a new nation state is a political challenge, and many ethnic groups or national minorities have had to take up arms and fight for their independence. Such has been the case in the violent breakup of Serb-dominated Yugoslavia, which was split into six smaller states between 1989 and 1992. However, some of these newly formed republics still have ethnic minorities. In southeast Serbia, for example, Albanian-speaking Kosovars fought a war of independence in 1999. The government of Serbia, dominated by Serbian-speaking Christians, later granted Kosovo autonomous status as a province. In 2008, Kosovars unilaterally declared their province an independent nation state, a status not (yet) internationally recognized.

Figure 12.7 The Kurd Nation Across State Borders
The Kurds—most of whom live in Turkey, Iran, and Iraq—are an example of a nation without a state. With a population of about 27 million, they are much more numerous than Australians, for example. In fact, the total population of the four Scandinavian countries—Denmark, Finland, Norway, and Sweden—is less than that of the Kurds, who have no independent country of their own.

Political Systems and the Question of Authority

Whatever a society's political system, it must find some way to obtain and retain the people's allegiance. In uncentralized systems, in which every adult participates in all decision making, loyalty and cooperation are freely given because each person is considered a part of the political system. However, as the group grows larger and the organization becomes more formal, the problem of obtaining and keeping public support becomes greater.

Centralized political systems may rely upon coercion as a means of social control. This, however, can be risky because the large numbers of personnel needed to apply force may themselves become a political power. Also, the emphasis on force typically creates resentment and may lessen cooperation. Thus, police states are generally short-lived; most societies choose less extreme forms of social coercion. In the United States, this is reflected in the increasing emphasis placed on *cultural* controls, discussed later in this chapter. Laura Nader (see the Anthropologist of Note) is well known for her anthropological research concerning issues of power, including cultural control.

Also basic to the political process is the concept of **authority**, claiming and exercising power as justified by law or custom of tradition. Unlike **coercion**, which imposes obedience or submission by force or intimidation, authority is based on the socially accepted rules or codified laws binding people together as a society. Without these rules and laws, however different in each culture, political rule lacks *legitimacy* and will be interpreted and perhaps openly challenged as unjust and wrong, opening the door to forced removal.

In a *monarchy*—a state headed by a single ruler—political authority can be based on different sources of legitimacy, including divine will, birthright in a royal lineage, or an election held among free citizens or a wealthy upper class (nobles). In a *theocracy*—a state ruled by a priestly elite headed by a supreme priest claiming holy or even divine status—legitimacy is embedded in sacred doctrine. In an *aristocracy*, on the other hand, the ruling noble elite claims legitimacy traditionally rooted in a ritual mixture of high-status ancestry and class endogamy, military dominance, economic wealth, and ceremonial capital.

Finally, in a *democracy* rulers claim legitimacy based on the idea that they act as representatives of the free citizens who elected them into office with the mandate to act on

nation A people who share a collective identity based on a common culture, language, territorial base, and history.

authority Claiming and exercising power as justified by law or custom of tradition.

coercion Imposition of obedience or submission by force or intimidation.

ANTHROPOLOGIST OF NOTE

Laura Nader (b. 1930)

Laura Nader has stood out among her peers from the start of her career in 1960, when she became the first woman faculty member in the anthropology department at the University of California, Berkeley.

Nader and her three siblings grew up in Winsted, Connecticut, children of immigrants from Lebanon. As she recalls, "My dad left Lebanon for political reasons, and when he came to the land of the free, he took it seriously. So we were raised to believe that you should be involved in public issues." They were also taught to question assumptions.

Both Nader and her younger brother Ralph have made careers of doing this. She is an anthropologist noted for her cross-cultural research on law, justice, and social control and their connection to power structures. He is a consumer advocate and frequent U.S. presidential candidate who is a watchdog on issues of public health and the safety and quality of life.

Laura Nader, a cultural anthropology professor at the University of California, Berkeley, specializes in law, dispute resolution, and controlling processes.

Courtesy of Dr. Laura Nader

Laura Nader's undergraduate studies included a study-abroad year in Mexico. Later, while earning her doctorate in anthropology at Radcliffe College, she returned to Mexico to do fieldwork in a Zapotec Indian peasant village in the Sierra Madre Mountains of Oaxaca. Reflecting on this and subsequent research, she says,

In the 1950s, when I went to southern Mexico, I was studying how the Zapotec organize their

lives, what they do with their problems, what they do when they go to court. And when I came back to this country, I started looking at American equivalents, at how Americans solve their consumer and service complaints.

Nader's first decade of teaching at Berkeley coincided with the Vietnam War, an era when the campus was in a perpetual state of turmoil with students demonstrating for peace and civil rights. Becoming a scholar-activist, she called upon colleagues to "study up" and do research on the world's power elite. "The study of man," she wrote in 1972, "is confronted with an unprecedented situation: Never before have a few, by their actions and inactions, had the power of life and death over so many members of the species."

To date, the results of Nader's own research have appeared in over a hundred publications. Among these are her numerous books, including *Naked Science— Anthropological Inquiry into Boundaries, Power, and Knowledge* (1996) and *The Life of the Law: Anthropological Projects* (2002).

Playing a leading role in the development of the anthropology of law, Nader has taken on specialists in the fields of law, children's issues, nuclear energy, and science (including her own profession), critically questioning the basic assumptions ("central dogmas") under which these experts operate. She presses her students to do the same—to think critically, question authority, and break free from the "controlling processes" of the power elite. In 2000, Nader accepted one of the highest honors of the American Anthropological Association—an invitation to give the distinguished lecture at its annual gathering.

Adapted from "Interview with Laura Nader." (2000, November). California Monthly.

---

the basis of collectively approved rules in the form of law. A democracy may have a king or queen as symbolic head. With an elected president as titular head, such a state is usually identified as a *republic.*

For example, as noted in this chapter's opening, the authority of the current emir of Kano in Nigeria is based on his royal ancestry and political-religious tradition. Like his predecessors, he is the son of an emir, was formally appointed by a group of high-ranking chiefs serving as "king makers," and was confirmed by the Nigerian state as his uncle's successor to the throne in 1963.

The emir's authority is also based on religion because Islam remains the basis of an emir's historic right as the

spiritual-political head of about 8 million Muslim subjects in his domain. As emir, he plays an active role as patron of Islamic scholarship. And because he made the pilgrimage to the sacred site of Mecca, he bears the honorific title *Alhaji.*

Beyond the legitimacy of his claim to rulership, the current emir's authority is also based on his personal achievements as an internationally educated diplomat, politician, and successful businessman whose great personal wealth gained him a reputation for generosity.

For purposes of symbolic display of his authority, the emir hosts *durbars* ("parades") celebrating his emirate's cultural heritage at public festivals in which his followers demonstrate their personal loyalty to him as their *sarki* ("king"). Finally, indicative of his prestige, the current emir has four wives (allowed by Islam) and about 60 concubines residing in his harem at the 800-year-old royal palace (Nast, 2005; Shea, 2007).

Politics and Religion

Clearly, as suggested in our discussion of the emirate of Kano, where Shariah (Islamic law) was instituted in 2000, politics is often intricately intertwined with religion. Frequently, it is religion that legitimizes the political order and leadership. Religious beliefs may influence or provide authoritative approval to customary rules and laws. For instance, acts that people believe to be sinful, such as murder, are often illegal as well.

In both industrial and nonindustrial societies, belief in the supernatural is important and is reflected in people's political institutions. Medieval Christian Europe well exemplifies the effect of religion on politics: Holy wars were fought over the smallest matter; labor was mobilized to build immense cathedrals in honor of the Virgin Mary and other saints; kings and queens ruled by "divine right," and they asked for the blessing of the pope (who claimed spiritual authority and political supremacy as head of the Roman Catholic Church) in all important ventures, marital or martial.

In Japan, until the mid-20th century, people were taught to believe they were subjects of a sacred king to be obeyed and worshiped as a divine ruler—not unlike the god-kings heading the ancient Egyptian, Inca, and Aztec empires. After defeat in World War II in 1945, Japan came under American military occupation for a number of years. As dictated by the U.S. government, their emperor was allowed to remain in office as a leader of his conquered nation, albeit no longer as a god.

Modern Iran was proclaimed an Islamic republic in the 1979 revolution that toppled the authoritarian regime of the shah; its first head of state, Ayatollah Ruhollah Khomeini, was titled the most holy of all Shiite Muslim holy men. As the highest-ranking religious and political authority of the country, he was pronounced its supreme leader, a position he held until his death ten years later. Since then, Iran has remained a theocratic republic with a high-ranking Shiite Muslim cleric, or grand ayatollah, as its most powerful authority. The country's democratically elected parliament and president are subordinate to the ayatollah (**Figure 12.8**).

VISUAL COUNTERPOINT

Figure 12.8 Church and State in Iran and Great Britain In contrast to countries such as the United States, where religion and state are constitutionally separated, countries such as Iran and Great Britain permit a much closer relationship between political and religious affairs. For instance, since 1989, a grand ayatollah named Ali Khamenei has held the title of Supreme Leader of the Islamic Republic of Iran, serving as the country's highest-ranking religious and political authority. In England, Queen Elizabeth is not only her country's nominal head of state but also the Supreme Governor of the Church of England, which entitles her to appoint the Anglican bishops in that state.

The fact that the president of the United States takes the oath of office by swearing on a Bible is another instance of the use of religion to legitimize political power, as is the phrase "one nation, under God" in the Pledge of Allegiance. U.S. coins are etched with the phrase "In God We Trust," many governmental meetings begin with a prayer or an invocation, and the expression "so help me God" is routinely used in legal proceedings. Despite an official separation of church and state, religious legitimization of government lingers. Similarly, for her coronation in 1953, Queen Elizabeth II placed her right hand on a Bible and kissed the sacred book when she signed the oath.